Lilian Baylis: A biography

THE SOCIETY FOR THEATRE RESEARCH

The Society for Theatre Research, founded in 1948, brings together those interested in the history and technique of the British theatre, and encourages research into these subjects. Lectures are held in London. Members receive the Society's illustrated journal, *Theatre Notebook*, as well as (at least) one book annually. The Society makes substantial Research Awards and in 1998 instituted the Theatre Book Prize. New members are welcomed. Details of subscription rates and a list of past publications appear on the Society's website – www.str.org.uk – or may be obtained by writing to: The Joint Hon. Secretaries, The Society for Theatre Research, c/o The Theatre Museum, 1E Tavistock Street, London WC2E 7PR

Lilian Baylis:
A biography

ELIZABETH SCHAFER

UNIVERSITY OF HERTFORDSHIRE PRESS
THE SOCIETY FOR THEATRE RESEARCH

First published in Great Britain in 2006 by
University of Hertfordshire Press
Learning and Information Services
University of Hertfordshire
College Lane
Hatfield
Hertfordshire AL10 9AB

British Library Cataloguing in Publication Data
A catalogue record for this book is available from the British Library

ISBN 1-902806-63-8 hardback
ISBN 1-902806-64-6 paperback

Design by Geoff Green Book Design, CB4 5RA
Cover design by John Robertshaw, AL5 2JB
Printed in England by Antony Rowe Ltd, Chippenham, Wiltshire, SN14 6LH

For Vincent Jones

Contents

List of Illustrations

Cover Illustrations

Front cover: Portrait of Lilian Baylis by Ethel Gabain (1936)
(Royal Victoria Hall Foundation). Photograph by
Vincent Jones

Back cover: Lilian Baylis as a Gypsy Reveller, Johannesburg
(Battye Library, Perth, W. A.)

Acknowledgements

This biography depends heavily on archival material, and staff at the following archives have been extremely helpful: the Bristol Theatre Collection, especially Frances Carlyon, Jo Elsworth and Rachel Hassall; the Mander and Mitchenson Theatre Collection, Jerwood Library of the Performing Arts, especially Richard Mangan; the Britten-Pears Library, Aldeburgh, particularly Nicholas Clark; the Royal Ballet School archive, especially Anna Meadmore; the Theatre Museum, especially staff at Blythe House; the National Portrait Gallery, especially Bernard Horrocks; the British Library Sound Archive; the Minet Archive, Lambeth; the English National Opera archive, especially Clare Colvin; the National Theatre archive; the Islington Local History Archive; the Shakespeare Centre, Stratford-upon-Avon; the Battye Library, Perth (Western Australia); the National Film archive.

Thanks are due to the Arts and Humanities Research Council (AHRC) for supporting several projects contributing towards this book, and to the International Federation for Theatre Research historiography working group. The Institute for Advanced Study at La Trobe University, Melbourne, also provided invaluable support in the later stages of my research.

Colleagues who have supported and sustained the project include Richard Cave, David Bradby, Jacky Bratton and Chris Dymkowski. My Head of Department at Royal Holloway, Katie Normington, was particularly supportive at all times. Thanks also to Robert Gordon, Kate Newey, Dave Ward, Jennie Clarke, Sarah Lenton, David Thurlby, Katherine Cockin, Rachel Barnett and Chris Wiley.

I would also like to thank the Vic-Wells Association, especially those who shared reminiscences and research with me: James Penstone, Eileen Hazell, Laura Probert and, most especially, Leo Kersley. Thanks to the Royal Victoria Hall Foundation, especially Valerie Colgan; and to Bryan Crimp; to Roy Waters who loaned me letters by Baylis; to Peter Davies, Warden of St Illtyd's, Oxwich, who provided me with images of the painting Baylis commissioned; and to Christopher Pearson at St Agnes, Kennington, for showing me round Baylis's church. My research assistants – Keira Roth, Kate Matthews and Tina Muir – have been exemplary in their attention to detail.

Kate Murphy gave the biography fresh impetus when it needed it most. Thanks also to George Green, Penny Warburton, Kirsty Dunseath, Jacqueline Korn.

I am particularly grateful to Vincent Jones, David and Rosemary Schafer and John Rogers, all of whom know more about Lilian Baylis than they ever anticipated they would. Madeleine Jones interrupted everything, wonderfully, and helped me keep a sense of perspective.

Notes
In quotations from manuscript and typescript material spellings and punctuation have not been normalised.

Records of governors' meetings and executive committees etc. are held in the Bristol Theatre Collection.

ABBREVIATIONS

M&M Raymond Mander and Joe Mitchenson Theatre Collection, Greenwich

OVEC Emma Cons collection, Bristol Theatre Collection, Bristol University

OVLB Old Vic Lilian Baylis collection, Bristol Theatre Collection, Bristol University

OVM *Old Vic Magazine* (References are by month and year, as the issue and volume numbering is inconsistent)

OV/M Annette Prevost collection, Bristol Theatre Collection, Bristol University

[1]

Introduction

On 6 January 1931, Lilian Baylis, manager of the Old Vic Theatre in London, opened her new theatre, the recently restored Sadler's Wells. A few days later, after a banquet held to celebrate this event, Baylis was involved in a serious car accident. She lay stricken, and badly hurt, but as someone identified her – 'It's Miss Baylis. Miss Baylis of the Old Vic' – Baylis roused herself, despite her injuries, and corrected them, '*And* Sadler's Wells.'[1]

This anecdote is one of the most frequently told stories about Lilian Baylis, a maverick and eccentric woman, who left her formidable and distinctive imprint not only on the theatres she actually managed, the Vic and the Wells, but also on her theatres' descendants: the British National Theatre, the Royal Ballet, and the English National Opera. She was an inspiringly successful, if unconventional, manager who ran two financially viable theatres housing a theatre company, a ballet and an opera company, all committed to bringing what was considered the very best of high culture – Shakespeare, Wagner, Mozart, *Giselle* – to working people, yet Baylis is often remembered nowadays primarily by means of comic anecdotes. These often portray her as a stingy caricature, and completely without tact. 'Quite a sweet little Goneril, don't you think?' was her crushing remark on an actress who had just performed that particularly unsweet role.[2] An unfortunate understudy emerging exhausted from playing a major role was greeted with 'Well, dear, you've had your chance. And you've missed it.'[3] Staff asking for a pay rise were told that Baylis would have to ask God, and God's response was always the same: 'Sorry, dear, God says No.'[4] And amongst underpaid Vic-Wells staff, Baylis's favourite prayer was reputed to be 'Dear

God, send me good actors but send them cheap.'[5] These anecdotes attest to undoubted truths about Baylis's management: last-minute, panic-stricken, under-rehearsed substitutions were common at her theatres; she did *not* flatter her performers; she underpaid actors of the calibre of Edith Evans and John Gielgud; and she was confrontationally public about her religious commitment. And yet the cumulative effect of the anecdotes very much suggests a tendency towards containment, as if the most effective way for many to deal with Baylis's unladylike, unorthodox but completely phenomenal success was to render her a joke.

Baylis herself, however, actively participated in the generation of some anecdotes. Malcolm Baker-Smith, a Vic stage manager who subsequently went on to become a radio producer, relates how once, after he had worked right through the night at the Vic, he caught a taxi home at 5.45 a.m. Baylis's response was not to thank him for going without sleep but to deplore the extravagance of taking a taxi, and to point out that working men's trains started running at six o'clock. To his shocked response of 'Oh really Miss Baylis,' Baylis laughed and commented, 'good story to tell'.[6] And as the Baylis anecdotes circulated over and over again, related with impeccable comic timing by such star performers as Sybil Thorndike, John Gielgud or Laurence Olivier, Baylis's two theatres acquired, as it were, a great deal of free advertising.

That Baylis may have deliberately encouraged the anecdote industry is suggested by the fact that she learnt the value of free publicity long before she became a theatre manager. Beginning in early childhood as a performer, a musician and dancer, first in London, and then later in South Africa, Baylis learnt the craft of marketing and playing to a very wide range of different and sometimes difficult audiences – London high society, inmates of lunatic asylums, gold and diamond miners in South Africa – and she learnt both to work audiences for all they were worth and to pitch her act very precisely. Evidence that Baylis's performance of the gruff, badly dressed, gauche but basically warm-hearted manager was not simply spontaneous abounds, although this is the persona that dominates the anecdotes.

The cultural work performed by the Baylis anecdotes is almost as important as their content, and theatre historian Jacky Bratton has recently argued for a more creative approach to the reading of theatrical anecdotes than is traditional. She suggests worrying less over whether an anecdote is 'true' in the sense that it can be documented, and instead being more attentive to what the anecdote is doing in terms of 'identity-formation' in relation both to individuals and to the groups and communities in which they seek to situate themselves.[7] Given this, it is instructive that Bratton identifies a tendency for certain theatre managers to be 'constructed by a stream of anecdotes as pillars of the performance community, bearers of a comically old-fashioned but valuable and authenticating set of attitudes and knowledge of the trade'.[8] Bratton is here discussing anecdotes about the theatre managers Thomas Dibdin and Sarah Baker, but many of the anecdotes surrounding Baylis operate in similar territory. And while historian Paula Backscheider maintains that

> [t]here must be reasons that an anecdote survives, is repeated, and regardless of how its veracity is questioned continues to be a compelling portrait of a person[,][9]

it is nevertheless important to note that some Baylis anecdotes, when read in terms of the theatrical hegemony of her time, can result in a construction of her success as *so* eccentric, *so* isolated and *so* unrepeatable that the implication is that no woman would ever achieve, or perhaps even want to achieve, similar success.

The anecdotes help keep Baylis's achievements in circulation, but it is not surprising that the Baylis who can be excavated from her own repeated attempts at autobiography and memoirs is quite different. Indeed, in her notes and unpublished autobiographical fragments she seems consciously to be trying to provide an alternative to the well-known public persona. Although Baylis never got round to completing her autobiography and telling her own version of her life story, she did want her biography written; indeed she expected that it would be written, because her chauffeuse and personal assistant Annette Prevost promised to write it.[10] After

Baylis's death, Cicely Hamilton, a much-published writer who had previously collaborated with Baylis on a book project, offered to write a biography of her, but the Vic governors informed her that Prevost was already at work.[11] Although Prevost did make occasional attempts to assemble material, to get letters transcribed and to make notes on the documentation she had access to, she never came anywhere near completing a biography.[12] What she did do was to cherish Baylis's personal archive, preserving personal notes, family letters and autobiographical sketches alongside more unexpected items such as shopping lists, veterinary bills, and Baylis's spectacles.[13]

The Baylis archive is very much the foundation of this biography, which I have tried to keep grounded in Baylis's own, and her family's, writings. I contend that Baylis has been rather ill served by her biographers so far, because none of them have taken serious account of her own writing. As a result, a very particular view of Baylis has been perpetuated: the Baylis who is familiar from the anecdotes, but not the Baylis she herself sought to present in her repeated attempts at autobiography. The only previous full-length biography of Baylis, written by Richard Findlater in 1975, is particularly problematic in this respect. Findlater records that Annette Prevost, who was then in possession of the Baylis archive, gave him invaluable assistance in his research, yet astonishingly laments the real 'dearth of autobiographical material' when in fact the archive is full of such writing.[14] It has to be assumed either that Findlater did not have full access to the archive or that he chose not to explore it fully.

An additional problem with Findlater's view of Baylis is that, although he was able to interview many people who had known her well, none of his interviewees met Baylis until she was already in her forties. Annette Prevost, whom Findlater relies on very heavily, only met Baylis in August 1932, five years before her death, when she was in ill health and slowing down.[15] Consequently it is not surprising that the older Baylis and the public persona dominate Findlater's biography, providing a stark contrast with Baylis's own autobiographical writings, in which she stresses her early life as if trying to suggest which experiences in her youth made her the woman she later became. Most critical of all, however, is the fact that none of the witnesses Findlater was able to interview had ever encountered the woman Baylis herself identified as the most inspirational and important influence in her life, Emma Cons, nor do they seem to have had much real understanding of the full extent of Cons's remarkable achievements (especially her role in the fight for women's suffrage).

This biography diverges in many places from Findlater's vision of Baylis. It takes Baylis seriously as a prolific (and published) writer, and also as a trained performer who knew how to work audiences and who used that knowledge very skilfully in the service of her theatres. It stresses Baylis the high-powered professional woman who enjoyed networking with other successful career women; Baylis the international traveller; Baylis the strategist who could (mostly) get what she wanted even when arguing about finances with economist John Maynard Keynes. This biography also challenges previous assumptions about Baylis's relationship with her mother, Liebe, who has hitherto been scandalously misrepresented; it highlights Baylis's and her family's commitment to the women's suffrage movement; it stresses the close and supportive relationships Baylis had with women friends such as Louie Davey and Cicely Hamilton; and it acknowledges Baylis's friendships with lesbian women.[16]

While I have attempted always to emphasise the influences that Baylis herself identified as important to her, and to acknowledge how significant Baylis thought her pre-Vic years were in making her the manager she eventually became, some caution is of course needed. Several of Baylis's autobiographical notes were made late in life, and she sometimes embroidered, elaborated, fantasised and forgot. When the significance of Baylis's early performance training, especially in improvisation, is taken fully into account, her attempts at autobiography offer a particularly rich negotiation of what theatre historian Thomas Postlewait identifies as the 'too neat' traditional dualisms that often operate around the autobiographies of professional performers: 'face and mask, presence and absence, private and public personality, life and art.'[17] However, I have tried to respect Baylis's own views on what she thought was worth recording of her life and, bearing in mind the old tenet that the personal is political, to treat Baylis's records of her private life, her family life, her spiritual life and her adventurous globe-trotting holidays as important in enabling her to achieve the public and well-documented theatrical triumphs of her later years.

Nearly seventy years after Baylis's death, it is important not to forget the extent of those unequalled triumphs. Under Baylis the Vic-Wells became an institution where dancers such as Alicia Markova and Anton Dolin, actors such as Edith Evans, Hollywood names such as Charles Laughton and singers such as Joan Cross would willingly work for dreadful wages. Stars in the making – Alec Guinness, Michael Redgrave, Alastair Sim, James Mason, Margot Fonteyn, Robert Helpmann – furthered their careers at Baylis's theatres. And under Baylis, the Vic-Wells also became a theatre which really inspired people; indeed it is difficult to find many significant British theatre practitioners in the mid to late twentieth century who were not influenced in some way by work done at Baylis's Vic. So, for example, in Britain during the 1950s, the Stratford Memorial Theatre – which later became home to the Royal Shakespeare Company – was dominated, and reformed, by the work of people like Anthony Quayle, Laurence Olivier and John Gielgud, who had acted at the Vic-Wells earlier in their careers. Meanwhile at the other Stratford, in East London, Joan Littlewood ran her Theatre Workshop fuelled at least partly by memories of the excitement generated by productions she had seen at the Vic in her teens: after Gielgud's *Hamlet* in 1930, the sixteen-year-old Littlewood 'didn't miss a production down the Waterloo Road.'[18] She wrote offering her services to the theatre (her mother intercepted the reply), and Littlewood could still describe enthusiastically, even sixty years after the event, the extravagant delights of Ernest Milton's performances in Shakespeare at the Vic.[19] And while Littlewood's work was crucial in the development of fringe theatre in Britain, some have seen Baylis's Vic, with its reckless, alternative, non-commercial and desperately poverty-stricken work, as a precursor to the Fringe.[20]

In addition to her work in London, Baylis took her message, that access to theatre, opera and dance was the inviolable right of all working people, wherever she went. Whenever her companies toured – to Manchester, Glasgow, Edinburgh, Portsmouth – she lectured local dignitaries on the importance of establishing lively and genuinely repertory theatres throughout Britain, or as Baylis herself often put it, an Old Vic in every town.[21] She constantly sought to inspire people with her vision of the Vic – the best live theatre possible at cinema prices – and her attempts to bring the best in opera, drama and ballet to working people continue to pose challenging questions for the theatre establishment today.

Baylis's own autobiographical writings go some way towards answering the question, 'How did she do it?' While a whole range of factors needs to be taken into account, for Baylis herself the explanation was simple: she was on a mission from God. But, in addition, she became what she became, very largely, because of her remarkable family.

NOTES

1   This anecdote is recorded in very many places, e.g. Russell Thorndike, 'Lilian Baylis: As I Knew Her' in Sybil and Russell Thorndike, *Lilian Baylis* (London, 1938), p. 187. For Baylis's own comments on the incident see Chapter 10. When anecdotes exist in many versions I have adopted the practice of only providing one source, as some anecdotes turn up in the memoirs of almost every performer who ever appeared at the Vic.

2   Val May, 'Tribute to the Lady', typescript, National Theatre archive.

3   Maurice Evans, *All This ... and Evans Too! A Memoir* (Columbia, South Carolina, 1987), p. 79.

4   Ninette de Valois, *Come Dance With Me: A Memoir, 1898–1956* (London, 1957), p. 82.

5   When opera personnel tell this story Baylis wants tenors cheap. Russell Thorndike, 'Lilian Baylis', p. 126 records his version of the anecdote in relation to a First World War *Henry V*.

6   Malcolm Baker-Smith, 'Lilian Baylis: A Portrait of a Great Lady', BBC radio 1952. Beatrice Wilson also feels confident that some

of Baylis's 'famous gaffes' were 'to keep up her reputation and to amuse people': see her contribution to Harcourt Williams, *Vic-Wells: the Work of Lilian Baylis* (London, 1938), p. 11.

7   Jacky Bratton, *New Readings in Theatre History* (Cambridge, 2003), p. 102.

8   Ibid., p. 119.

9   Paula R. Backscheider, *Reflections on Biography* (Oxford, 1999, reprinted 2001), p. 110.

10   See, for example, Lilian Baylis, 'Myself When Young', c. 1936, OVLB/000157 (unpaginated autobiographical essay dictated to Annette Prevost) and 'Autobiography', c. 1936, OVLB/000156 (unpaginated autobiographical essay dictated to Annette Prevost).

11   OV/M/000057/1–2 is a letter from Cicely Hamilton to Prevost dated 23 December 1937 in which Hamilton acknowledges that Prevost was 'engaged in collecting material for an autobiography at the time of dear friend's death' and suggests that they collaborate; however, Hamilton insists that she won't 'butt in'. The Vic-Wells governors' minutes for 10 December 1937 discuss the matter.

12   Annette Prevost did produce a two-page article entitled 'A Great Lady and her People: Lilian Baylis and the Vic-Wells Era' for *Country Life* in 1974. Richard Findlater, *Lilian Baylis: The Lady of the Old Vic* (London, 1975), p. 12 states that Prevost did not write the biography because of the illness of her husband George Chamberlain.

13   At Prevost's death, in 1983, the archive went to the Royal Victoria Hall Foundation and most of it is now on loan to the Theatre Collection, Bristol University. Some personal effects, such as appointments diaries, however, are lodged in the Mander and Mitchenson Theatre Collection.

14   Findlater, *Lilian Baylis*, p. 12. The archive at Bristol is, of course, much easier to use now it has been catalogued.

15   See ibid., pp. 15–16. The letter offering Prevost her appointment is dated 29 August 1932 (OV/M/000041/1).

16   Liebe's main detractors are Richard Findlater, and Tyrone Guthrie in 'A Portrait and Two Profiles: Lilian Baylis', *In Various Directions: A View of Theatre* (London, 1965). Rosemary Auchmuty first suggested that Baylis's relationships with lesbian women should be studied but did not investigate the Baylis archive. See 'By Their Friends We Shall Know Them: The Lives and Networks of Some Women in North Lambeth, 1880–1940'

in Lesbian History Group (ed.), *Not a Passing Phase: Reclaiming Lesbians in History 1840–1985* (London, 1989).

17 Thomas Postlewait, 'Autobiography and Theatre History' in Thomas Postlewait and Bruce A. McConachie (eds.), *Interpreting the Theatrical Past: Essays in the Historiography of Performance* (Iowa, 1989), p. 259. See Maggie Gale and Viv Gardner, *Auto/biography and Identity: Women, Theatre and Performance* (Manchester, 2004) for a recent discussion of the particular issues that arise in relation to women theatre workers' autobiographical writing. Gale and Gardner (p. 2) survey important work in the field but still note the comparative lack of work looking 'at autobiographical writing in relation to women actors' or other female theatre workers' lives'.

18 Joan Littlewood, *Joan's Book: Joan Littlewood's Peculiar History as She Tells It* (London, 1995), p. 51.

19 Ibid., pp. 57–8. Littlewood spoke of her memories of Milton at the Vic in an interview with the author in June 1996.

20 See, for example, Norman Marshall in 'Lilian Baylis and the Old Vic', a chapter in his *The Other Theatre*, 2nd impression (London, 1948), which offers a history of theatres Marshall applauds for their risk-taking and experimental qualities.

21 See, for example, Lilian Baylis, interviewed in 'The Theatre of To-day and To-morrow: Lilian Baylis Wants An Old Vic in Each Town', *Era*, 5 September 1934.

[2]

Beginnings: 'Housing and Music, Music and Housing'[1]

In an autobiographical essay entitled 'Myself When Young', Baylis is in no doubt as to the major influences on her during childhood: social housing and music. In asserting this fact Baylis is also signalling who she considered to be the most important people in her life during her early years: 'housing' meant the influence of her aunt Emma Cons; 'music' meant the influence of her parents Newton and Liebe Baylis. In later life Baylis would claim Emma Cons as the more important influence, and one anecdote that Baylis enjoyed telling about her early life emphasises this. In 1881, Queen Victoria's cousin, Princess Frederica of Hanover, visited the Vic, then managed by Emma Cons. The seven-year-old Baylis was chosen by her aunt to present a bouquet to the Princess. Baylis did not believe that the Princess was really a princess because she was dressed in black, in mourning, so she insisted on presenting the bouquet to a lady-in-waiting, who was dressed in what Baylis considered to be a proper princess colour, pink.[2] A week later one of the official guests, Canon Horsley, met Baylis again and, half-recognising her, asked who she was: Baylis replied that she was 'Auntie's niece'.[3] And in many ways, as manager of the Vic, Baylis *was* Emma Cons's niece, disciple and heir. However, she was also Liebe Baylis's daughter and even when she was most in denial about her mother's achievements, Baylis was still reacting to her mother's life choices, often by trying to do the complete opposite.

Lilian Mary Baylis was born on 9 May 1874 at 19 Nottingham Street, Marylebone, London, the eldest child of Elizabeth Baylis, née Cons, who usually called herself Liebe or Libby. Liebe was a professional singer, a contralto and pianist, whose professional debut at Margate was followed by a year-long tour of the UK and Ireland with Clarance Holt, the actor, manager and entrepreneur.[4] In this entertainment, which was entitled 'A Night with Dickens and Shakespeare', Liebe played the piano and sang in between Holt's appearance as, amongst others, Shylock, Hamlet, Macbeth, Jaques, Touchstone and Mark Antony. After this tour ended in 1873, Liebe married. Her marriage to Newton Baylis resulted in ten full-term pregnancies in fifteen years, yet remarkably Liebe managed to keep her career as a musical performer and teacher going despite her fluctuating health and the emotional trauma associated with the deaths of four babies and her seven-year-old son, Francis.[5] In persisting with her career, however, Liebe was flouting convention as well as putting huge pressure on herself, and it is hardly surprising that Baylis, who as the eldest child was first in line when help was needed, had a complex relationship with Liebe. Baylis describes her mother as temperamental: servants often left, and Baylis had to look after her younger brothers and sisters in what 'was never a tranquil household'.[6] Baylis's claim that Liebe had 'scant time for the care of her young family' is probably true:[7] Liebe's music teaching would have meant less time focused on her family, but her passion for music did mean that she ensured all her children received enthusiastic and rigorous musical tuition from an early age. As they progressed in their music studies, the children also frequently performed in orchestras made up of Liebe's pupils, who regularly demonstrated their skills in exhibition concerts, and Baylis's first solo performance as a singer took place when she was five years old.[8]

Liebe's more pragmatic side as a mother perhaps can be seen in the Baylis family's decision to send two of their six children, Violet and Ray (then aged thirteen and nine), to live with Liebe's childless elder sister, Esther Forrest, and her husband, Robert, in Western Australia.[9] This decision carried with it the serious possibility that Liebe and Newton might never see Violet and Ray again, although in 1889 the Baylis family were considering following their two children to Western Australia, and Newton Baylis was thinking about applying for work there.[10] Initially it was Baylis's aunt Eliza who in 1888 had been invited to Australia by Robert Forrest to look after her sister Esther, 'a lover of horses and a keen horsewoman' who had 'unfortunately met with an accident whilst out riding and seriously injured her back'.[11] Since Eliza was caring for Violet and Ray at this time, the invitation was extended to include them. By the standards of the day, for Liebe and Newton Baylis to send two of their children to live with wealthy but childless relatives was not aberrant behaviour: Robert Forrest owned the Koombana Flour Mill, whilst his family was one of the most powerful and influential in Australia at the time. Indeed, Esther Forrest's brother-in-law, Sir John Forrest (later first Baron of Bunbury and the first native-born Australian to become a baron), was at various stages of his career acting premier of the state of Western Australia and acting Prime Minister when Alfred Deakin was overseas.[12]

Deciphering Liebe's relationship with her eldest daughter Lilian is also complicated by the fact that on some occasions Baylis blamed Liebe for the paralysis that clearly marked Baylis's face and gave her mouth a lopsided look. Working in a profession where most women were expected to be conventionally beautiful, Baylis was always acutely aware of this disfigurement. At various times and to various people Baylis related several, completely mutually exclusive accounts of how this paralysis originated. Most of these narratives have the paralysis resulting from some kind of trauma, often from a dangerous swimming incident. In one account Baylis claims the paralysis took hold on a seaside holiday at Broadstairs in Kent. Baylis got into difficulties swimming, was ill afterwards, and Liebe decided not to pay for a doctor.[13] On other occasions, however, Baylis blamed the paralysis on losing consciousness in a rough sea in South Africa; on falling off a bicycle; on an encounter with a South African murderer; on the disappearance (and presumed death) of her ex-fiancé.[14] It seems as if Baylis, always an inveterate performer, could not resist playing to individual audiences with gusto, and supplying whichever version of events she thought would best fit a particular audience at a particular time.

It is in this love of performance, and in the emphasis in Baylis's education on practical music, that Liebe's influence is most apparent. Baylis often characterised herself as uneducated and claimed that she felt handicapped by this. Certainly she was particularly prickly and defensive in the company of people she felt were better educated than she was. In fact, the Baylis family did have the benefit of a governess, whom they shared with the children of a Mrs Jones, and Baylis learnt some German and French.[15] As a robustly church-centred family, the young Baylises also engaged in Bible studies, which necessarily entailed a good standard of literacy, and Baylis intermittently attended St Augustine's school, Kilburn. Nevertheless, under Liebe's auspices music did dominate Baylis's education and created an imbalance.

When she was seven Baylis began learning the violin and was being groomed for public performance. Her first teacher was a retired 'regimental band-master', named Holst, and she then became a pupil of John Tiplady Carrodus, who from 1869 until his death in 1895 played principal first violin at Covent Garden.[16] Carrodus was famous for setting extremely high standards in his own playing and in that of his pupils, and for improving the standard of string playing in English orchestras of his time.[17] Baylis's tuition with him continued until her family left for South Africa in 1891.[18] Before long Baylis's musical studies had progressed rapidly enough for her to begin supervising her mother's pupils doing piano practice, particularly scales (which the pupils predictably hated). By the age of eleven she was teaching her own violin pupils, she began regularly playing in concerts and became involved in what she claims to be the first of its kind, a Ladies' Orchestra; and at sixteen she was teaching violin at a school in Croydon.[19] Her education might not have been comprehensive, but musically speaking Baylis was learning fast, in performances and concerts as well as in classes. Five days after her twelfth birthday, in 1886, she was reviewed in *The Stage* magazine. The critic describes Baylis and her nine-year-old brother Willie as 'two mere children' and comments of their execution of the 'violin soli from *The Barber of Seville* and *Faust*' that 'though they both gave some signs of promise, they are not yet sufficiently capable to appear in public'.[20] By November *The Stage* is applauding Baylis's 'marked improvement' and, in 1890, is describing her as 'a clever young lady' who 'sang with much spirit and expression "In Old Madrid"'.[21] Once Baylis was competent enough Liebe also started delegating considerable responsibility to her: if two bookings were in the offing, Liebe led one concert party and Baylis, from her early teens, led the other. It is small wonder that Baylis matured quickly, and she looked so much older than her years that she had to carry documentation to ensure she could get a half fare on the train from the age of twelve.[22]

Something of the strength of the affection between mother and daughter can perhaps be gauged from letters written by Liebe to Baylis during the late 1890s, early in their first lengthy separation. Baylis, then aged twenty-three, had left her parents in South Africa and returned to England: she was recuperating from an operation, but she and her younger sister Ethel also wanted to get away from what was quite clearly beginning to turn into all-out war between British and Dutch South Africans. During the South African War, Liebe wrote frequently to Baylis and Ethel, even though it was extremely difficult to get letters through in war conditions. In her replies Baylis signs herself 'Ever your loving daughter',[23] while Liebe's letters are addressed to 'Dearest Lil', 'Dear Child', 'Dear Lilian' and are invariably signed 'Your Affectionate Mother'. The tone suggests love and respect between mother and daughter. Liebe is concerned about her children's health and in one letter anxiously instructs her son Willie, who was then in another part of South Africa, to look after himself, adding, 'I know the girls are all right as Aunties will see after *them*.'[24] However, it was perhaps inevitable that during this period of separation (which lasted seventeen years, until 1914) that Liebe's influence on Baylis would begin to wane. Meanwhile, as she lived and worked alongside Emma Cons, Baylis really started becoming 'Auntie's niece'.

When Baylis's then elderly parents returned to England in 1914, with the start of the First World War, they had been living in South Africa for twenty-three years. Their daughter was running the Vic single-handedly, and was about to embark on a major period of empire building. Baylis records, 'In the spring of 1914 my mother lost the sight of one eye and was told her only chance of saving the other was to leave South Africa and return at once to England for a special operation.'[25] An additional consideration may have been Liebe's German nationality (her paternal family were German and Liebe was born in Hanover). This had proved a great advantage during the South African War, when Liebe had far greater freedom of movement than her English husband, but in 1914 German nationality had the potential to prove embarrassing. Returning 'home' to Britain, where two of her children – Ethel and Ray – were in military service, was circumspect.[26]

From 1914 on Liebe and Newton would depend on Baylis's support for the rest of their lives; they were no longer the reckless adventurers or indeed the performers they had once been when they set off to South Africa, but they both worked hard for the Vic. Indeed, during the First World War, when Sybil Thorndike was busy combining childbirth with playing Shakespeare leads at the Vic, she remembers the support Liebe offered her and that she 'was very kind when I was a bit off colour'.[27] Given her own experiences of trying to keep a career going through successive childbirths, Liebe could presumably sympathise with Thorndike's predicament.

Liebe's determination to persist with her career as a performer and teacher, rather than to succumb to Victorian ideals of domesticated womanhood, was very much in keeping with the ethos of her immediate family. The Cons sisters were all professional women who did not let traditional notions of decorous feminine behaviour stand in the way of their success. Liebe's four elder sisters were all career-minded: Esther, the eldest, who emigrated to Fremantle, Western Australia, in 1869, worked as a teacher before settling in Bunbury and marrying Robert Forrest in 1875; Eliza (Lila) worked as a clerk before travelling to South Africa then finally settling in Western Australia, where she founded a mission to seamen; Emma was an artist, social worker, suffrage worker and local government adviser, and effectively the founder of the remodelled Vic; Ellen (Nell) tended to live in Emma's shadow, but worked with her sister and provided vital support for her, living with her until Emma's death in 1912. The Cons sisters were hard-working, and inculcated with a very strong sense of duty towards those less fortunate than themselves. Their attitudes, their social awareness and their pragmatic feminism were all absorbed by the young Baylis.

As a child, Baylis spent a great deal of time with Emma and Ellen Cons. Every time Liebe was due to give birth, Baylis went to stay with her aunts, but she also went on holidays with them. On one holiday her life was saved by Ellen Cons, who, seeing Baylis fall into the sea from a breakwater where she was playing with her doll and buckets and supposedly being supervised by a nursemaid, immediately dashed into the sea to rescue the child, despite being unable to swim herself. Both aunt and niece were swept out to sea and high drama ensued as a rescue was mounted.[28] Baylis also became accustomed from a very early age to accompanying Emma and Ellen to committee meetings on social housing.[29] These meetings were often held in very wealthy London homes, and were dominated by unmarried career women of great determination who were dedicated to improving the appalling slums of London. One house Baylis visited very often as a child was that of the leading housing reformer, co-founder of the National Trust, and radical social worker Octavia Hill. At Hill's home, Baylis would sit in the housekeeper's sitting room while the Cons sisters and Hill planned rent collection, the acquisition of new buildings, or trips for tenants to the countryside to pick flowers to sell. Baylis vividly remembers sitting with her 'dolls and picture books' while slum management was discussed around her. Baylis didn't understand everything that was said but it is clear she was not impervious to the debates: once her aunts and their friends were discussing how to help a woman whose baby had measles and who was worried her other children would catch the potentially lethal disease. Although Baylis had no idea what the word 'isolation' meant, her doll immediately developed measles and went into isolation just as her aunts had suggested the woman's baby should. Perhaps the crucial point is that from an early age Baylis learnt to take for granted the idea that energetic and committed women could put the world to rights.

In a letter of 18 December 1900 Liebe mused, 'it is strange that a Family so divided in different parts of the world should all be mixed up in musical and philanthropical affairs'.[30] However, there is considerable evidence that there were also major differences of opinion within the Cons family, whose passionate commitment, directness and sheer energy probably made family disagreements almost inevitable. Such disagreements may be the reason that the Cons sisters had nothing to do with their brothers, Frederick and Charles, and in this Baylis followed her aunts' lead. In rough notes made around 1910, Baylis records that 'The Pianoforte makers at Camden Town must be my uncle Frederick Cons, we know nothing of them. My uncle Charles Cons died about 2 or 3 years ago and left some children I believe.'[31] Baylis's lack of interest in her uncles is all the more remarkable given the fact that at various times she did try to assemble information about her family antecedents: she claims in her notes that prison reformer Elizabeth Fry was called 'Aunt' by 'Grannie' and that railway engineer Robert Stephenson was 'Grannie's cousin'.[32]

'Grannie' was Esther Cons, née Goodair, who was descended from rich industrialists from Manchester and Chorley. She was 'the daughter of a mill-owner and cotton-spinner' whose home had been attacked by the Luddites, and in 1926 Baylis published an account of how Esther Goodair's mother

> received the news that the mills had been set on fire and the mob was making for the house. The old coachman hurried the family into the carriage – and as they drove over the brow of the hill, they looked back to see their home in flames.[33]

The Goodair family connection included a coincidence. Baylis's cousin, Colonel Goodair of Ashton Park, Lancashire, married a daughter of Victorian actor-manager Samuel Phelps: it was Phelps who in the mid nineteenth century resurrected the Sadler's Wells Theatre, the theatre Baylis was to reopen in 1931.

During Baylis's childhood 'Grannie' lived with her daughters Emma, Ellen and Liebe, after the death of her husband Frederick Cons senior in 1870. Frederick had shown great promise early in his career: he came from a family of reputable piano manufacturers, he made a good living for a significant part of his life and he 'made the ivories for most of the first English pianos'.[34] Baylis proudly records Frederick's ingenuity when he and a fellow apprentice, John Brinsmead, set about making a new prototype piano (which eventually became the first Brinsmead piano) in the basement kitchen of Frederick's home. On suddenly realising they would not be able to move the piano out by the kitchen door, the young men heaved up paving stones in the pavement outside in order to get it through the kitchen window.[35] At some stage Frederick experienced a major reversal in fortune, lost his money and, in Baylis's words, 'became an invalid and remained so until his death'.[36]

Overall, the Cons family background offered Baylis a combination of northern industrial wealth, feminist working women, and musical instrument manufacture. The Cons family were full of adventurous, outspoken and occasionally conflicting personalities. The family were very proud of their German origins, and they preserved the passport that permitted their forefather Elias Konss to move from Germany to England, via France, in the eighteenth century. Liebe, sensibly, often deployed the German spelling of her maiden name for performance publicity, thus exploiting the contemporary association between Germanness and musical genius.

While the Cons sisters were clearly the dominant influence on Baylis as a young girl, the Baylis family input was also important and the family's various claims to fame are carefully documented in notes made by Baylis's father, Newton.[37] Newton's father, William, was a jeweller in London; his paternal grandfather, from Gloucester, had made a lot of money in the jewellery business but 'fooled it away in his old age'.[38] On his maternal side Newton claimed that his great-grandfather was an Irish gentleman, Carter, who was supposedly involved in the 'old rebellion' of Bonnie Prince Charlie. After the Jacobite collapse, Carter had to leave the country but he was reputed to have run the Southampton Arms in Mornington Crescent near Camden Town, which, in those days, was a country hotel.

What was crucial about the Baylis family's influence on Lilian Baylis was that Newton and his mother Mary, after whom Lilian Mary Baylis was named, were passionate about music. Newton was an enthusiastic baritone singer, who worked as a book-keeper for Gillows furniture business for eighteen years but yearned to make his living by professional performance. His mother Mary

> was a clever musical and literary amateur. She was in the chorus of the first Handel Festival also for years a member of John Hullah's Choir at all his Oratorio concerts at the Old St Martin's Choir and as a child of 6 [Newton] began to attend them all.[39]

Mary Baylis also connected with the world of theatre because of her very close friendship with the famous actress Fanny Stirling and the novelist and playwright Charles Reade.

Newton describes his mother, Fanny Stirling and Charles Reade as 'inseparable pals' and claims 'almost all Reade's books and plays were read and criticised by my mother before they were printed'. While Stirling had had a successful career as an actress before she met Reade, she became particularly famous for her comic performance as Peg Woffington in *Masks and Faces*, originally acted in 1852, which Reade wrote and developed as a vehicle for her. Newton claimed that both his 'father and mother were present at the original reading of the play by Charles Reade, to Mrs Stirling and Mr. Ben Webster'. Stirling, however, was Bohemian company for a respectable jeweller and his wife: Reade was only one of many men who besieged Stirling, and although she had separated from her husband around 1838–9, she had had a daughter in 1842 and later lived for many years with the eminent civil engineer Sir Charles Hutton Gregory before marrying him not long before her death in 1895.[40] Newton benefited from his mother's friendship with Stirling when he chose not to follow his father and grandfather into the jewellery business but instead became an articled engineer working for Gregory.

Newton Baylis built up his musical experience by singing enthusiastically in many church choirs, particularly at All Saints Margaret Street, just off Oxford Street.[41] While church choirs are by definition amateur, doing their work for love, All Saints was no ordinary church. It was the centre of the Oxford Movement, which worked for a Catholic revival in the Church of England and was distinguished not only by its High Church ceremony and ritual but also by its rigorous standards in the performance of music.[42] Baylis herself always tended towards the Anglo-Catholic end of the Anglican church spectrum, but it was probably All Saints's musical reputation which attracted Newton Baylis to the church where he and Liebe were married and where their first eight children were christened.[43]

Newton met Liebe Cons when 'she studied at the L[ondon] A[cademy] of M[usic] three days a week and School of Art three days' before she 'finally decided on the musical profession'.[44] After his marriage, Newton supplemented the family income by promoting, managing and participating in Liebe's concert parties, which performed at venues as diverse as cathedrals, churches, lunatic asylums, servants' halls, workhouses, lung hospitals, tennis parties, embassies and aristocratic socials, and visited 'almost every cathedral city in England and most of the big towns'.[45] Newton estimates that his family's concert party played in twenty-eight different lunatic asylums, which he regarded as providing particularly good audiences.[46] The use of music and drama for both entertainment and therapy in the treatment of asylum inmates was becoming more popular at this period, and the Baylis family were part of this initiative, although they were not sentimental about playing to patients. Newton breezily records mixing with patients at private asylums and 'often having letters given us to deliver to friends outside, which we took and afterwards destroyed'.[47] The concert party's repertoire included ballads, instrumentals, excerpts from operettas, and Gilbert and Sullivan. Occasionally the party went as far as a full costume recital of an opera; for example, an early success was a costume recital of Flotow's *Martha.* Several incidents from these asylum tours appealed very much to Newton and he made great efforts to record them, sometimes writing down the same anecdote over and over as if to get the narration just right: once, because of a mix-up with a doorman, Newton was nearly mistaken for a patient and locked in an asylum himself;

The Gypsy Revellers (before 1890). Lilian Baylis is second from right, back row. Willie Baylis is on the left holding the cello. Liebe Baylis is seated second from right next to the toddler, Ethel Baylis. Courtesy of the Royal Victoria Hall Foundation and the University of Bristol Theatre Collection

one patient the family played to had been involved in a notorious divorce case; one doctor they dealt with paid them twice, so they voted him 'a real good Mad Doctor'; another doctor, at Hanwell, went mad himself.[48]

The importance of professional performance in Baylis's early years becomes even clearer with the history of the Gypsy Revellers. This concert group was started by Liebe and Newton in 1889 and it employed, amongst others, Lilian, Willie and Ethel Baylis. The Gypsy Revellers enjoyed fashionable status for a while at high-society engagements and became, according to Baylis, the 'rage' of the London season. The group dressed in what they described as eighteenth-century Neapolitan Gypsy costume and performed 'Gypsy' music and dances, accompanied by violin, cello, mandolin and guitar. The party size ranged from six to twenty and Newton recounts that 'we worked this show successfully for 2 seasons and in 1891 took it to S[outh] A[frica]'.[49]

Perhaps the most prestigious Gypsy Revellers concert took place in Piccadilly in June 1890, where the audience included the Prince of Wales, the future Edward VII. The event was a party given by the Duke of Devonshire, and it was reported in newspapers of the time. Newton himself describes one incident enthusiastically:

> We were placed in a charming dell in the grounds. The Scots Guard band ... on the steps near the house played a selection off and on with us when they finished we did a turn down in the ground and when we finished they did another there were 3000 to 4000 guests including various foreign Ambassadors and diplomats in London. Edward (then Prince of Wales), and Princess Alexandra came down the grounds to hear us, there was a sort of impromptu reception in front of us, it was very curious that the Prince and Princess arrived by us as we were singing Glover's Gypsies Laughing Song ... Miss Lilian Baylis was singing a solo bit and our girls whispered to her, bow Lilian but she did not notice the royalty – then I sang a solo "I am your King"... and while doing so I looked the Prince of Wales full in the face – he laughed heartily at the fun of it.[50]

While it is difficult now to establish precisely how good the Gypsy Revellers were, the group would not have secured and survived high-society engagements like this one if they had not performed at least competently.[51] Contemporary reviews differ in their assessments, and this may reflect whether the Gypsy Revellers were present in force, performing a single concert, or splitting resources and doing two concerts at the same time. One reviewer, in the *Era*, certainly encountered the Gypsy Revellers in crisis management mode at Ladbroke Hall:[52] when the concert was due to start, the main concert party were still at a garden party in Dulwich. Newton Baylis had to keep the show – and some music – going until the rest of the Gypsy Revellers arrived and were ready to perform. The newspaper comments that the 'scenes from gypsy life' were 'idealised a little, of course' but the reporter seems to have enjoyed the entertainment. On another occasion the Gypsy Revellers became stranded in Chester, when the local performer with whom they were sharing the bill 'cleared off' with the takings; then most of the grown-ups in the party had

Newton Baylis in old age. Courtesy
of the Mander and Mitchenson
Theatre Collection

to pretend to be children in
order to get back to London on
children's fares, as they didn't
have enough money for adult
tickets.53 Meanwhile Baylis
became used to playing the
audience like a professional,
unfazed by any event, not
necessarily the most consummate
performer of her generation, but
determined to entertain, and that,
come what may, the show *would* go on.

Baylis's experiences as a Gypsy Reveller
clearly fed into her shoestring theatrical management style,
but in addition the operas that furnished songs and
instrumentals for the Gypsy Revellers and Konss-Baylis concert
parties were those that dominated early operatic performances
at the Vic. Most of these works – 'light' or ballad operas such as
The Bohemian Girl – are no longer performed, but Baylis felt
confident from her concert experiences that they would be
popular with Vic audiences. A context, if not an excuse, for the
sometimes unreasonable demands Baylis made of her
performers at the Vic is also provided by the sometimes
punishing performance and teaching schedules of her own
teenage years. For example, in one day Baylis had three
engagements: she started at Brighton Aquarium in the
afternoon, then caught a cab and train to Victoria and played
at a big church charity concert, and finally went on to an
Embassy reception at 11 p.m. as a Gypsy Reveller. She was back
again in Brighton for an engagement the next day.54 On
another occasion, Baylis was due to play violin at the People's
Palace:

> The performers were conveyed to Mile End in one of the
> old "knifeboard" horse buses, and the child violinist, of

course, chose to sit on the top next the driver – and had to run the gamut of rotten apples and tomatoes cheerfully flung at the then unexpected apparition of a bus among the stalls in the Mile End road.[55]

Baylis claims that 'in the season my mother, brother and I as a trio often made three appearances in 24 hours' and describes her voice as 'a small, but quite pleasant, soprano' which she accompanied on the 'guitar or the banjo'.[56]

Another Vic legacy from the training ground of Baylis's early performing career was the notorious deputy system, which Baylis had been used to from a very early age. If a musician was offered a last-minute engagement that was better paid (which was not difficult given the rates of pay Baylis offered at the Vic), they could arrange to send a deputy to perform at their original engagement. The problems inherent in this system are obvious – the deputies had to learn tempo on the job, they would be under-rehearsed, not used to the orchestra they were playing with and perhaps not used to the venue. Yet even as late as 1930 Baylis was still using the system and declaring, 'Unfortunately, it will be quite impossible to pay the orchestra the doubled salaries demanded by the Musicians' Union if the "deputy" system is to be eliminated.'[57] The deputy system encouraged a nerve-racking, 'we'll-get-by' approach to performance which prevailed at the Vic until very late in Baylis's reign there, and there is a fund of anecdotes based on last-minute dashes across London to cope with sudden crises. In one story, the actress Beatrice Wilson was asked to play Viola in *Twelfth Night* at a moment's notice because Viola Tree, who was playing the part, had suddenly fallen ill. Wilson suggested that she should play Olivia instead of Viola – as Olivia's first entrance comes later in the play. She then raced across London, without any dinner, and arrived at the Vic minutes before curtain up. She dashed onstage in costume just in time for Olivia's first cue.[58] Beatrice Wilson's account stresses the kindness and care offered to her by Baylis in this emergency and it seems almost churlish to point out that an effective understudy system would have reduced the need for Wilson's heroics.

Other childhood experiences may have helped Baylis develop a cool head in a crisis. In one autobiographical essay Newton Baylis reflects 'I may say I have led a somewhat adventurous life', but although he was thinking here of his time in South Africa, Newton records plenty of hair-raising adventures before the family left England.[59] For example, one family holiday was disrupted when the train the Baylises were travelling on was involved in a serious accident at Sittingbourne. The corpses of those killed were laid out in the waiting room, Liebe's dress was covered in blood, the children were understandably upset and the next passing train was not prepared to stop and rescue the marooned survivors. Newton, in effect, had to hijack the train and make it stop to pick up his family.[60]

Overall, life for Baylis as a child seems to have been slightly chaotic, full of variety, unpredictable, and, as she herself stresses, dominated by music and housing. When she was seventeen, however, her life suddenly changed completely; social housing receded as an influence and music took over completely when the Gypsy Revellers left England and went off to tour South Africa.

NOTES

1   Baylis, 'Myself When Young'. OV/M/000073 suggests this essay was commissioned by Frederick Miller Publishers.
2   Baylis, 'Autobiography'.
3   Lilian Baylis, 'Emma Cons, the Founder of the Vic' in Cicely Hamilton, *The Old Vic* (London, 1926), p. 251.
4   Holt (1826–1904) made his London debut in 1843 but performed successfully in Australia and New Zealand before running the Duke's Theatre, London (1878–80), and touring Theatre Royal, Drury Lane melodramas.
5   Liebe's pregnancies followed in quick succession. She gave birth to: 1874 Lilian Mary Baylis; 1875 Violet Esther Baylis; 1877 William Robert Baylis; 1879 Ray Hope Newton Baylis; 1880 Margery Alice Baylis (died 1880); 1881 Hugh Dean Baylis (died 1883); 1883 Francis Baylis (died 1890); 1886 Arnold Newton Baylis (died 1886); 1887 Herbert Aidan Baylis (died 1888); 1889 Ethel May Baylis. Seven-year-old Francis Baylis's death is

recorded in Liebe's diary for 16 February 1890 (M&M) and she cancelled engagements in the wake of this event.

6   Baylis, 'Autobiography'. Baylis adopted a more supportive attitude towards the challenges facing working mothers when she confided to Louise Morgan, in *Everyman* 22 April 1933, that one of her ambitions 'has always been to have a crèche'.

7   Baylis, 'Myself When Young'.

8   Baylis, 'Autobiography'. The *OVM* for October 1919 states that Baylis was seven, that the party was in Drury Lane and that her first professional engagement was three years later.

9   At this stage young Francis Baylis was still alive so the children remaining with Liebe and Newton were Lilian, Willie, Francis and Ethel. Violet is not listed on the family musical bills, but Verna Glossop's history of the Baylis family in Australia describes Violet as 'Possessed of a very good singing voice' and someone who 'gave a lot of pleasure as a soloist at many concerts' (OVEC/000269).

10   OVEC/000072. Liebe and Newton were reunited with Ray when he was in England serving during the First World War.

11   OVEC/000269, p. 3.

12   Colonial prejudice has resulted in the high status of Baylis's Australian relatives by marriage, the Forrests, being insufficiently appreciated in most discussions of her life, but when Baylis visited Australia in 1910 (see Chapter 5), she was wined and dined by some of the most powerful people in the country.

13   The commonest retrospective diagnosis is that Baylis suffered from Bell's palsy, which usually clears up, without treatment, after a couple of weeks. With Baylis, however, the disfigurement was permanent.

14   Findlater, *Lilian Baylis*, p. 82 surveys these stories.

15   Baylis, 'Autobiography'.

16   Baylis, 'Myself When Young'.

17   For Carrodus see Stanley Sadie (ed.), *The New Grove Dictionary of Music and Musicians*, 20 vols. (London, 1980).

18   Baylis, 'Autobiography'.

19   Ibid.

20   *The Stage*, 14 May 1886. Reviews are collected in the scrapbooks OVEC/000111 and 112.

21   *The Stage*, 12 November 1886, 25 July 1890.

22   Baylis, 'Myself When Young'.

23   The only letters by Baylis to her parents from this period that

have survived are those that were returned to sender as mail was
suspended (OVLB/000025/1, 2).

24 OVLB/000012/3.

25 OVLB/000139, p. 2.

26 See OVLB/000012/2 for Liebe's discussion of her German
nationality.

27 Quoted in Peter Roberts, *Lilian Baylis Centenary Festival 1974:
Souvenir Programme* (London, 1974), p. 17.

28 Baylis, 'Autobiography'.

29 Baylis, 'Myself When Young'. Information in the following
paragraph is taken from this document.

30 OVLB/000012/20.

31 OVLB/000101/2 – Baylis's notes are made on the back of a
letter from John J. Myres.

32 OVLB/000101. I have been unable to corroborate these claims.

33 Baylis, 'Emma Cons', pp. 255–6.

34 OVEC/000232/2.

35 Baylis, 'Emma Cons', p. 255. For John Brinsmead (1814–1908),
who founded his piano making firm in Windmill St, London, in
1835, see Sadie (ed.), *The New Grove Dictionary of Music and
Musicians*. As Frederick Cons was born in 1810, the two men
would have been close in age.

36 Baylis, 'Emma Cons', p. 257. The illness is unknown and
Frederick's death is not recorded in the General Register,
although he was buried with some dignity in the family tomb in
Highgate Cemetery (Findlater, *Lilian Baylis*, p. 37). A will made
by Frederick in 1853 (OVEC/000139) indicates he was still
then a man of substance. Letters from a Cons family cousin,
Julia Pfeiler (OVEC/000218), indicate his family's grief at
Frederick's death in 1870.

37 Newton was christened Edward William Baylis but, according to
Findlater, *Lilian Baylis* (p. 67), used Newton as a stage name
because he claimed descent from Isaac Newton.

38 Information on Newton's family in this paragraph is taken from
OVLB/000029/1, a letter from Newton dated 13 December
1912.

39 OVEC/000001. Information in this paragraph is all taken from
this document. Hullah (1812–84) was a friend of Charles
Dickens and devised a new method of teaching music which
became very popular in the 1840s and adopted in many schools
(see Sadie (ed.), *The New Grove Dictionary of Music and
Musicians*).

40 'Victorian Notes' by B[en] G[reet], programme for *Richard III*, March 1918. See also Percy Allen, *The Stage Life of Mrs. Stirling: With Some Sketches of the Nineteenth Century Theatre* (London, 1922) for information about Fanny Stirling.

41 Newton also sang in the choir at St Augustine's, Queensgate, where he was directed by Lisson, a particularly well-respected choirmaster.

42 The church was designed by William Butterfield, had its foundation stone laid in 1850 by Dr Edward Pusey, and was consecrated in 1859. The church was thus from the beginning associated with the Puseyite movement.

43 OVLB/000139, p. 1.

44 OVEC/000001.

45 Baylis, 'Autobiography'.

46 As evidence Newton cites the fact that after a performance of Grossmith's *Cups and Saucers*, he and Liebe were surprised one day when an 'attentive and appreciative' lunatic asylum audience at Hanwell laughed on a line where they had never got a laugh before. When Newton examined the script afterwards he found what he describes as 'a fine bit of veiled humour' that he'd never spotted previously (OVEC/000001). Liebe's engagements diary for 1890 (M&M) contains details of bookings for that year as well as money received, expenditure, travelling expenses, etc.

47 OVEC/000001.

48 OVEC/000001. Irene Beeston describes Newton Baylis late in life as 'an indefatigable raconteur' (Harcourt Williams, *Vic-Wells*, p. 52).

49 OVEC/000001.

50 OVEC/000001.

51 Findlater, *Lilian Baylis* (p. 81) quotes from 'one senior citizen' in South Africa in the 1950s saying of the Gypsy Revellers: 'As musicians they were just mediocre – all right for those old mining-camp days, but they would not pass muster now.' The 'senior citizen' is discussing performances that took place sixty years earlier in the early 1890s. Closer to the time, in 1897, Harry Raymond, *B.I. Barnato: A Memoir* (London, 1897), p. 162 comments of white South African performance: 'the audience of diamond diggers was rough, but most critical.' Such audiences were hardly likely to be polite if they thought a performance below par.

52 *Era*, 19 July 1890.

53 OVEC/000001.

54 Baylis, 'Autobiography'.

55 *OVM*, March 1937.

56 Lilian Baylis, 'Prayer – and One's Hour of Destiny', *Daily Sketch*,
13 July 1931.

57 *OVM*, December 1930.

58 In Harcourt Williams, *Old Vic Saga* (London, 1949), p. 59.
Wilson's earliest rendition of this story (*OVM*, April 1933)
includes the detail that someone forced her 'to swallow a raw
egg' presumably to help her keep her energy up, and that Ellen
Terry was in the audience.

59 OVEC/000009/1.

60 OVEC/000009; Baylis, 'Autobiography'.

[3]

South Africa: Baylis's Adventures
1891–1897

> If anyone ever writes the life of Lilian Baylis, quite a big
> slice of it will have to be devoted to her girlhood's
> adventures in South Africa, because memories of it occupy
> so big a corner of her heart.[1]

South Africa gave Baylis her distinctive accent, which some
misrecognised as Cockney, and Baylis loved to talk about her
adventures there. Some of her stories were Rabelaisian, some
tended towards 'The Perils of Pauline', some were pure Mills
and Boon.[2] Forty years after the original events took place,
Baylis still enjoyed regaling listeners with tales of her life as a
pioneering heroine, the tough conditions she'd survived, and
the thrills and spills she had experienced in what was a
dangerous and contested outpost of the British Empire. When
she came to plan her autobiography, Baylis dictated extensive
notes on her life in South Africa, drawing heavily on family
journals and letters written to Baylis by her parents during the
turmoil of the South African War. By the time war finally broke
out, Baylis was back in London, but she clearly felt it was
important to document the dangers her parents faced, which,
if nothing else, would give an insight into the life she was
leading in London, full of anxiety, not knowing for long
periods if her mother, father and brother were still alive.

The South Africa Baylis lived in was a complex country, with
native Africans being dispossessed by British and Dutch
settlers, and vast fortunes being made by white men in
diamond fields and gold mines, particularly around
Johannesburg. Johannesburg itself was in the process of
growing rapidly from a tent city inhabited by miners equipped
with dynamite and guns into a more permanent, solid and

Lilian Baylis as a Gypsy Reveller, Johannesburg. Courtesy of the
Battye Library, (649B) Perth, W.A.

respectable settlement. Baylis remembered Johannesburg as a
town with only one two-storey house, and some of the Anglo-
South African mining communities she encountered were
dominated by bars and brothels.[3]

Newton and Liebe Baylis decided to go adventuring in
South Africa because the theatre impresario Ben Wheeler

offered them a nine-month contract for the Gypsy Revellers to tour the country. Wheeler engaged the Baylises on 15 August 1891 and the family of five – Liebe, Newton, Lilian, Ethel and Willie – plus five ladies and a tenor vocalist sailed for South Africa on the Roslyn Castle, which the family nicknamed 'the Rolling Castle' because the ship rolled so much it made everyone seasick.[4] They arrived in Cape Town on 2 September 1891, having spent much of the voyage keeping in practice by entertaining fellow passengers. They then travelled by steamer to Durban, where embarkation was 'in a basket sack' which was 'slung up and dropped on the deck of the steamer', which made all the girls scream.[5] They travelled on to Port Elizabeth and then 'up country', where the tour began.[6]

Ben Wheeler's planned tour was ambitious given that travelling in South Africa was often extremely difficult: distances between concerts were long, and communications were erratic. When the tour eventually ran into financial trouble, Wheeler offered every member of the company the choice of the fare back home to England or £40 in cash. The Baylis family stayed, while the rest of the Gypsy Revellers went home. Several factors could have affected the family's decision: Baylis herself was ill with gastric fever and thus unfit to travel; the family had rented out their London home as a furnished let and so they had no home to return to;[7] they also seem to have acquired a taste for touring the exciting and dangerous country they found themselves in. They decided to set off trekking around the country in bullock wagons, and they began performing in any makeshift theatre space they could find: pubs, a courthouse, a roller-skating rink.[8] Baylis recalls that she 'worked every town of any importance in South Africa ... I made a tour of most of the small towns and dorps, playing in the Court House or dining room of the only hotel if that was the largest room in the place.'[9] Profit was not so important: Newton Baylis commented that his family were delighted to make some money on their visit to Zululand, as they 'expected to cover expenses' and were willing to play not for profit but 'just to see Zululand'.[10]

Newton was the Baylis family's baritone, manager and publicist, and his journal records details of how the concert tours operated: he used to send advertisements ahead to the postmaster of the next town the Baylises were due to visit; the postmaster would arrange for 'native kaffirs riding bareback on Basuto ponies' to ride around handing out handbills; Newton himself 'went on about a week before and boomed up the show' and 'At our shows usually I used to sit at the receipt of customs and take the tickets & money for the first quarter of an hour or so while the overture was played & one or two numbers given.'[11] Young Ethel Baylis was particularly popular with her playing of the mandolin and her singing of 'little songs such as, "I'm called little buttercup", "I live with my grannie on yon little green"'; she once earned £10 in tips by singing 'I'm John the gentleman's son la-di-da' sitting on a hotel counter 'with her small top hat on', money which she spent on promotional photographs 'which she sold afterwards at the show'. The nine-year-old Ethel was also curious as to why, in one town, 'B.A.R.' was written on every window.[12]

In general the Baylis family displayed versatility and an energetic preparedness to cope in a crisis. Once, when arriving at the hotel where the Baylises were booked to play, the family found the proprietor and his family had rushed off to a gold field. After being served a very poor dinner by the skeleton staff left at the hotel, the young Lilian Baylis commandeered the kitchen, and ran it for the duration of the family stay.[13] Newton once even took a church service when the vicar didn't turn up.[14] Wagons frequently got stuck and had to be hauled out of the mud, and Newton estimated that, in total, he and his family covered about 4,000 miles in their travels playing to audiences that ranged from 'the roughest miners to S.A. millionaires'.[15]

Baylis describes how the family were

sometimes playing in the townships that were just beginning to flourish, while the natives crept to the side of their waggon entranced as they practised their classical trios round the camp fire. Mr. and Mrs. Baylis also did sketches (George Grossmith's "Cups and Saucers" was one of the most successful, and Mr. Grossmith, who was a great admirer of Mrs. Baylis, rehearsed it himself), operettas, and duets and trios from Gilbert and Sullivan operas.[16]

The image of 'natives' 'entranced' by classical trios is Victorian in its high colonial mindset, but these reminiscences are important in indicating how Baylis learnt hands-on theatre management, serving, in effect, an apprenticeship under her father in South Africa. Many of the publicity tactics Newton used became central later on to Baylis's approach to marketing the Vic. Her longstanding resistance to advertising in newspapers and her preference instead for relying on green bills, which contained details of the Vic repertory and which were handed out to all and sundry, could certainly be seen as a legacy from her days of touring South Africa.

The Baylises toured for a total of two years, although they sometimes settled for brief periods, and they made a special trip to Pretoria to see the arrival of the very first train there.[17] In 1892 Baylis took on an engagement to play violin in the orchestra for Miss Sidney's pantomime of *Beauty and the Beast*, which ran for around a month in Durban before moving on to Maritzburg. This production included Baylis appearing in her Neapolitan Gypsy dress for a palace scene, and it was during the run of *Beauty and the Beast* that, the story goes, Jack Webster, Baylis's fiancé, fell in love with her.[18]

Baylis's love life in South Africa is full of puzzles, but Jack Webster was undoubtedly important in her life for some time. A letter from Baylis written in 1893 and addressed to Jack's sister Harriet Webster in London confirms that she has just become engaged to Jack.[19] For many years Baylis owned a brooch containing the claws of the first lion killed by Jack Webster;[20] the claws were

> mounted on the first gold brought up, from a mine [Webster] prospected, on 9th May, 1893, and called The Birthday Mine in honour of Lilian Baylis, whose birthday it was. Webster was for 3½ years engaged to Lilian Baylis ... She broke off the engagement because she could not see herself as "a hausfrau on the Veld" ... Webster, broken-hearted, set out on a caravan with his young brother, but without escort. Neither has been heard of from that day to this. They are presumed ambushed and killed.[21]

Yet on her return to England Baylis gave this brooch away to

Harriet Webster, whom Baylis 'supported, financially and morally' and who often stayed with Baylis in London.[22]

A rather more startling account of Baylis's romantic adventures in South Africa, however, appeared in the *Star* in 1937, which describes

> a tempestuous and upsetting affair with an associate of Cecil Rhodes during her South African days.
>
> Now and then, in moments of intimacy, she would tell a tale or two about this brusque, masculine man who would wade across rivers with her flung across his shoulder.
>
> He wanted her to give up the stage and the concert hall.
>
> There were stormy quarrels. Both the lovers were energetic and adventurous, and both could express their sentiments in the rough language of the Rand. In the end the lady renounced her man.
>
> "I would not go through it all again for anything," she said years afterwards. "Love is the most upsetting thing in the world."[23]

It is not at all clear that this 'brusque, masculine man' was Jack Webster: it may well have been another of Baylis's admirers, Howard Robinson.

Letters from Howard Robinson were kept by Baylis all her life. Robinson, who worked at the Jupiter Gold Mine, wrote to Baylis when she was back in England, wishing she would return to South Africa soon, longing to go out with her for 'a good gallop', chatting about horses, horse racing, polo, about Liebe, Newton and Willie, and stating:

> You had better think of returning soon you have had a nice holiday now. I am sure foggy London will kill you if you stay much longer. Try to get back before the Winter sets in and let us have some fun again.[24]

Robinson laments, 'I have no Guardian Angel now to look after me – I wish you were back.'[25] The following year he is asking 'When are you coming back?', demanding '*Come back soon*', and always signing off with a long row of kisses.[26] Baylis was also kept informed of Howard Robinson's activities by means of the letters written during the South African War by her mother, Liebe. Howard Robinson's energetic participation in the hostilities is discussed, and Liebe often comments on what a nice chap Howard is, but tellingly she also states, 'I for one should be very sorry for you to marry into that family', which suggests that such a marriage had indeed been mooted. Liebe adds that Robinson's family are 'so jealous its quite silly – suppose they think you want him'.[27] Elsewhere Liebe says Howard Robinson is saving to travel to the Paris Exhibition next year and that he is going around saying 'he expects to go alone but have a companion back'.[28] Howard Robinson was generally sporty and full of high spirits: once when drunk on peach brandy, he tried to ride two horses, one after another, into the shop that Liebe and Newton had recently opened. He often went to the theatre with Baylis in South Africa but abandoned theatre going once she returned to England.[29]

It seems significant that none of the Jack Webster memorabilia ended up as part of Baylis's own personal archive, whereas the letters from and concerning Howard Robinson did. However, there is yet another complication in that the feminist stockbroker (Beatrice) Gordon Holmes claims her maternal uncle Jack was also a contender in Baylis's love life. Holmes first met Baylis when Holmes was only twelve and Baylis had recently arrived back in England from South Africa,

> bringing with her a banjo belonging to my grandmother's youngest son, Jack, who had recently died in Johannesburg. He had been in love with Lil and she with him – but she didn't realize it fully till his sudden death.[30]

This 'Jack' must be someone other than Jack Webster. Holmes's uncle died in Johannesburg, whereas Jack Webster disappeared in the South African bush; Holmes's mother's maiden name was Coqui, not Webster. When Holmes and Baylis eventually became close friends, Baylis 'used to murmur' to Holmes, 'You know, dear, if I'd married your Uncle Jack you'd have been my niece!'[31]

Perhaps the crucial point about Baylis's South African romance or romances is that, in the end, she made a definite choice not to become a wife and mother. She may have had Liebe's experiences of childbirth and infant mortality in mind, or she may have changed her mind over Jack Webster, or Howard Robinson or Jack Coqui. Nevertheless, the population statistics in South Africa at the time make it plain that – to put it brutally – Baylis as a young white woman would have been in a strong negotiating position if she *had* been interested in marriage. Because white men vastly outnumbered white women, Anglo-South African men looking for Anglo-South African wives had to offer something special, and the women could afford to be choosy. If she had wanted to marry, Baylis had ample opportunity to do so while she was in South Africa.

The imbalance in the male-to-female ratio in the white population in South Africa at the time is also reflected in some of Baylis's 'white woman in peril' stories. For example, at Jeppestown, when the family rented a furnished bungalow, the local hotel owner asked Liebe Baylis if she could accommodate overflow guests for a while.[32] She agreed, but one night, when Baylis was sleeping with her sister Ethel, an intruder appeared in the room and tried to get into bed with Baylis. Liebe was convinced that the intruder was one of the hotel guests, but Baylis claims she saw a 'kaffir' face and responded by catching the man by the neck and attempting to strangle him. Uproar followed: the other hotel guests and Liebe all came running in to the rescue, but the assailant escaped. A similar story relates how at eighteen Baylis was subjected to an outbreak of passion by a young postmaster who smothered her with kisses 'again and again'.[33] Baylis came to her senses when she mysteriously heard the voice of a former schoolmistress saying 'Lilian, Lilian' in 'surprised and disappointed tones', and she dashed back to her parents.[34] Baylis 'later found out that this teacher', a nun from St Augustine's school, Kilburn, 'had died on that date'.

Despite all this excitement, Baylis was still very career-centred and, once the Baylis family stopped touring, she began a new career in teaching dance. Whilst settled for a while in Doornfontein, Baylis and her mother came to the rescue of the local Christmas show, which looked as if it was about to collapse because the performers who had been engaged to appear had failed to turn up. The wife of the theatrical entrepreneur responsible for the show, Mrs Chapin, asked

Baylis and Liebe to go on and play instead. Baylis also danced in the show, and she did this so well that Mrs Chapin persuaded her she should start dancing classes for children. Baylis soon had so many classes that she needed a bicycle to get around from one class to another. She thus became, she claimed, only the second woman to ride a bicycle in South Africa. Her pioneering spirit here was put to the test by one Dutch family whose children used to shout out 'Devil on a wheel' and throw tins at her as she cycled past.[35] Baylis eventually opened a studio and she comments of her dance classes: 'when everyone else who danced used to do high-kicking people seemed to like my graceful dancing'.[36] Baylis was not teaching the can-can but the Sir Roger de Coverley.

In an article Baylis wrote in 1931, looking back nostalgically to her time in South Africa, she suggests that it was here that she really learnt her love of working an audience:

> Jo'burg loved us, and you can have no idea what marvellous audiences those rough miners made. When I sang them "Old Folks at Home" I moved them to tears, and as the banjo tinkled and my small clear soprano hovered over the tense silence of that great rough crowd, I felt that I had some kind of power.[37]

Baylis also claims that

> I had lost much by leaving England. I might have been a great violinist, but in the Colonies I could not get tuition.[38]

Whatever her real potential as a violinist, it is indubitably true that Baylis had sacrificed the opportunity for further tuition by teachers as highly regarded as John Tiplady Carrodus, her teacher in London, by moving to South Africa. Overall Baylis made a good living from teaching fiddle, banjo and mandolin; she also led several orchestras, including a banjo orchestra of bank workers and an orchestra of the wives of such millionaires as Randlords Barney Barnato and his nephew Solly Joel. As Barnato was then Cecil Rhodes's main rival in the struggle to gain control of the South African diamond fields, Baylis was here mixing with people with very powerful connections. Mrs Barnato learnt guitar from Baylis and Mrs

Joel learnt mandolin; the latter's children came to dance class in a goat cart, with a large Zulu man in attendance.[39]

While the Baylis family were in Johannesburg successfully running 'The Rand Academy of Music, and Art School', and while Baylis was earning as much as £50 a month with her teaching, the Jameson Raid took place.[40] This turned their lives upside down. The ongoing struggle between Cecil Rhodes (representing British interests) and Paul Kruger (representing Dutch interests) spurred one of Rhodes's associates, Dr Leander Jameson, to lead a posse of 400 men into the South African Republic in December 1895. The men headed in the direction of Johannesburg, and claimed they were intent on saving Anglo-South African women and children from Dutch oppression. The expedition was a military disaster: Jameson and his men surrendered in Krugersdorp, near Johannesburg, and were taken to Pretoria and thrown into jail. Jameson was sent back to England for trial, but several death sentences were handed out to those who were tried in South Africa, sentences which were commuted eventually by Kruger, who turned the entire incident into a propaganda coup for the Dutch. For those Anglo-South Africans, like the Baylises, living in Johannesburg, these were extremely tense times. A Jameson victory could have heralded a new period of British dominance in Johannesburg, but in the immediate aftermath of the failed raid, all Anglo-South Africans were suspect. The fathers of eight of Baylis's pupils were sentenced to death.[41] Not surprisingly in such volatile times, the demand for music lessons plummeted, and Baylis's income dropped from £50 to 30/- a month. However, the Jameson raid was also the reason Baylis met Mark Twain, who was then on a lecture tour of South Africa. The tour began to flounder because of the general panic, and, with time on his hands, Twain came to one of Baylis's dancing classes. After observing the children dancing, 'he asked permission to take a little boy's place' and was 'not very good' at the Lancers, whereupon Baylis 'made him go through them properly'.[42]

Baylis wrote detailed notes about her experiences at the time of the Jameson raid, notes which give a vivid impression of excitement, panic and danger.[43] Baylis had been away with a large group of young people on a holiday that consisted of lots of picnics and horse riding, but the holiday ended on a sour note when someone, presumably Dutch, joked that the only English flag they had seen recently was the 'white flag of truce.' On her return to Johannesburg, with the prospect of Jameson's invasion seeming very real, Baylis records 'scenes at station' that were 'terrible' as Dutch families tried to escape:

> people sitting in trains all night hoping to get away. Terrified by rumour that English would enter town & do wholesale slaughter ... All shops shut and barricaded people flocked to town & camped there – all the servants had to be sent away being Kaffir. Father and brother joined defence league & had to go off and guard property – left 3 women all alone in lonely house.

Baylis actually 'went out to meet Jameson' and 'Saw dust rising & army marching – not Jameson who was by then in Pretoria jail – this was victorious Dutch coming with news of defeat.' Shortly after this a truck of dynamite

> standing in poor quarter exploded ... The vibration of explosion lifted roof of our house but it came back again exactly – room full of dust. Tore out into street to see what has happened only in petticoat; followed by agitated dress maker with table cloth – horrified at my dishabillée.

Around this time Baylis had to have a kidney operation which resulted in her spending seven weeks in bed. Whilst lying down and recuperating she carried on playing the banjo, something which was very popular with her fellow patients.[44] Nevertheless, in an autobiographical fragment entitled 'Shakespeare for the People', Baylis talks of this period as one of breakdown, brought on by the stress and panic generated in the Anglo-South African community by the Jameson raid. Emma Cons then offered to pay for a return fare so that Baylis could travel to England for six months' convalescence away from a country that was clearly heading towards all-out war. Consequently in 1897 Baylis left South Africa, taking her sister Ethel with her so that Ethel could go to school in safety in

England. Newton and Liebe stayed in Johannesburg 'teaching singing & voice production & instrumental teaching with a little occasional touring' and opened 'a bookselling and music store'.[45] Baylis's music pupils were taken on by her brother Willie (who, judging by his surviving letters, was a lively chap who cheerfully dismisses the Forrests, the relatives in Australia who had adopted Violet and Ray Baylis, as mean with their money, and frequently tells his big sister Lilian to stop fussing). War finally broke out on 12 October 1899. Newton comments stoically, 'when war was declared I elected to try & stop in Johannesburg & stick by my stuff. Of course in the end I lost everything.'[46]

In England Baylis recovered quickly and was soon hard at work helping Emma Cons run the Vic. Initially Baylis was given £1 a week pocket money, which seemed a pittance compared with her usual income in South Africa. As the situation in South Africa worsened, communications began to break down, the postal services were severely disrupted, and censored. At one stage Baylis went for over six months without any news of her parents. When letters did arrive, they were months out of date and often smuggled out via Germany (Newton was sending letters to his cousin Gilbert Dalziel in envelopes addressed to an obliging German firm which agreed to forward the correspondence). The uncertainty and worry on both sides is very clear: on 16 October 1899 Newton is trying to reassure Baylis, 'Dear girl try & not to worry over us up to now considering ... this awful state of things we have done wonderfully well.'[47]

Baylis wrote an account of her parents' wartime adventures, which was published in the *Old Vic Magazine* after Liebe's death and which was closely based on Newton's notebooks and Liebe's letters.[48] Although most British citizens left Johannesburg in a hurry once the war had started, Newton took on a disguise, passing himself off as Mr Pryce-Jones of Chicago. He

> shav[ed] his beard and dress[ed] in his old sweater of the Thames Rowing Club, he stayed; and was nearly betrayed by his own collie dog. But his wife swiftly evolved some

story about an American porter and man-of-all-work that saved him.[49]

Newton's son, Willie, commented, 'I did not think Dad had it in him to do as he did.'[50] Liebe sent Baylis a photograph of Newton in disguise, adding, 'Dad ... is not so bad in the photo but in life – well!' and 'when I opened the door & saw him I sat down & laughed so I think I should be really ill – it was the first laugh I had had for weeks'.[51]

Newton's 'Diary of the Dutch Occupation of Johannesburg from the Declaration of War Thursday Oct. 12th. 1899', which blames all the hostilities on Kruger, offers a detailed account of the progress of the war:[52] the crises; the boredom of waiting for action; his and Liebe's attempts to revive their dancing classes without infringing the various curfews. Meanwhile Baylis was following South African events closely via the British newspapers. Indeed she notes on one letter 'Mafeking is Relieved Rule Britannia.'[53] Baylis's continuing focus on South Africa can also be seen in the Vic's hosting of a concert, on 6 December 1899, in the presence of Queen Victoria's youngest daughter, Princess Henry of Battenberg, in aid of a fund for the wives and children of reservist soldiers there.[54]

Liebe's letters to Baylis during this period complain of censorship, curfews and the price of food; she describes troops departing for the front, the excitement of victory and the trauma of bomb explosions. She updates Baylis on how friends are getting on and who has been killed or wounded in the war; almost every letter written by Liebe contains some news of Howard Robinson. Liebe's letters also worry about the likelihood that her outspoken daughter's letters will be stopped by the censor and she comments in a letter to her son Willie:

> I am so anxious to hear from you to & know if you've heard from Lilian – if you have heard and think it safe to send on her letters to me – do *not* do so *if* she has made any of her Lilly remarks therein – or they will be stopped at Pretoria.[55]

At least one of Baylis's letters was opened and read by censors, as a comment of Newton's shows: 'the Govt officials have amused themselves with it & fastened up again ... glad you put in no treason'.[56] Meanwhile Liebe and Newton passed most of their music business on to Willie and concentrated on running their general store.[57] Despite the war, they did good business for a long time.[58] Liebe and Newton also continued to organise dances in their dance hall, to teach dancing and to give private music lessons.[59] They carried on supporting the local church choirs, even though congregations were sparse, as so many British had left town, and some churches had lost their minister. But when their shop was severely damaged by a bomb explosion around the end of April 1900, a badly shaken Liebe was almost ready to give up.[60] A few weeks later she writes that she has 'got over the explosion a bit', but she and Newton have moved home as the Baylis shop was a ruined shell and 'it was like living & sleeping in the street'; Liebe comments, 'talk about a 3 vol novel – I could fill 20 vols with what we have gone thro'.[61] By September 1900 Lord Roberts had overcome the Dutch South Africans, and the South African Republic had become the new British colony of the Transvaal. Liebe was jubilant over the British victory, but she approved when the local minister preached 'one of the most beautiful sermons I've ever heard – full of sorrow for the poor Dutch'.[62]

After the war, life continued to be difficult. Liebe got the dance classes restarted, but Newton comments:

> Those who ran away from her[e] in panic or could not stay on most venomous to us who in spite of all stuck to our stuff & remained & the few who now manage to get back say if you were a sound Britisher you would have left & gone out & fought for your country (though most of them did not fight themselves) & many other bitter nasty things – I think 53 years of age is rather late in life to start as a soldier.[63]

However, as fighting and looting were still taking place, Newton volunteered and joined the Rand Rifles to help keep the peace. He acted as a cyclist orderly and despatch rider for ten months '& did a lot of intelligence work as I well knew all the haunts of the bad men'.[64] Newton was particularly keen to expose the doings of 'the Anti Britishers, Irish Americans'.[65]

The South African War was clearly the critical reason why Baylis did not return to South Africa after her convalescence in England, as had originally been planned. Although Baylis's sister Ethel returned to South Africa in 1902, Baylis had by then been persuaded to stay on to manage the Vic and work alongside Emma Cons. At the time, however, this was a very difficult decision for her to make. Howard Robinson was begging her to return, and Baylis thought long and hard about her options. She wrote to a respected friend, Mrs Van Den Berg, to ask for advice and was told to stay on in London.[66] Mrs Van Den Berg's reply stresses the settled, certain career path which seems to lie before Baylis in London, in contrast to her uncertain prospects in South Africa. She describes the current teaching market in South Africa as unpredictable, suggests it would be difficult for Baylis to pick up the pieces of her former career after the upheavals of the recent years, and reminds her that she had been finding the climate of Johannesburg (which is high in altitude) difficult before she left. The letter argues that even though Baylis may not be finding life in London as 'merry' as the life she was used to in South Africa, she should nevertheless stick with it. It also praises her for earning enough money in England to pay for Ethel's education as well as to help her parents with the debts they had incurred after their shop had been destroyed. What is absolutely clear from this letter is that in 1899, when the letter was written, Baylis was still very seriously considering returning to South Africa.

In fact Baylis didn't actually revisit South Africa until 1924, when she was on a four-month, supposedly recuperative, holiday from the Vic. But she always welcomed visiting South Africans to the Vic with open arms, and South Africa remained for her a romantic place, a place of adventure, of pioneering travel, of performances in shanty towns, and of coaching the wives of millionaires. Baylis spent six very impressionable years in South Africa: she arrived there aged eighteen and she left aged twenty-four, and the country gave her a lifelong love of travelling, of adventure and of camping.[67] When she left South Africa, Baylis left behind her family, a host of friends and a lover, but she was persuaded to give all this up for the opportunity to work alongside her redoubtable aunt, Emma Cons.

NOTES

1 *OVM*, May 1924.
2 'Rabelaisian' is Evelyn Williams's description in Harcourt Williams, *Vic-Wells*, p. 33.
3 OVLB/000156, 'Part II, Africa'.
4 OVEC/000004/2.
5 OVEC/000004/3.
6 OVLB/000156.
7 Ibid.
8 Ibid.
9 Lilian Baylis, 'Women's Contribution'. Baylis also states that her South African experiences were 'useful' when it came to running the Vic in 1898 (OVLB/000146/5).
10 OVEC/000004/13. This jars with Richard Findlater's conviction that the Baylis family's tour of South Africa was a 'desperate venture' (*Lilian Baylis*, p. 77), dogged by 'The grumbling ineffectuality of Mrs Baylis. It was she, no doubt, who insisted that the touring should end' (p. 78). Findlater's 'no doubt' has no evidence whatsoever to back it up.
11 OVEC/000004/5, 8.
12 OVLB/000156.
13 Ibid.
14 OVEC/000004/7–8 (7).
15 OVEC/000009/1.
16 *OVM*, December 1925.
17 OVLB/000156. The Delagoa Bay railway line reached Pretoria in 1895.
18 Information taken from OVLB/000156.
19 The letter was dated 26 May and is referred to in Roberts, *Lilian Baylis*, p. 6. A photograph of Jack Webster is also reproduced here. Roberts comments that two later letters to Harriet, written after Webster's death, 'throw more light on [Baylis] as a busy music teacher than they do as a troubled lover.' Findlater, *Lilian Baylis*, p.79 also quotes from the Webster letters. The catalogue of the Lilian Baylis Centenary exhibition, Leighton House, records the display of a 'Telegram sent by Jack Webster, then

her fiancé, to Lilian Baylis, announcing his safe arrival at
Victoria, 25th May, 1893.'

20 Annette Prevost bequeathed the brooch to the British Theatre
Museum on 9 May 1974 (OV/M/000044/3).

21 Catalogue of the Lilian Baylis Centenary exhibition, Leighton
House, 1974. The text here is by Annette Prevost.

22 Catalogue of the Lilian Baylis Centenary exhibition. Harriet
Webster gave the brooch to Prevost in the 1940s. Findlater,
Lilian Baylis, p. 293 records a fascinating comment on Harriet
Webster by Baylis: 'I wish I didn't hate her so', something which
again suggests complexity in the Baylis/Jack Webster story.

23 *Star*, 26 November 1937. Baylis had published an essay on the
Vic-Wells opera in the *Star* the previous week and enjoyed good
relations with the newspaper, but the appearance of this racy
account in the same issue that announced her death is startling.

24 OVLB/000138/2, 10, letter dated 28 December 1898,
continued 29 December. The letters are addressed to 'Jini' but
the contents – references to Ma and Pa Baylis, Willie and Ethel –
indicate that Baylis is the addressee.

25 OVLB/000138/2–3.

26 OVLB/000138/12, 14, letters dated 21 August 1899, 18
September 1899.

27 OVLB/000012/12, letter dated 20 March 1900.

28 OVLB/000012/4. A letter from Baylis's brother Willie,
OVLB/000033, also comments on 27 April 1900, 'I often
wonder where Howard is[,] he is not a prisoner.'

29 The attempt to ride into the shop is described in
OVLB/000012/10. For Robinson's theatre visits see
OVLB/000138/11. It is possible that it is Robinson who is the
subject of Richard Findlater's undocumented story (*Lilian
Baylis*, p .243) that Baylis considered marrying a former admirer
from South Africa in the late 1920s, primarily so that she could
have a chauffeur. Clearly the man in question could not be the
deceased Jack Webster or Jack Coqui.

30 Beatrice Gordon Holmes, *In Love With Life: A Pioneer Career
Woman's Story* (London, 1944), pp. 137–8.

31 Ibid., p. 138.

32 OVLB/000156.

33 OVLB/000155/1.

34 'and disappointed' was later crossed out.

35 OVLB/000156.

36 *Star*, 25 November 1937.

37 Baylis, 'Prayer – and One's Hour of Destiny'.

38 Ibid.

39 OVLB/000156. For Barney Barnato's love of theatre see Raymond, *B.I. Barnato*, pp. 161–4.

40 OVEC/000011/11 advertises the Academy's services: private lessons in piano, violin, banjo, mandolin, guitar, singing harmony and drawing (15/- to £1 1s a month), also classes in voice production and dancing.

41 Baylis, 'Prayer – and One's Hour of Destiny'.

42 Interview in the *Star*, 12 April 1937. See also Baylis, 'Prayer – and One's Hour of Destiny'. Mark Twain/Samuel Clemens's tour lasted from 4 May to 14 July 1896 and, in the company of Baylis's acquaintances Mr and Mrs Chapin, he visited the prison where the Jameson Raid prisoners were being held. See Mark Twain, *Following the Equator: A Journey Around the World*, vol. I (London, 1925).

43 OVLB/000156.

44 OVLB/000055/8.

45 OVEC/000004/20.

46 Ibid.

47 OVLB/000012/2.

48 *OVM*, December 1925. If this article was not actually penned by Baylis, which is likely, then it was certainly supervised by her.

49 *OVM*, December 1925.

50 OVLB/000033/14.

51 OVLB/000012/16.

52 OVEC/000007, 8.

53 OVLB/000028.

54 John Booth, *The "Old Vic": A Century of Theatrical History. 1816–1916* (London, 1917), p. 67. Satin souvenir programmes were produced for this occasion.

55 OVLB/000012/10.

56 OVLB/000012/2, letter dated 16 October 1899.

57 OVLB/000012/1 states that Willie has been given a bass (purchased by Baylis), an organette, a guitar, he has 2 banjos, a cello and violin, his parents' music stand and 'all our Dance Music' plus Liebe's jewellery and £5 10s – Liebe comments 'he seems quite happy & fallen on his feet as usual'. Willie taught banjo and mandolin in Durban but fell on hard times when he became ill and by July 1906 was very short of cash. Willie died of consumption that year aged twenty-eight.

58 It is worth stressing this, as Findlater is convinced that the

Baylises were financial disasters all the time they were in South Africa. Liebe's and Newton's letters do not support this argument at all. In OVLB/000012/13 Liebe talks of sending money to Baylis in England (in 1900) but she has been told that money is taken off people as they cross the border. She talks of stock running low but not of financial difficulties and in OVLB/000012/15 is offering to cable money for Ethel's passage to South Africa. In OVLB/000012/19, dated 1 June 1900, Liebe is looking for a new room to rent for a dance school and states of the financial situation 'I've a good bit in hand.' The crucial event in the decline in their fortunes seems to have been the explosion wrecking their shop.

59 OVLB/000012/13 reports that around 6 April 1900 the Baylises had thirty people for a dance. They managed eleven or twelve dances between 7.15 and the 9 o'clock curfew.

60 See OVLB/000012/14. Newton describes their home as 'pretty well smashed up' (OVLB/000028).

61 OVLB/000012/16.

62 OVLB/000012/19.

63 OVLB/000012/21.

64 OVEC/000004/35.

65 OVEC/000009/4.

66 OVLB/000016. This letter is dated 22 April 1899. Dora Northcroft in her account of Baylis's life in *Girls of Adventure* (London, 1944), pp. 109, 111 is also very clear that six months after returning to the UK from South Africa Baylis 'began to make her preparations for returning' to her 'happy-go-lucky' family, and that staying in the UK was not at all her original intention.

67 For Baylis's love of camping see Sybil Thorndike, 'Lilian Baylis: As I Knew Her' in Sybil and Russell Thorndike, *Lilian Baylis* (London, 1938), p. 64.

[4]

Lilian Baylis and Emma Cons

For Baylis, her aunt Emma Cons was an emotional and political inspiration, a career mentor, a godmother and a close friend. Baylis inherited far more than the Vic Theatre from her aunt: she inherited many of Cons's attitudes, especially her determination, and her conviction that theatre must always include social work. The primary source for information on Cons's life and career is Baylis's own biography of her, in the chapter she wrote for Cicely Hamilton's 1926 history of the Vic.[1] It is extremely revealing as a niece's portrait of a loving and beloved aunt, as a tribute from one successful career woman to another, and as a clear indication of what impressed Baylis herself most about Cons's achievements.[2]

Born in 1838, Emma Cons was identified at an early age as having artistic potential and studied art under Madame Holliday and Louisa Ganne before joining the Ladies' Co-operative Art Guild in Fitzroy Square. The Guild was supported by the Christian Socialists and run by Caroline Hill, mother of the future housing reformer and founder of the National Trust, Octavia Hill. Baylis comments of Caroline Hill's management:

> this was an enterprising step in 1851, the era of rigid Victorian convention, when a girl who thought of adopting a profession was supposed to forfeit her right to the status and dignity of gentlewoman. Mrs. Hill's new venture defied tradition and had, for one of its objects, the finding of employment for ladies with artistic ability.[3]

The Guild helped Cons get paid work as an illuminator, and she restored manuscripts for John Ruskin, who 'became interested in the work of the two girl-friends, Octavia Hill and

Emma Cons. Courtesy of the Royal Victoria Hall Foundation and
the University of Bristol Theatre Collection

Emma Cons'.4 Then, after a holiday in Switzerland, when she
observed women working as engravers and decorating the
backs of watches, the young Cons set up a similar business,
priding herself on making every single watch she engraved
completely unique.5 The business flourished until male
competitors realised they were losing contracts, and beat up
the delivery man who worked for Cons. After this incident,
commissions dried up. Baylis believed that this experience
'only strengthened in Emmie her already firm conviction that

women had a right – as well as men – to carve out careers for themselves', a conviction that was still comparatively unusual in the late 1850s.[6]

Cons also experienced work-place harassment in her job as a designer of stained glass windows for a company called Powells, a company that put her to work for two years on stained glass for Merton College, Oxford. At Powells, male workers sabotaged Cons's work, deliberately smudging colouring and cracking the glass. Cons's effective and assertive resistance to this harassment contributed, Baylis felt, to her ability to 'control the refractory men she had to deal with in after life'.[7] In addition, after Cons had blazed the trail for women at Powells, other women also started working for the company, including Emma's sister Ellen.[8]

Cons abandoned her career in applied art when she moved full time into social housing as a direct result of her intense and passionate friendship with Octavia Hill, a relationship which Baylis describes as 'strong and intimate'.[9] From 1864 Cons officially worked for Hill as a rent collector and, although the two women were close in age, Hill saw Cons as a protégée, and trained her in her own particular enlightened methods of rent collecting. Hill's energy, coupled with a determination to succeed that sometimes led her to the brink of total collapse, can also be seen mirrored in the similarly totally committed work ethic of her disciple Cons. However, Cons and Hill did have differences of opinion: Baylis claimed that Hill evicted bad tenants whereas Cons wanted to persevere with them; and when a young social worker, Andrew Carthews, attempted to plead for a tenant Hill was about to evict, she responded:

> if I thought I had a mission to improve people I had better go and work for Miss Cons. Miss Hill would never allow rent to run when I was working for her, but Miss Cons frequently allowed it to run for months.[10]

Cons was not a soft touch as a manager, however, as one of her workers, Mrs Maclagan, makes clear:

> I worked at first under Miss Emma Cons, the most genial and kindly of women, and I may add the most courageous.

I have seen her plunge into a street row, and forcibly separate combatants, men and women who slunk away from her indignation like whipped hounds.[11]

There were other differences of opinion between Cons and Hill: Cons was in favour of women's suffrage and practical politicking whereas Hill was not; and Cons was far more fervently committed than Hill to the notion that art, and particularly music, should be available to the poor. Very early in Cons's slum management career, records appear of concerts for tenants by Antoinette Sterling, an American Quaker contralto who sang for Cons without taking a fee and later became one of Cons's most steadfast supporters at the Vic. Cons started a brass band to encourage music making among her tenants; in the year of Baylis's birth, an operetta for Cons's tenants at Barrett's Court was arranged by Liebe Cons and her friends.

One aspect of Cons's social housing career that Baylis was especially proud of was her commitment to taking parties of her tenants to the countryside. Baylis describes how:

[M]y aunt took her people from the slums of Drury Lane, Marylebone and from Surrey Lodge into the country for the day. She was one of the first persons to organise such excursions; and very often we were about 1,000 strong. All tenants who had paid their rents regularly – fathers, mothers, and the children – met at Liverpool Street and we went to Epping Forest for the day … Miss Ellen Cons made a wonderful lemon syrup – many bottles of it; and this was packed in boxes; cricket stumps, gifts, a large skipping rope which also served for starting the races which came at the end of the day – all these packages were put in Bob's charge; and he also saw that great cans of water were ready to mix with the syrup. The tenants brought their own lunch; but we all sat down to a big tea about three o'clock.[12]

One particularly favourite spot for such visits was Chippens Bank, at Hever in Kent, the home of Cons's great friend Ethel Everest, daughter of the surveyor who had had the Himalayan mountain renamed after him. Cons spent most of her weekends with Everest, whose home became a real retreat for her. Although the train station of Hever is conveniently nearby, even today the house is still remarkable for its quietness and for the beauty of its surroundings. Baylis once described Cons's life as 'a crusade against ugliness', and this crusade can certainly be seen at work in Cons's passion for taking London slum dwellers to visit Hever.[13]

Cons started her career as a professional rent collector at Barrett's Court, near Oxford Street, but later she focused her energies on south London, and in 1879 she established the South London Dwellings Company around Surrey Lodge, Lambeth, near to Waterloo Station. The old Surrey Lodge was pulled down and rebuilt at a cost of £33,000 on a ¾-acre plot of land which included play areas and flower beds.[14] Each two-roomed tenement had its own dustbin, washing room and 'sanitary arrangements', and 600 people lived in the building.[15] Cons introduced sensible management practices of her own, such as creating spaces on the tenement roofs for washing to dry.[16] Surrey Lodge was where Emma and her sister Ellen chose to live (and where Baylis came to live when she returned from South Africa), amongst the tenants Emma was managing. Baylis describes the relationship between these two sisters, Emma and Ellen, in the following terms: 'we used to say that Emmie was like the strong husband and Ellen the devoted wife', and Cons 'could never have accomplished the half of what she did, without Ellen's loving care at home'.[17]

Cons's work in south London began after a traumatic break with Octavia Hill. The relationship between Hill and Cons had become very close, something indicated clearly in surviving letters, but Edmund Maurice, Hill's brother-in-law, drawing on family recollections, claims that Hill's sisters and friends 'were rather startled at the attraction which her new friend [Cons] had for her,' even though Maurice is sure that Hill 'saw the real power concealed for the time under [Cons's] hoydenish ways'.[18] Hill was certainly better connected than Cons: her circle included Tom Hughes, author of *Tom Brown's Schooldays*, Charles Kingsley, Lord Shaftesbury, Robert Browning and Elizabeth Barrett Browning. Hill's brothers-in-law included

George Eliot's stepson, and Hill's housing courts were visited incognito by Queen Victoria's daughter, Princess Alice.[19] While Edmund Maurice describes Cons as 'given to romps', full of 'high girlish spirits', Baylis herself comments that Cons had 'certain tomboyish tastes … she always carried a knife and a piece of string in her pocket, even when she was wearing evening dress'.[20] Beatrice Webb writes in a similar vein: although Cons was clearly '[n]ot a lady by birth,' she had 'the face and manner of a distinguished woman, almost a ruler of men'; Webb adds that Cons had

> [a]bsolute absorption in work; strong religious feeling, very little culture or interest in things outside the sphere of her own action. Certainly, she is not a lover of fact or theory.[21]

Webb also comments that Cons, 'one of the most saintly as well as the most far-sighted of Victorian women philanthropists, deserves to be more widely known'.[22]

Despite their closeness in age, Hill saw herself as Cons's guide and mentor. Partly this mentoring was intellectual, and it was certainly due to Hill's influence that Cons began to attend public lectures and to debate socialism, philanthropy and theology so energetically. Suddenly Hill realigned the relationship, however, and she seems to have engineered this rather coolly:

> Unfortunately, Miss Hill, in seeking to divide the two spheres of labour, and compel Miss Cons to assume the sole charge of one of them, and obtain her own workers, did not explain her object, with the result that Emma saw her act and decisions only as evidences that she was to be "got rid of", and banished from the larger coterie of devoted adherents who had gathered round Nottingham Place …
>
> Then arose strained relations, and "she said", "they said", and "we said" made matters worse. Emma used to come down to Whitechapel in an agony of pain, and a letter after one such visit will show the depth of her love, the simplicity of her nature, and amid all her grief, the utter selflessness of her outlook.[23]

The writer here is 'Yetta' (Henrietta) Barnett, a close friend of Cons who became famous in her own right for her social work and outreach.[24] Yetta was nineteen when she met the thirty-two-year-old Cons; the letter she refers to, which is dated 2 March 1875, belongs to a period about five years after they first met. In it Cons writes to Yetta:

> I fear I was possessed by the devil this evening till you sent me to prayer (the only real comfort in this world), and I cannot go to rest until I have confessed, and thanked you for all your love, kindness and truly friendly thrashing. The fact is I was nearly mad with all this confusion of facts and the continual strain and re-actions of the day, etc. All last evening and night being in a high state of excitement and expectation of such big results from your great influence with O.H. and then on going to her this morning full of hope and getting stabbed through and through (may you never feel such). Oh. it was almost too much ...
>
> You or no-one has the least idea of how I love her.
>
> After a great struggle with the demon, I think I can safely promise you to follow your advice and will (D.V.) lay self entirely and make a fresh start ... My principal dread has been her not wanting me.[25]

This impassioned letter, which Baylis chose not to refer to in her biography of Cons, is a typed copy, not the original. It is not clear whether the two ellipses are Cons's personal style or the typist, copyist or an editor (possibly Baylis?) making choices about what, in the documentation of this relationship, was being left to posterity. Baylis certainly bluntly states in a letter to her parents that after Cons's death she went through all of Cons's private papers censoring them and burning a great deal.[26]

Yetta's account of Cons's character is distinguished by its frankness and directness:

> Her personality was arresting though often vexing; especially to one, who like myself, had been reared in close obedience to the early Victorian tenets that young ladies should speak softly, walk with short steps, agree with most

things that were said by their elders, and be modestly subservient to the male members of their families. At 32 Emma Cons spoke loudly and often aggressively, strode as if she were measuring a plot by yard steps, disliked, positively disliked, the male sex, and questioned the wisdom of many of the standards of conduct and thought accepted by past generations. Moreover she dressed badly, really badly, was untidy and abnormally often in a great hurry.[27]

Yetta's stress on Cons's dislike of the male sex is definitely missing from Baylis's account. This omission may well have been because Baylis did not believe it to be true, and Cons certainly had a track record of being able to work amicably with men during her long career. Overall, however, Yetta is very appreciative of Cons:

> I delighted in her, but some of her helpers whom Octavia and not she had selected could not see the valuable timber of the trees because of the brushwood of manner ... I can visualise her now; mounting ladders, mixing colours, ordering and laughing at the men, who when too inexperienced, backward, or perhaps indolent, would show resentment at, or disinclination for, the job, were made ashamed and also encouraged by seeing Miss Cons seize the brush and give an excellent lesson in distempering, painting or washing down.[28]

From a twenty-first-century perspective it is almost inevitable that the question has to be posed as to whether Emma Cons's woman-centred lifestyle and her resistance to social norms for women suggest lesbian identity. Prevailing Victorian attitudes towards intense, romantic friendships between women need to be taken into account here, and it is extremely difficult to decipher these relationships now. Respectable Victorian women were expected to form romantic friendships with other women, but they were also expected to believe that 'Good women had no sex drive.'[29] Historian Rosemary Auchmuty is confident she can claim Octavia Hill as a lesbian and comments:

Emma and Ellen Cons at Letchworth Garden City,
before 1912. Photograph by Lilian Baylis. Courtesy
of the Royal Victoria Hall Foundation and the
University of Bristol Theatre Collection

A passionate affair with the pioneer doctor Sophia Jex-
Blake, when both were in their early twenties, was ended by
the intervention of Hill's mother. Hill lived for the last 35
years of her life with Harriot Yorke, and they are buried
together in the churchyard at Crockham Hill, near
Edenbridge, Kent.[30]

However, perhaps what is most crucial in relation to Lilian
Baylis is the simple fact that Emma Cons offered Baylis a
liberating lifestyle model in being so radically woman-centred,
and in associating so closely with so many high-achieving and
successful career women.

Cons first encountered several of the women she worked

and socialised with as a result of her very active participation in the campaign for women's suffrage. Cons helped to organise meetings, lobbied extensively among her acquaintances and generally worked hard to raise the profile of the moderate suffragists' campaign. Most crucially of all, Cons helped ignite an important and ultimately decisive crisis over the role of women in local government.[31] In 1889 Cons became the first ever woman alderman on the London County Council (LCC), working alongside the first elected women members Jane Cobden (elected for Bow and Bromley) and Lady Sandhurst (elected for Brixton). The election of Lady Sandhurst was instantly challenged by the anti-suffragist Beresford Hope, whom Lady Sandhurst had defeated. *Beresford Hope v. Sandhurst* reached court on 18 March 1889 and went to appeal in May of that year: Lady Sandhurst was ruled to have been illegally elected and Beresford Hope took the seat of Brixton. By contrast, Jane Cobden's defeated rival was a Liberal, who was in favour of women's suffrage, and he chose not to contest her election. Emma Cons's position was more difficult to contest because she had not been elected (indeed she had refused to be nominated for a constituency), but she had been specifically asked by the LCC Progressives to become an alderman.[32] Supporters pointed out that if Cobden and Cons managed to avoid any challenges for twelve months, the law stated that they could not be ousted until the next election, and so for twelve months they both kept a low profile. Their anomalous and unprecedented position was much discussed, however, and once the twelve months were past, and the women started voting at Council meetings, the Tory Sir Walter de Souza filed writs demanding they be fined £250 each, at a rate of £50 a vote. *De Souza v. Cobden* reached the Court of Appeal in 1891 and it bizarrely declared 'Cobden's membership of the council valid but her participation in that council invalid'.[33] Both women had thus helped prove that the law was an ass, but they were in fact both liable for the fines demanded by De Souza. Cons stayed hidden at a friend's house until an LCC meeting because she wanted the summons actually served at the LCC.[34] Various attempts to rescue the women were made via Parliament, with three bills introduced in the Lords and one in the Commons. Lobbying over Cons's and Cobden's position took place at the very highest political level – Lord Meath supported them in the Lords, Lord Granville, Lord Salisbury and Gladstone were sympathetic – but it was clear to many that allowing women to serve in local government would be setting very important precedents, and the bills were defeated by the anti-suffragists.

Cons outlines the reasons for her actions in a letter to *The Times*.[35] She sees it

> as a protest on behalf of the ratepayers, men as well as women, against the restriction of their right of free choice of representatives; as a protest on behalf of women against the ignoring of their rights of citizenship; and because the majority of the councillors themselves (presumably a body of experts) had decided to avail themselves of the 30 years of experience gained by me in hard and practical work for the improvement of the houses and amelioration of the lives of the poorest classes.

Despite the fact that she feels uncomfortable at becoming 'a subject of public dispute and discussion', Cons argues that her work has given 'the public an opportunity of judging for themselves as to the competency of women to discharge the duties required by the County Council', something which before Cons began her work as an alderman 'could only have been argued theoretically'. She then declares:

> My feelings on the subject of women councillors are as strong as ever, and I shall neglect no means in my power to secure a perfect freedom of choice to the ratepayers, and equal municipal rights for women as for men. It is a bitter experience when one for the first time fully realizes that even a long life spent in the service of one's fellow-citizens is powerless to blot out the disgrace and crime (in the eyes of the law) of having been born a woman.

Cons indubitably proved her case, to anyone prepared to listen, in terms of demonstrating how effectively women could work for the LCC: she served on six committees and eleven sub-committees covering Housing of the Working Classes,

Council Chamber and Offices, Asylums, Industrial and Reformatory Schools, Parks and Open Spaces, Sanitation and Special Purposes, and Theatres.[36] Also indicative of Cons's phenomenal capacity for work is the fact that in order to take on these council duties she had to pay two women to do her own work. During this period Cons also became more and more active on the Committee for the Return of Women as Councillors, the Committee that paid Cons's and Cobden's fines, which were eventually reduced to £5 per vote. Cons was also beginning to work extensively with the Women's Local Government Society (WLGS), and at one stage became vice-president. The Liberal-dominated WLGS has been described as 'one of the least known, yet one of the most effective women's organizations in the late nineteenth century' and a 'formidable lobbying machine'; when it finally celebrated the legalised election of women to local government in 1907, Cons was a guest of honour at the banquet.[37] Cons's ongoing interest in the cause of women in local government can also be gauged from a letter to Baylis written in 1909 during a stay at Hever, when her 'head is too bad today to do anything but growl because I cannot go to London and vote in the Election for women on "Borough Councils". This is too hard on me when I have worked for 20 years to get them on … I am savagely disappointed!!'[38]

At the time Cons started pushing back the legal boundaries, establishing precedents and being discussed by the leading politicians of the day, Baylis was fifteen, an age at which it would have been difficult for her to be unaware of her aunt's political misadventures and the implications for women in general. In her biography of Cons, Baylis refers to this as 'the historic County Council episode', and although she was not a suffrage activist like her aunt, she did take as self-evident certain assumptions about how unjust the political system was to women.[39] In a letter written in 1912 to thank the committee of the London Society for Women's Suffrage for their condolences on the death of Emma Cons, Baylis explicitly identifies with the suffrage cause:

Her loss is irreparable, but the remembrance of her

brightness and hopefulness must help us all to fight on in the Cause *so dear to us* and for which she laboured unremittingly [my italics].[40]

Baylis and her family took support for the suffrage cause almost for granted: indeed Baylis's father, Newton, matter-of-factly comments of his family's friendship with Nina Boyle, 'who was at that time an active suffragette' in South Africa, 'of course we were pals'.[41]

Baylis saw another of Cons's passions, temperance, as an extension of her feminist politics: although she suggests that this was 'the one subject on which this exceptionally broad-minded woman was intolerant', she identifies the origins of Cons's commitment as her anger at the alcohol-fuelled domestic violence against women that she witnessed among her tenants.[42] Baylis records that 'the man who came home drunk and began to beat his wife always had Emmie to reckon with; even if the row took place at midnight, she was out of her cottage on the instant'.[43] Social reformer Ellen Barlee also recalls that Cons was 'not above descending from her bed in dressing-gown and slippers in the small hours of the morning … to restore order'.[44] Because Cons had chosen to live amongst her tenants, her home could provide a temporary refuge: 'frightened mothers and children were always welcome to shelter in her cottage when "farver came home boozed"'.[45] In this period, however, when drinking water was often unsafe and few working-class homes could afford to offer the comforts – lights, warmth, entertainments – supplied by the music hall or pub, the challenge Cons faced in tackling alcohol abuse was daunting. And yet it was her enthusiasm for the temperance cause that inspired Cons to take over the Vic.

At this time the Vic had sunk to a low point in an already chequered career. Founded in 1816, it was named after Prince Leopold of Saxe-Coburg, who married the heir to the throne, the ill-fated Princess Charlotte, who was to die soon afterwards in childbirth. The Coburg Theatre became the Victoria in 1833, in honour of the then heir to the throne, Princess Victoria. The theatre always suffered from being on the 'wrong', that is the south, side of the river Thames, away from London's entertainment centre, and during the Victorian period it became notorious for blood-tub theatricals, scurrilous music hall acts and making its money from alcohol sales. It also hosted stars such as Eliza Vestris, Edmund Kean, Paganini and Grimaldi, but it was not, generally speaking, seen as a high-class establishment. Local girls confided to Cons that 'having gone with their boy sweet-hearts, or in pairs together, to the "Vic.", they had been treated to drink, until, taking glass after glass, they had lost all knowledge of their whereabouts and had become an easy prey to profligacy'.[46] Cons determined to act, and when the Vic became available she proposed opening it as a coffee-house theatre, a high-profile temperance zone. This would build on the experience Cons had already acquired in the hospitality business with the establishment of the successful Coffee Tavern Company, which had created a series of alcohol-free cafes in London. After a meeting of supporters in the august surroundings of the Jerusalem chamber in Westminster Abbey, the Vic project was agreed upon. After extensive cleaning – 'literally sacks' full of shrimps' heads and tails, periwinkle shells, nut-shells, and dried orange-peel' had to be dug out of the pit – the coffee-house style Vic was reopened on Boxing Day 1880.[47] Baylis was present at the official opening and vividly remembers 'as a child of six, standing on a chair in the committee box of the "Old Vic." and seeing the audience rush in at the Webber Street entrance on the opening night'.[48]

Cons ran an entertainments programme centred around what a contemporary described as 'comic songs, clog-dancing, hornpipes, acrobatic performances, nigger minstrelsy, performing animals, comic ballets ... cleansed from objectionable matter'.[49] She soon found it was very difficult to run a theatre without the sale of alcohol to boost the finances, and as the Vic began losing money fast she tried to solve the problem by hiring several theatre managers in quick succession. The most effective of these was William Poel, who began work at the Vic in 1881. Later in his life Poel would be one of the most influential, if maverick, theatre theorists and practitioners of his generation. Poel's ideas on staging, in particular the importance of staging Elizabethan and Jacobean plays on an open stage with minimal scenery, were to influence many major theatre practitioners of the early twentieth century, including several directors who worked at the Vic. Emma Cons, however, wanted Poel to improve the Vic's financial fortunes, whilst still adhering to its strict moral code.

Poel introduced opera concerts and tableaux, which were very popular, with singers and dancers who were recruited from Camberwell's Church of the Sacred Heart. He also established a weekly programme: variety shows took place on Monday and Saturday; Tuesday was devoted to a lantern lecture, usually scientific in nature; on Wednesday the hall was closed or let; Thursday and Friday offered a ballad concert and a temperance meeting respectively. The ballad concerts featured singers like Antoinette Sterling; they became popular, if not great money-spinners, and even attracted royalty until the artists' agents started banning them from singing for nothing. Enterprisingly Poel then got the Life Guards band to play, but overall he found trying to make the Vic pay its way a disheartening struggle. The major obstacle to a coherent artistic policy was the fact that the Vic didn't hold a full theatre licence, and so could not produce plays or operas in their entirety, only excerpts or tableaux. Poel left the Vic, very disenchanted, around Christmas 1883.

Poel's brief tenure at the Vic suggests that Cons, like Baylis, had great skill in picking out those who had a lot to give to the Vic, although, famously, she turned down local boy Charlie Chaplin:

> it was one of his ambitions to appear at the Old Vic. He actually wrote in twice but received no reply. He did not know that Miss Cons never answered a letter which did not contain a stamped, addressed envelope.[50]

But after Poel's departure, in 1894, Emma Cons decided to take over the management of the Vic herself, and she continued to act in this capacity until she persuaded Baylis officially to take over in 1900.

Cons's theatre management style owed much to her experiences of managing slums and Baylis remembers Cons at the Vic 'in her delicate little lace bonnet, facing and quelling a gang of roughs in the gallery' but also managing to give 'a smiling greeting to regular patrons'.[51] Some of Cons's methods were carefully copied by her niece: for example, one of the most distinctive aspects of Baylis's management of the Vic, the tradition of throwing parties, can certainly be traced to Cons.[52] Baylis saw that these parties brought people together, promoted community spirit and could also help build an audience. They generated good will, and distributing free Christmas presents to local poor children also publicised the Vic, as did the fact that on Tuesday afternoons Baylis

> used to collect all the children from the tenements, where she lived with her aunt, and from the New Cut. They were then taught such games as 'London Bridge is Falling Down' and 'Oats and Beans' by voluntary helpers on the Old Vic stage.[53]

Such activities certainly helped the Vic reach out to the local community.

Another aspect of Cons's management style which Baylis emulated was in running the theatre as a matriarchy. Cons's commitment to the employment of women was a constant in her life, and was presumably partly fuelled by the prejudices she had encountered when attempting to earn a living in her early teens. However, Cons's style of theatre management was decidedly her own. The rules for artistes appearing at the Vic clearly stated:

> IV. – No Artiste shall, by inference, direct or indirect, innuendo, or by attitude, or by-play, or by the words of any dialogue or song, introduce anything obscene, or demoralizing in idea or otherwise, or make any jocular allusion to Religious Subjects …
> X. – Artistes must go on the Stage properly and decently attired.[54]

On one occasion when a performer started singing a bawdy song Cons 'boldly ordered the curtain to be dropped upon the singer'.[55] But perhaps the most problematic aspect of her eccentric management of the Vic was Cons's ongoing and steadfast opposition to the theatre applying for a full theatrical licence. This entrenched position was probably a result of a humiliation that she felt very deeply: the successful prosecution of Cons in January 1886 for breaking the protectionist theatrical licensing laws by the performance at the Vic of an entertainment entitled *King He's A Bore; The Pride of His Mama.*

The Theatre Managers' Association used the licensing laws to preserve their monopoly on the production of drama and to prosecute non-legitimate theatres which infringed this law. They argued that *King He's A Bore* broke the terms of the Vic's music hall licence, and while the fine was a nominal 2/6, the humiliation for the upright Cons of being convicted of wrongdoing must have been considerable. Cons's close friend Caroline Martineau comments on this 'very unpleasant episode' and claims that because the entertainment concerned had cost a lot of money to stage, 'it was really no trifle, and the consequent worry had a good deal to do with a dangerous illness which soon after obliged Miss Cons to be absent many weeks together'.[56] However, William Poel remembered that on at least one occasion Cons made the licensing limitation work in her favour when she persuaded Cardinal Manning to speak on temperance at the Vic. When the Cardinal informed Cons that he could not appear at a theatre, Cons pointed out that the Vic was not licensed as a theatre, and so he agreed to speak there.[57]

Cons was also fervent on the subject of women's right to an education, perhaps partly because she felt her own education had suffered. Her friend Sophia Lonsdale records that Cons found writing letters difficult, as she 'knew very well what she wanted said, but her powers of expressing herself on paper had never been developed'.[58] Cons helped found Swanley Horticultural College, the first such college for women, in 1892; she also helped found Morley College for working men and women on the same premises as the Vic as a direct result of the Tuesday lecture series there.[59] In 1882, Willliam Lant Carpenter gave the first lecture on the subject of 'The Telephone' and the lectures quickly proved very popular. When a group of students asked Cons if the programme could be extended, Cons agreed, and soon students were able to sign up for a range of courses;[60] by 1893 classes were being offered in subjects such as reading and writing, arithmetic, languages, electricity and magneticism. Cons subsequently persuaded the Bristol-based millionaire and philanthropist Samuel Morley to endow a college for working men and women by purchasing the Royal Victoria Hall's lease with a £1,000 donation.[61] The fledgling college was housed in what would normally have been the theatre's dressing room spaces, plus spaces below and above the stage (all separated from the theatre by fireproofed walls and doors). Cons was able to do this because the programmes then running at the Vic – temperance lectures, concerts, music hall acts minus the rude jokes – did not need large backstage areas for scenery and costume changes in the way that a conventional theatre would. However, once the Vic under Baylis started expanding and housed full theatrical productions, this sharing of space became more and more intolerable, and Baylis had to spend enormous amounts of time and energy trying to solve what for her was the problem of Morley. Morley College continued to thrive and famous names taught and lectured there – Ralph Vaughan Williams, Virginia Stephen (later Woolf), Vanessa Bell, G.K. Chesterton, Arnold Bennett, Sir Ernest Shackleton and Gustav Holst (who conducted the orchestra for many years) – but it took until the 1920s for Baylis to be able to relocate Morley College and reclaim the Vic's backstage. In the meantime she used Morley as a source of 'supers': Morley College students who volunteered to help out in productions were rewarded 'with a cup of coffee and a slice of cake'.[62]

Cons's great friend Caroline Martineau, who was Principal of the college, wrote a history of its foundation in the Morley College magazine for October 1894.[63] Although initially the college was aimed primarily at working men, very early on women were not only permitted to study but also dominated the board, and Morley's commitment to gender equality was made very explicit. Caroline Martineau comments: 'The women stand on a precisely similar footing to that of the men' and 'not the slightest difficulty would be made if a man wished to learn Cooking, or a woman Machine-drawing'.[64] The foundation decreed that at least three members of the college council should be women: for Cons and Martineau, Morley

College was a success not only because it advanced the cause of education for the working class, but most particularly because of the new opportunities it offered to women.

Cons's achievements were also remarkable in other areas: she founded the Working Girls Home, a hostel in Drury Lane; she established crèches and clinics; she worked with 'the Home for Feeble-Minded Girls at Bodmin';[65] she was on the executive, and later became Vice-President, of the Women's Liberal Federation; in 1908 she became the first woman to address the Institute of Directors; she raised funds to secure Vauxhall Park as a public park; she travelled to Canada to visit ex-tenants. Cons also devoted one autumn holiday in Cyprus to helping refugee Armenians who had fled from persecution in Turkey. Commenting that 'there is no object in repeating over and over again the sickening details of butchery which everyone has been reading in the papers', she recounts her attempts, 'with fair success, to form small committees of the leading inhabitants, in various parts of the island, to act as a labour bureau'.[66] She describes how readers of her report can help the refugees, without unduly disrupting the local labour market; she denounces the Sultan of Turkey for his treatment of his Armenian subjects; and she claims that England is under a particular obligation to help the refugees given that 'Cyprus came into English hands by means which are open to much criticism from the Great Powers of Europe'.[67] In her outspoken and intensely pragmatic approach to such problems, Cons, over and over again, set Baylis a practical example of the importance of getting on with solving problems others felt were insoluble.

The impression of Cons that emerges from the extant correspondence between her and Baylis is that she was a lively, encouraging, loving and attentive aunt.[68] In 1905, when on holiday with her friends Hester and Julia Sterling in Falmouth, Cons writes to Baylis a letter full of cheerful exclamations and emphatic underlinings. Later, in 1908, Baylis is sending Cons balance sheets for her to check; Cons responds with 'Hurrah' and praise for Baylis's work, which she 'will soon be able to do ... without me.' In another letter she instructs Baylis to ignore 'the cold water Miss M pours on your efforts ... we should have done nothing if I had listened to her croakings – you go on and win! As you did with your Wireless lecture.' To have a woman as able, as caring and as determined as Cons cheering her on to win through must have made a very significant impact on Baylis.

Cons was also crucial in enabling Baylis to achieve what she did simply because Cons made Baylis independent financially. During her life Cons amassed a fairly substantial amount of money, and in her will she left £4,233 before tax.[69] The bulk of this money came to Baylis via Cons's sister Ellen. Some sense of Cons's financial position can also be gauged by the fact that in 1902 she intended to buy a house for Baylis; in January of that year she is writing to Frances Haseldine – a woman to whom Cons had lent money because Haseldine's husband was ill and couldn't work – explaining that Haseldine's failure to repay the loan over several years had cost Cons dear:

> I had promised to my niece Miss Baylis to buy her a country house and now she has had to wait more than a year and has lost the purchase of two properties. It really is very troublesome and disappointing that a sacrifice on our part to do you a kindness should prove a disagreeable incident between us and only make bad feeling instead of good.[70]

Generally, Cons's philanthropic lifestyle didn't leave much time for spending money, and as Emma Cons worked nearly all the hours God sent, presumably much of her wealth simply accumulated from her wages over the years. What should not be underestimated, however, is the significance of this money in terms of Baylis's career. Cons's money meant Baylis never needed to worry about her own personal income; as a result, she could dedicate her working life to an enterprise, running the Vic, that often seemed destined to be permanently in the red.

Baylis's gratitude towards her aunt and her commitment to ensuring Cons's achievements were remembered are perhaps most evident in her attempts to commission a biography of Cons. Initially Baylis wanted the biography to be written immediately after her death in 1912, and several friends and supporters of Cons felt this was appropriate. Baylis also met with opposition, however:

the friend whose home in the country she shared, well knowing EC's dislike for publicity, was so against any record of her life being published, that the matter was dropped for the time being. This friend died two years afterwards.[71]

That friend was Ethel Everest, and after Everest's death, Baylis was too embroiled in launching her Shakespeare Company whilst the First World War raged around her to be able to concentrate on the Cons biography.

Baylis returned to the project, however, in the early 1920s and she asked her closest longstanding friend, Louie Davey, who had worked with Cons, to help her. Baylis and Davey contacted many who had known Cons and asked for their reminiscences in preparation for producing a full biography (this is when Henrietta Barnett was asked to write her introduction to Cons's character). Baylis attempted to track down several of Cons's artworks, but was unsuccessful in trying to locate the stained-glass windows that Cons worked on in Merton College, Oxford. In 1923 she approached Reginald Blunt to write the Cons biography;[72] she got the book costed – and Williams and Strahan agreed to publish a book of 35,000 words for £21.[73] In the end the book project was abandoned, but Baylis's and Davey's research clearly provided the foundation for Baylis's essay on Cons in Cicely Hamilton's history of the Vic.

The early 1920s was a period when Baylis was so busy that many thought she was pushing herself to the edge of breakdown.[74] This makes it all the more significant that she nevertheless made time to research and write her account of Cons's life. Some of her investigations were extremely frustrating: in 1922 Baylis was anxiously trying to find out whether the portrait of Cons as an alderman – which had been commissioned as a tribute to her pioneering political work – would be hung in the new County Hall, and all she obtained were non-committal answers.[75] But in producing a pen portrait of her aunt, Baylis also revealed a lot about herself in her admiration for Cons's resilience and perseverance; for her commitment to the poor, to women's right to work, to education and to women's suffrage; and for her 'love of beauty'.[76] Baylis's portrait of Cons is not a hagiography, however, and it includes comic defeats as well as feminist triumphs, recounting several anecdotes of Cons being outwitted by independent-minded slum dwellers, resisting Cons's determination to 'improve' their lives. One family managed to convince Cons that the father had just died, and she 'emptied her purse' into the poor wife's hand before leaving.[77] Discovering she had left her umbrella behind, Cons returned to pick it up and found the 'corpse' and his wife celebrating their good fortune by drinking gin.

Emma Cons died on 24 July 1912, of a cerebral haemorrhage, at Ethel Everest's home, Chippens Bank, and it was here that her ashes were scattered.[78] The Bishop of Southwark presided at her funeral, and the King and Queen sent a telegram of condolence. The loss to Baylis was immense, and it is hardly surprising that the year of Cons's death, 1912, was pivotal in many ways for her. In that year she lost a close friend, a source of inspiration and a role model. But Baylis also finally gained full control of the Vic.

NOTES

1   This chapter is the major source of information used here. Judith Leighton's 'An Analysis of the Life and Work of Emma Cons (1838–1912), Manager of the Old Vic Theatre, London', M.Phil. dissertation, Middlesex University, 1996 is another source of information. Baylis was not the only woman whose working career was inspired by Cons, as Sophia Lonsdale's testimony makes clear (see Violet Martineau (compiler), *Recollections of Sophia Lonsdale* (London, 1936), pp. 160–5).

2   Baylis also made several attempts to create a physical memorial to Cons. Her efforts eventually resulted in a large wall medallion in bronze (still to be seen in the Vic), a stone inscription, and a shelter for those queuing for gallery seats. Several times over the years the *OVM* carried articles, presumably by Baylis, reminding readers of Emma Cons's work.

3   Baylis, 'Emma Cons', p. 257.

4   Ibid.

5   Sophia Lonsdale in Violet Martineau, *Recollections of Sophia Lonsdale*, p. 162.

6   Baylis, 'Emma Cons', p. 260.

7   Ibid., p. 261.

8   Ibid.

9   Ibid., p. 257.

10 OVEC/000171, letter dated 10 February 1924.

11 Quoted in Gillian Darley, *Octavia Hill* (London, 1990), pp. 135–6.

12 *OVM*, February 1931.

13 OVEC/000233.

14 Ellen Barlee, *Pantomime Waifs or, a plea for our city children* (London, 1884) p. 195. For a colourful description of Lambeth's state of depravity slightly earlier see John Hollingshead, *Ragged London in 1861* (London, 1861), who characterises the Waterloo Road district as the haunt of prostitutes, thieves, and tramps (pp. 166–7), and the Victoria Theatre as full of '[h]alf the evil, low-browed, lowering faces in London' (p. 180).

15 Barlee, *Pantomime Waifs*, p. 195.

16 Baylis, 'Emma Cons', p. 274.

17 Ibid., p. 256.

18 C. Edmund Maurice, *The Life of Octavia Hill As Told in Her Letters* (London, 1913), p. 15.

19 E. Moberly Bell, *Octavia Hill: A Biography* (London, 1942).

20 Ibid.; Baylis, 'Emma Cons', pp. 258–9.

21 Beatrice Webb, *My Apprenticeship*, vol. II (Harmondsworth, 1938), pp. 315–16.

22 Ibid., p. 315. Her admiration for Cons did not extend to performances on offer at the purified Vic: 'To me a dreary performance, sinking to the level of the audience, while omitting the dash of coarseness, irreverence and low humour which give the spice and reality to such entertainments' (p. 321).

23 OVEC/000231/5–6.

24 Yetta (1851–1936) was known publicly as Mrs Samuel A. Barnett, and later Dame Henrietta Barnett. She and her husband established and ran Toynbee Hall. Barnett is also remembered for her philanthropic work with children, for her campaign for the preservation of Hampstead Heath, and her contribution to the planning of Hampstead Garden Suburb.

25 OVEC/000175.

26 OVLB/000017.

27 OVEC/000231/1.

28 OVEC/000231/2–3.

29 Lillian Faderman, *Surpassing the Love of Men: Romantic Friendship and Love between Women from the Renaissance to the Present* (New York, 1981, reprinted London, 1985), p. 156. Faderman argues that where the twentieth century would expect sexual activity to take place between lesbian women, cultural conditioning meant that many woman-centred Victorian women simply would not have envisaged a sexual dimension to even the most intense of relations between women. However, the late twentieth-century notion of a 'political' lesbian allows for a focus on the woman-identified woman without the distraction of trying to establish whether any sexual activity with another woman ever took place. For a critique of Faderman see Sheila Jeffreys, 'Does It Matter If They Did It?' in Lesbian History Group (ed.), *Not a Passing Phase: Reclaiming Lesbians in History 1840–1985* (London, 1989), pp. 19–28.

30 Auchmuty, 'By Their Friends We Shall Know Them', p. 80. Nicky Hallett, *Lesbian Lives: Identity and Auto/Biography in the Twentieth Century* (London, 1999) also discusses Octavia Hill in terms of lesbian relationships, and her relationship with Emma Cons is analysed (see pp. 88–90).

31 The clearest account of this battle appears in Patricia Hollis, *Ladies Elect: Women in English Local Government 1865–1914* (Oxford, 1987).

32 See Emma Cons, 'Women and the County Council', letter to *The Times*, 1 December 1890 for her refusal to stand for a constituency. OVEC/000233 stresses that Cons had been specially asked to serve as an alderman by the LCC.

33 Philippa Levine, *Feminist Lives in Victorian England: Private Roles and Public Commitment* (Oxford, 1990), p. 122.

34 OVEC/000233/3.

35 *The Times*, 1 December 1890.

36 Anonymous account, OVEC/000249.

37 Hollis, *Ladies Elect*, p. 317. A fragment of Cons's engagements diary from 1906 exists (M&M) and her ongoing interest in political issues is documented: on 18 October she is part of a deputation to 12 Downing Street; details of the LCC motion of 16 October are noted.

38 OVLB/000047/6.

39 Baylis, 'Emma Cons', p. 281.

40 Women's Library, London, Autograph Letters, vol. I (1912).

41 OVEC/000004/21. Boyle stood, unsuccessfully, for Parliament

in England in a by-election in 1918.

42 Baylis, 'Emma Cons', p. 271. In addition the Cons family connection with Preston, via the Goodairs, might be significant, as Preston was the centre of the most militant temperance movement of the times.

43 Ibid., p. 270.

44 Barlee, *Pantomime Waifs*, p. 196. Given this, it is hardly surprising that Cons rarely started work before 10.30 a.m. (see Lonsdale in Violet Martineau, *Recollections of Sophia Lonsdale*, p. 163).

45 Baylis, 'Emma Cons', p. 283.

46 Barlee, *Pantomime Waifs*, pp. 198–9.

47 For the cleaning operations see ibid., p. 204. Sophia Lonsdale (Violet Martineau, *Recollections of Sophia Lonsdale*, p. 165) testifies to the fact that Cons failed to get rid of the Vic's fleas.

48 *OVM*, October 1919.

49 Edwin Hodder, *The Life of Samuel Morley* (London, 1887), p. 433.

50 Raymond P. Mander, 'The Old Vic Fifty Years Ago', *The Vic-Wells Association Newsletter*, 82 (November 1953) relates that Chaplin told this story to Hugh Hunt, artistic director of the Vic during the early 1950s.

51 Baylis, 'Emma Cons', p. 252.

52 OVLB/000156 records that Cons's Christmas party involved 500–600 tenants.

53 Reminiscences of Grace and Violet Marfleet, dancers at the Vic 1903–22, quoted in Mander, 'The Old Vic Fifty Years Ago'.

54 Emma Cons, 'The Royal Victoria Coffee Music Hall Rules', M&M.

55 Barlee, *Pantomime Waifs*, p. 206. Barlee specifically records (p. 207) that dancers had to have ankle-length skirts and children had to be chaperoned by their parents – the latter was a particular point in Cons's favour for Barlee, who campaigned against the exploitation of child performers in Victorian theatres and circuses.

56 Caroline Martineau, 'A History of the Royal Victoria Hall and Morley Memorial College' (pamphlet reprint of article first published in the *Morley College Magazine*, October 1894), pp. 9–10.

57 *OVM*, December 1930.

58 Sophia Lonsdale in Violet Martineau, *Recollections of Sophia Lonsdale*, p. 163.

59 Baylis, 'Emma Cons', p. 281. Morley College still flourishes and offers courses to some 15,000 adult students.

60 OVEC/000206. J.G. Sparkhill records that it was he and Percy Eyre who asked for more lectures after a lecture on astronomy by Mr Maclure.

61 Other donors included the Martineau family, and Julia and Hester Sterling, whose grandfather, Captain Edward Sterling, was the original 'Thunderer' of *The Times* and who earlier had bought property in Walmer Street and Walmer Place, which Cons managed.

62 Denis Richards, *Offspring of the Old Vic: A History of Morley College* (London, 1958), p. 198. Richards's account is very dependent on Caroline Martineau's 'A History of the Royal Victoria Hall and Morley Memorial College'.

63 All information here on the history of Morley College is taken from Caroline Martineau, 'A History'. The *OVM* of February 1923 contains an article by Guy Martineau, who had just joined the Vic as an actor, explaining that Caroline's famous aunt 'Harriet Martineau, was also interested in Miss Cons' work'. The same issue of *OVM* comments that 'The theatre still receives from the executors of Miss Harriet Martineau, a small annual subscription.'

64 Caroline Martineau, 'A History', p. 16.

65 Baylis, 'Emma Cons', p. 281.

66 See Emma Cons, 'Armenian Exiles in Cyprus', *Contemporary Review*, 70 (July–December 1896), pp. 889, 891.

67 Ibid., p. 895.

68 All references in this paragraph to the letters are catalogued at OVLB/000047.

69 See OVEC/000137 and OVEC/000142/2.

70 OVEC/000184.

71 OVEC/000232/3.

72 OVEC/0000164.

73 OVEC/0000213.

74 The governors of the Vic almost had to frog-march Baylis into going on holiday in 1924, and insisted on paying for her trip to South Africa.

75 OVLB/000010.

76 Baylis, 'Emma Cons', p. 273.

77 Ibid., p. 266.

78 OVEC/000252. Ethel Everest actually left twenty-six acres of her land to the National Trust as a memorial to Cons, but the National Trust were not willing to take it on.

[5]

Personal Matters

During the First World War Lilian Baylis became a public character and this event can be dated fairly precisely. When Zeppelin raids began, leading actor Philip Ben Greet

> used to go on directly the warning was received, and would tell the news to the audience so that they could go if they wished. One night he went on in a rather ghastly make-up prepared to die very early in the play, and so alarmed members of the audience that they fainted. After that the Manager went on herself. "It was my first effort at speech making," she says.[1]

Baylis made her speech with gruff abruptness, and was an instant success with the audience. From then on she quickly began to develop her act, and became very adept at working her audience and responding to their laughter. Indeed Vic audiences soon came to expect and to enjoy Baylis's comic speeches; however, this also meant that many who met her after these performances began looked for (and often found) the public persona – the caricature Baylis. The woman that Baylis was immediately *before* she started playing, exploiting and possibly being trapped by her public performance of 'The Manager of the Vic' began to disappear from view, and that is why it is particularly important to acknowledge the private Baylis, the Baylis that she herself wrote about: a woman who travelled the world; a woman who experienced religious visions; and a woman who struggled to cope in the aftermath of the death of her aunt Emma Cons.

One of the longest extant pieces of continuous prose written by Lilian Baylis is a letter she wrote providing an account of Emma Cons's final days for Baylis's parents, who in

1912 were still far off in South Africa.[2] This letter demonstrates unequivocally that Cons's death hit Baylis very hard because, quite apart from her own feelings of loss, nearly everyone around her seemed to collapse emotionally, especially Emma's younger sister, Baylis's aunt Ellen, and Emma's close friend Ethel Everest, at whose home Cons had died. Baylis was particularly disgusted with the behaviour of 'Miss E', her 'madness and badness', and blamed her lack of sustaining religion.[3] Everest added to Baylis's work at this time by complaining about the nursing Cons had received, and demanding that Baylis contact the press to correct inaccurate reports about Everest.[4] Baylis enjoyed funerals ('I would rather go to a funeral than a last night of the season, because I *do* believe in the Resurrection') but she had to organise a big public funeral for Cons, as well as her cremation, and in addition, deal with Everest's enquiries as to who was going to buy Cons's shares in the Hampstead Garden Suburb.[5]

Baylis's letter to Liebe and Newton Baylis provides striking evidence of her emotional turmoil, and of her private sorrow. The detail is intimate although there is also a strongly pragmatic streak: because Cons had asked to be cremated and cremations were a new thing in the family, Baylis pays particular attention to explaining the details of this process. The letter speaks volumes about what Cons meant to Baylis, and is worth quoting at length:[6]

Surrey Lodge, Lambeth Road July 29 1912

Dear Mother and Dad,

… Your opinion mother of Emma was so true, the danger was a relapse. When I look back I have not a thing to regret, God gave me strength to do all possible for her, after the convulsion Sun[day] morn[ing] she never recovered consciousness, the Dr. thought she must go before Tues[day] and yet it was 8.20 Wed[nesday] the 24 in the evening she died. Nurse who had been such a little beast the 1st week got better and better, she loved Emma so, when these laboured breaths and death rattles started Mon[day] and continued 3 days she was quite knocked Tues[day] night she comforted me, Wed[nesday] she had red eyes all day and every time she'd tried to sleep or been out of the room she sat down by Emma & said "poor sweet soul, oh dear, dear soul, this is dreadful, how long it is lasting, this breathing is cruel." I kept worrying if aunty could feel anything but Dr. and nurse said no, she was conscious of nothing, nurse meant it was cruel to us nursing her, but I seemed to get above it. When I was alone at 1st with her, if nurse and aunt Nell had been in the room & just gone out, I felt if I let myself go I'd simply never leave off sobbing & weeping, but I know my work will be awful and I must not give way, directly I feel I'm going to, I clutch the cross round my neck and calmness returns. The last half hour her breathing had changed from noisy to gentle sobbing kind, a long drawn out sob like a tired child that has been unhappy & was cuddling down to sleep against its mother, a long sobbing breath & then a sort of echo of it, I counted 5 between the sob and the echo, & it comforted me this happy relief from the laboured breath ...

I left off trying to feel her pulse, it only bothered me, & my hand came from hers as if from a pool of water, her head was burning, her dear leg went 1st all horrid colour and then her hands ... I never thought I could so long for her to go ...

when nurse was sure she had gone I took aunt Nell and put her in the easy chair in our bedroom & put her feet up. I'd thought to ask Dr. to leave a tonic & nurse when Emma's breathing got quiet gave aunt Nell a dose. She was quite calm, but v[er]y shaky, I left her resting & returned to nurse & helped wash my Emmie for the last time, I never Mother in all these weary weeks had held her poor body over & turned her in bed without feeling unhappy until this laying out ...

I was awake at 4 felt I must be on the go, tore up letters & packed up ...

I'd wanted the Vicar or someone so badly all Mon[day] and Tues[day] Wed[nesday] I read all the prayers for the dying out loud to Emma when we were alone & the hymn

[77]

"On the Resurrection Morn" which has always helped me buck up since Willie died ...7

One night after I'd helped change the drawsheet & pillow which were soaked with perspiration & then sat watching till after 5, I felt if I didn't have an hours sleep I could never nurse all day ...

I went in to Emmie, nurse came & removed the clothes, she looked most lovely, her beautiful silver hair we had done as during her illness in 2 plaits tied with white ribbon, her hair sort of half curled down each side of her forehead, it looked full of life, her whole face was smiling & most peaceful, I laid one of her favourite roses on her breast, kissed her and flew off to church. When I returned I found pressmen on the doorstep & it was one whirl of rush & work from that moment ...

I alone received [the undertakers], the men asked me if I'd rather go out, but I felt I wanted to know her body was being gentle handled so I took off the sheet that covered her & a little water had run as Nurse feared it would as we'd given medicine 4 hours before death by the rectum, so I just let the top sheet drop over the damp patch as they lifted her gently into the coffin ...

I ran up to Town on Fri[day] left Hever 6.40 broke my journey at Edenbridge for the death certificate, caught the 7.40 up to Town, found I could wear an almost new black coat & skirt of Emma's, just had it lengthened, & my black Tulle hat ...

I felt I must have someone with me as I never knew if I was going to pitch on my head or my knees give way ...

sometime I'll tell you what madness & badness we'd had to put up with at Hever Miss E[verest] loves Aunt Nell but simply torchured her if she could get her alone, poor darling I am so sorry for her, she is desolate, no God or helpful Faith to cling to, only Miss Tricky who puts low ideas into her head, we can seldom speak without a row, but I love her all the same & only hope her mind won't get more unhinged & she be shut up ...

the body of the church was quite full, 100's were disappointed at not knowing, I hurried it for Sat[urday] so that the working people could come. 3 of the Coffin Bearers hurried direct from work to the Church ...

the beautiful aloe that Emmie planted some years ago which had blossomed Miss E[verest] cut and laid all along the coffin, but it got so to one side she asked me to carry it ...

The horses walked all the way to the Vic, right down the Cut, we stopped a minute at the Stagedoor, then all our men Miss Ellis & many poor folk followed down Oakley St. behind us. I had the aloe in my hand, around Surrey Lodge we went & stopped again for many of the tenants to fall in & then to Lambeth Church, the crowd round the church was great ...

I followed the coffin up. Kissed the aloe & placed it right down the coffin, all the other flowers were left in the hearse ...

it was a beautiful service ...

when I got to the top of the steps leading down to the S[tree]t the crowds of people, I felt a sudden tremble and believe I should have collapsed only the Bishop stood at the bottom & simply held my eyes with such a dear Fatherly smile & gave me courage to go on ...

we went slowly to the Tube where numbers took tickets to Golders Green & we drove quickly across London. I felt strange at the Crematorium, never having been in such a place before. The chapel was almost full of the Walmer Street & Bill Street people ...[8]

Its a square marble Hall with a large sq[uare] platform up 3 steps ...

After the committal prayer the coffin slides away through the wall & the stones meet again, the flowers remaining on the table. Mr. Briant gave me his arm & I went up the steps across this platform through an iron door in the wall & to the left near where the coffin was standing as it came through the wall, in the centre was this huge chamber, a furnace, the door was opened & one could not see where the fire came from only glorious flames like an angry sunset red & gold, the coffin shot off this table right into this glorious flame, I just saw the coffin catch round the edge, the aloe was caught in the flame and seemed full of life and magnified just as if there were a hundred lilies, the door shut & I heard the roar of the furnace & I suppose I felt sick … I decided to wait for the ashes myself. This chapel was full of people who loved Emmie, about 20 men or more from Morley College. I did not know what to do with all the flowers & suddenly thought how Emmie would love them all to take some away, so said to the men who'd carried the coffin all old servants, to divide up the flowers …

eventually all left, but faithful Miss Tyte and Davey. Davey made me go & have tea while Miss Tyte kept watch, then we walked round the beautiful grounds & then the ashes were ready …

I saw the furnace door open & you could see the shape of the coffin in ashes …

they raked them all up in a heap & then they dropped into a tray below & then onto a huge marble slab, with 2 bronze shovels, 2 men sorted out the long nails & took the ashes up into the simple urn …

We take them today to Hever.

Post going so goodbye my dear ones

Ever your loving

Lilian

Davey, the woman who so sensibly made Baylis go and have a cup of tea after the cremation, was one of Baylis's closest and dearest friends. Davey had worked for Emma Cons in social housing after studying at Oxford (without taking a degree, as Oxford then still debarred women from graduating).9 Davey was

a source of great pride to Emma Cons, who envied the young girl the ease with which she acquired the "college" education which was denied to most women of Miss Cons' own generation.10

The friendship between Baylis and Davey was to last for thirty-three years, and in a letter written in 1923 Davey recalls, 'I cannot remember exactly when I first came to Surrey Lodge, but I had been there at least some months in May 1904 so it must have been in 1903 or early 1904, probably the former,' which establishes that the twenty-three-year-old Davey first met Baylis when the latter was around thirty years of age.[11] Davey's letter has been cut, almost to pieces, with scissors, but other uncut letters indicate that Davey spent much of her later life looking after her wheelchair-bound father.

Davey also accompanied Baylis on many of her holidays: significantly, it was Davey who travelled with Baylis when she went on the longest and most extravagant holiday of her life – a world cruise in 1910. Indeed one of the most relaxed-looking photographs of Baylis in existence is of her and Davey, sitting together after their return from this holiday (see p. 82).[12] Baylis kept a journal of their travels, but it is very much a record of what she saw, places she visited and landscapes she admired. As she states in a letter written from Sydney, 'Time flys [*sic*] so, if I am to see any of the interesting places I can't write letters. I've tried to make short notes for you to read on my return.'[13] The idea that the journal constitutes 'short notes' might explain some notable omissions: Baylis is completely silent on how she felt on meeting up in Australia with her sister Violet and brother Ray after over twenty years apart. Presumably she felt she was unlikely to forget such an experience and needed no *aide memoire*; she kept several photographs taken during her visit, as well as a group of photographs of 'Ray's child' in three different moods in ten minutes.[14] Yet all Baylis records in the journal is 'Vi met me.' Despite the conciseness of her travelogue, however, it still offers a vivid portrait of Baylis as sensitive, fun-loving, and romantic.

Baylis's love of beautiful scenery is particularly conspicuous. She describes landscapes at length and with great enthusiasm, although she will often compare the landscape she is encountering to what she already knows: the Canadian Prairies are like the Transvaal; Banff is like Switzerland; the Blue Mountains, New South Wales, like Norway; Manly beach in Sydney like Ramsgate or Margate; the Sahara Desert like 'the Margate sands stretching for miles and miles in width as well as length'. Baylis also comments extensively on trees and

Louie Davey and Lilian Baylis at Ethel Everest's home, Chippens Bank, Hever, 1910. Inscription in Baylis's handwriting 'Davey and Lilian at Hever The Cottage'. Courtesy of the Royal Victoria Hall Foundation and the University of Bristol Theatre Collection

flowers, and when she visits cities she will often make tracks for parks or botanical gardens to see more flowers and trees. While the whole holiday, which lasted for four months, was almost constant movement, Baylis still found time to linger over sunsets and sunrises; she noted that on the trip it was mostly men who were taking photographs, but she herself was energetic in her use of the camera and often attempted to photograph majestic scenery, particularly in the Canadian Rockies, even when rattling along on a train.

The trip began with a crossing to Ireland and then on to New York, Niagara, Toronto, Winnipeg, Calgary, Banff. The Rockies so impressed Baylis that she missed lunch in order to remain on her own in the observation car watching the scenery. Vancouver was followed by Victoria, then Hawaii. Baylis loved Hawaii, where she rushed out to see and collect night-blooming irises by moonlight. She put three in her washbasin and, knowing they would close again by morning, she writes 'I hated to go to sleep. I longed to sit and gaze at these wonderful flowers.' She swam at Waikiki, watched Hawaiian canoeing and surfing, 'fished for sharks and should have died with fright if we'd got one', and commented overall, 'I should have liked 2 or 3 weeks in Honolulu and the surrounding Islands.'

After Hawaii, Baylis visited Fiji, Brisbane and Sydney, from where she travelled up to the Blue Mountains and the Jenolan Caves. This massive network of caves, embellished with extraordinary stalactite and stalagmite formations, really caught Baylis's imagination. She spends pages describing the caves in overwhelming detail. Later on, in Melbourne, Baylis mixed with the Australian ruling elite including Lady Forrest (her aunt Esther's sister-in-law). 'Lady Forrest motored down to the Quay to meet me', but

> a dreadful railway accident had just occurred & as we passed the big railway station Flinders St. crowds were standing watching the ambulances bringing out the injured, then as Lady Forrest motored me to the Botanical Gardens, we passed the station where the accident happened and saw the people swarming up the railway banks, it seemed dreadful.[15]

Baylis then lunched with the Forrests at the Grand Hotel, visited Government House, and met several Australian statesmen with whom she had a 'jolly chat'. As the Forrests knew the officers and the captain of Baylis's ship, they were all invited to dinner, with music and dancing up in the Forrests' private drawing room. Baylis then went on to Adelaide and

Fremantle, and the rolling of the ship whilst crossing the Australian Bight caused much hilarity. Baylis records:

> I never remember laughing so much as I did at my last breakfast on the Moldavia, everything ran from you … when wanting butter, it was at the far end of the table, butter please, & as a big roll came, the butter dish slid all down the table almost onto your lap and the same with the milk jug and everything. We told the steward he could take a holiday the things ran down to us unaided. I've never heard such smashing, £1s & £1s of crockery must have gone that morn. Everything in the cabin went from one side to the other, I could not attempt to pack, I did nothing but laugh, until we'd almost sighted Fremantle.

In Fremantle Baylis met her sister Violet. Rains and floods meant Baylis did not see the nearest city, Perth, at its best but she reported in detail on crops, flowers and fauna, and wrote down a description of Bunbury (where her immediate family were based). Baylis and Davey then travelled on to Colombo, Aden and Port Said before sailing for home.

The itinerary for this world cruise is astonishing when Baylis's reputation for frumpy parochialism is considered. In fact, unsurprisingly after her adventures in South Africa, Baylis loved travelling: she visited the Matterhorn; she cycled in France; in 1900 she saw the Passion play at Oberammergau, visited the Rhineland and also travelled around Norway (including the far north, where very few visitors ventured and very little English was spoken).[16] Baylis's journal for this holiday, which begins on 12 July and ends on 1 September, relates that Baylis and her sister Ethel were the only women on the trip, which was full of beautiful scenery but dangerous in places.[17] They examined wild flowers, brought some home 'for verification', climbed mountains, picked up shells, crossed the Arctic circle 'in the most exquisite tints of rosy morning light' and visited an 'encampment of the Laplanders' – although they were slightly worried when sitting next to some Lapp women in church, as they had been told 'they were very dirty underneath their outer clothing'.[18] They saw 'the interesting tho' horrible sight of cutting up the whales for making oil' but

[84]

decided not to go whale catching as the weather was too rough.[19]

Baylis the traveller is almost the antithesis of the Baylis of the anecdotes, a creature who could not be imagined longing to stay up to watch Hawaiian night irises bloom before they faded and died. What is more, the sheer extravagance of the round-the-world trip is incongruous alongside the penny-pinching, gauche Baylis of legend.[20] Baylis's voice in the journal is that of a woman who at thirty-six can still be open-eyed with wonder, excitement and enthusiasm, a woman who enjoys taking physical risks, like the hair-raising car journey she describes, speeding back to Sydney from the Blue Mountains. The cruise holiday lasted from June to September, and during this time Baylis and Davey in effect lived together, on ship and in the various places they stopped and visited. This is the kind of ongoing close companionship that really makes or breaks a friendship.

While Davey's support for Baylis in the aftermath of Emma Cons's death must have been crucial, Baylis also mourned by throwing herself into work. However, while she constantly fought to uphold what she reported as Cons's mission statement on her deathbed, that 'the Vic must help poor children', in other ways Baylis knowingly betrayed Cons's vision.[21] Indeed, in 1912, almost as soon as her aunt's ashes were scattered at Hever, Baylis in effect broke faith with her by immediately applying for a full theatre licence. This disregard of Cons's well-known opposition to the Vic changing its licence can only have made Baylis's grieving more complex, and it seems significant that 1912 was also something of a watershed for Baylis spiritually. In this year she went on a religious retreat where she met the priest who was to become her spiritual adviser for the rest of her life, Father Andrew Hardy.[22]

Baylis's immediate family had always been enthusiastic churchgoers, and particularly focused on the musical side of worship. Yet in her time of working with Emma Cons, Baylis's own religion does not seem to have been conspicuously on display in the way that it often is in the comic anecdotes about her. This may have been because, despite the theological disputes with Octavia Hill in her teens, Emma Cons was someone who, according to her friend May Hughes, 'seldom talked religion, unless her feelings were very much wrought upon'.[23] Another friend, Sophia Lonsdale, suggests a darker side in her recollection of Cons looking down at the Thames from Lambeth Bridge and saying:

> When one thinks of all the sin and misery there is in London what's to prevent one's throwing oneself over there, except one's faith? I wish I were in Heaven with the gate shut.[24]

It is clear, however, that for Cons faith meant good works. By contrast, the Baylis of the comic anecdotes parades her religion, claims 'I've the Almighty in my pocket', and berates God for not helping the Vic quickly enough.[25]

The period in which Father Andrew became important in Baylis's life was a time when she may have been particularly vulnerable as a result of Cons's death, but she was certainly not alone in allowing Father Andrew to direct her spiritual life. He was a charismatic and supportive priest, and the mere fact that Kathleen Burne's *Life and Letters of Father Andrew*, published in 1948, was on its fifth impression by 1951 suggests something of his influence in the mid twentieth century. Father Andrew's self-published book of prayers for wartime also notched up impressive sales figures – 14,000 copies – for a time of rationing.

Father Andrew was an Anglo-Catholic who in 1894, along with James Adderley and Henry Chappel, founded the Society of the Divine Compassion, a Franciscan-style community which eventually made its base at the church of St Philip's at Plaistow. This church is where, in accordance with her expressed wishes, Baylis's ashes were eventually scattered. At Plaistow, Father Andrew worked amongst dockers, the dying, the drunk, the unemployed, as well as establishing a reputation for himself as a leader of retreats. In 1914 the community struck out radically and established the foundation that was to become Baylis's favourite charity: the St Giles home for lepers at East Hanningfield, Essex. Baylis's enthusiasm for St Giles's led her to pressgang famous performers to go there and entertain those suffering from leprosy, and while some performers groaned about this as an imposition, the fact remained that those suffering from leprosy could not, because of their illness, visit a theatre and expect a welcome, and Baylis's support for St Giles's deserves credit. Indeed when the home was first established it was so hated and feared that local inhabitants protested vigorously and even organised a boycott of Percy Pettit, the only local trader willing to supply the home with essential goods.[26] Leprosy was seen to render sufferers complete pariahs, and Baylis's ongoing and high-profile support for the St Giles home – which often included benefit nights at the Vic – helped the home very significantly.[27]

Although he felt called to work amongst the very needy, such as the St Giles patients, Father Andrew was also an artist, primarily a watercolourist, who had had some success in his occasional theatrical endeavours. From 1894 on he had produced series of religious tableaux, some of which became phenomenally popular. Father Andrew also moved into playwriting with *The Hope of the World*, which was directed at the Vic in 1919 by Russell Thorndike, and he wrote several other plays that were produced in religious environments. At a later stage in his life Father Andrew gave up going to the theatre. As he wrote to Baylis,

> I am sure you know that there is hardly a bigger sacrifice that I offer to God in my life than the sacrifice of coming to the Vic as I used to. I believe there is no one who loves the theatre more than I do, or who is more completely happy in its atmosphere and in the appreciation of dramatic art; but that good thing God, I believe, asked me to offer up as a sacrifice and I have done it.[28]

Father Andrew's influence on Baylis became a great source of speculation amongst Vic personnel.[29] Robert Atkins, Baylis's artistic director at the Vic in the early 1920s, describes Father Andrew as a 'tall and massive figure, in a monastic robe, with a skull-cap crowning one of the most arresting yet sinister faces I have ever seen'; he was

> always gliding in and out of the Vic and Miss Baylis was very much under his influence. One morning, inadvertently, I

entered the office and found them at prayer. Though put at ease by an invitation to join her, I made a dignified retreat.[30]

Edward Dent also characterises Father Andrew as gliding:

> He haunted the theatre, and haunted is here indeed the right word, for his tall and sinister-looking figure would sometimes glide silently into the shadows of the Governors' box during a performance, draped in some sort of monastic habit, and suggesting a Grand Inquisitor escaped from the score of some forgotten opera by Mercadante or Donizetti. I do not remember that I ever had the honour of being introduced to him, but I was told that in private life he was considered to be a man of great kindness of heart.[31]

Many at the Vic found Father Andrew disconcerting but there is no doubt that he was someone to whom Baylis could always turn, who would offer prayer, calm, and peace in times of crisis – in marked contrast to the habitually frenetic rhythms of theatre life. Father Andrew's advice to Baylis was often simply that she should slow down: one letter to Baylis says 'Don't try to go to Mass so much your work has to be your mass, I am sure our Lord would say "Lilian stop in bed!" I am certain of it.'[32] At the same time Father Andrew certainly saw the Vic as an opportunity for witness and Baylis may have been caught in the middle occasionally between her religious commitment and financial imperatives: one (undated) letter from Father Andrew states wistfully, 'I should be awfully hurt if you didn't do my Nativity Play next Winter.'[33]

Baylis's spiritual life, however, was not all centred around Father Andrew's teaching, and she experienced several profound and intense religious visions, which she recorded with scrupulous care.[34] It is unclear whether Baylis documented these experiences for her own benefit, to return to in moments of crisis, or whether they would ever have formed part of a published autobiography, but they undoubtedly sustained her, and so are important in understanding her success. Yet by their very nature such experiences are unlikely to mean much to others, simply because the actual vision, euphoria, or sense of transcendence was crucial, and to reduce these events to a verbal narrative is almost inevitably trivialising.

Baylis's spiritual record establishes her absolute belief that she had encountered miraculous intervention by God, sometimes in quite mundane circumstances. In one account she records how once at the Vic 'a ne'er do well brother of a dear friend of hers' called at the theatre to try to borrow money and 'began to make violent love to her', quickly becoming 'more and more amorous'.35 Although people were around outside the office Baylis 'felt ashamed that they should know she was being insulted' and so she prayed, whereupon there was a sudden 'violent knock at the door and the handle turned imperatively as if someone was at once entering the door'. There was actually no one there, but the knock stopped the young man in his tracks even though he was 'mad with passion'. It is typical of Baylis's scrupulousness in recording her religious experiences that she includes tiny details in this slightly breathless narrative: it was a Friday and 'pay night'; people waiting outside, who heard nothing of the miraculous knock, included the dresser who was packing opera costumes away, a young singer who was looking through an opera score and the Vic messenger, Bob, who 'was waiting to have his weekly petty cash till passed'.

Baylis was also scrupulous in recording the circumstances surrounding her visions. In 1921 she was suffering great pain, particularly in her knee, from a cycling accident when 'A motor going at express speed in the same direction as myself knocked me off my bike'.36 Baylis tried 'to keep the seriousness of the accident from her aged parents';37 nevertheless she describes the pain as 'beyond words', with 'a sort of rigour' setting in, her 'whole body shaking', and her feeling 'cold and dreadfully ill'. In addition, very alarmingly, 'her leg occasionally shot upwards and it had to be dragged down forcibly on to the bed'. In the midst of this Baylis

> suddenly felt as if she were being lifted up on most lovely downy pillows, a soft beautiful bed of ease. All pain left her;

all the cold shivers disappeared and perfect comfort of body came to her.

She was first conscious of a quiet peace and then the ceiling of her room vanished and one unending sea of silver took its place; a glorious silver Dove was directly over her and radiating from this Dove, (the Holy Ghost) was this wonderful sea of silver light, reaching far, far into the distance.

Eventually 'just one silver streak like an angel's wing was left'. The comfort of this experience helped Baylis soldier on at a time when the hunt to find new premises, and funding, for Morley College was exerting huge emotional pressure on her.

An experience in a similar vein took place in 1924 when Baylis was about to depart for South Africa. What the Vic governors had desperately tried to insist was to be a complete holiday had already metamorphosed into more of a business trip because of the number of speaking engagements she had accepted. Baylis knew she was 'very overtired' and began to panic over her ability to stick to her punishing schedule. She then heard 'a strong voice' say 'My Grace is sufficient for thee', relaxed and fulfilled all the engagements.[38]

Baylis also recorded two occasions on which she witnessed a vision of Christ. Once, when staying with friends at Shell Ness on the Isle of Sheppey, Baylis was bitterly disappointed at missing communion because someone had blocked her car in overnight.[39] Despite making frantic efforts to get to a church in time, Baylis ended up at 'the beautiful old church at Eastchurch' too late in the service, she felt, to take communion. She knelt near the door and 'feeling very disappointed, wept'. The priest suggested she pray in the Lady Chapel where he had left the blessed bread and wine which he was going to use later in the day to give communion to a woman who was dying. As Baylis prayed, she 'saw our Lord kneeling against the little table facing her. They seemed to say the Our Father together and when she opened her eyes again, He was not there'.

A year later Baylis was still pondering over these events, and she returned to the church to check if a trick of sunlight on the stained glass windows might have caused her vision. She concluded it could not but she also found that the friendly priest was dead, and indeed had been very ill when she had met him. She decided that the priest 'was so near Christ and so longed for prayer by the Blessed Sacrament, that our Lord came to that little chapel at the good priest's desire – and that L.B. saw Him also'.

Baylis also saw 'a very wonderful and glorious picture of our Lord' and a 'glorious golden picture of the face of Christ' once when she awoke from sleep in her summer house.[40] She was looking 'into the bedroom of Dr Mary Smith who lived next door' and at first assumed her vision was actually a picture hanging on Smith's wall. However, 'when asking her friend about this glorious picture she had in her room Dr Smith said she had no picture of our Lord'. Baylis actually went into Smith's bedroom to 'see what could have been transformed by the early morning sun. But the wall by the bed was bare'; she therefore decided her vision was real.

What is startling about this record is how far Baylis's sense of spirituality and ecstasy here are from the famous 'Sorry, dear, God says No' response to any request for a pay rise. This document offers private, almost embarrassingly intimate snapshots from Baylis's spiritual pilgrimage: in particular, her sense of complete desolation at missing communion is remarkable and provides a counterbalance to other accounts in which she comes across as a pious prig – such as the occasion on which she rebuked assistant stage manager Madge Whiteman for not attending church and was then actually put out to be told by Whiteman that she *had* been at church, it was just that Baylis hadn't noticed her.[41]

Baylis chose to make some of her spiritual experiences public, and one story she often told relates how God performed a miracle for the Vic:

> The Manager was at her wits' end to know how to keep the theatre alive; and to crown everything she was threatened with serious eye trouble, and arranged to pay a visit to a Harley Street specialist.[42]

While waiting for her prescription Baylis went into All Saints, the church where she had been christened:

This was the only time I remember entering a Church and
not kneeling to pray. I sat and groused to the Almighty. I
could hardly shoulder the burden of my aged dear ones
with my normal health: my work was bristling with
difficulties: my wonderful aunt, who had founded the Vic
and had always been such a pillar of strength to me, had
passed on some months before. I told God even the Daily
Telegraph, who seldom failed to note my musical
programmes, had taken no notice of our last Wagner
performance. I had no praise or thanks in my heart – just
one hateful grumble.[43]

God helped the Vic by sending Baylis Nellie Melba:

That evening Madame Melba, who had the night before
arrived in England, paid a surprise visit to the Old Vic, and
the daily paper of which the Manager was thinking
chronicled the event in three columns.[44]

Such free publicity at such a crucial time was miraculous as far
as Baylis was concerned.

Another insight into Baylis's spiritual life can be gained
from the letters she wrote to a young Anglo-Catholic, Ivy
Smithson, in the last years of the First World War.[45] Unlike
Baylis's brief essays on her spiritual experiences, these letters
are intensely private, and written very specifically to be read by
someone who had explicitly asked her for religious guidance.
Baylis takes for granted that the reader will be deeply steeped
in Catholic tradition, terminology and iconography, and she
makes practical suggestions about spiritual exercises which
would mean little to anyone from other traditions.

Baylis stresses the importance of quiet days at retreat
centres. She herself is 'an associate of 2 religious communities
& that is as much as I can manage'.[46] She recommends
friendships with members of religious communities as 'once
you make a big pal' they sustain you with prayers and letters.
Baylis encourages Smithson to use a Rosary, to meditate on the
Stations of the Cross, Devotions to the Precious Blood and the
Joyful and Sorrowful Mysteries, even though she herself finds
this 'more than I could think of'. She takes Smithson through

the Mysteries in detail, and she comments of Easter meditation that 'you feel if Easter was not so near with all its joy, your own sorrow would finish you off'.

Pragmatically speaking, the Smithson letters reveal very precisely how Baylis's religious practices informed and sustained her work at the Vic. For Baylis, the thought that religious friends will be praying for her is vital:

> then I feel all will be well & my worry ceases, I just pray about it in the morn. for a minute and leave it with God … Never look back, dear, just look ahead. When you fail, pick yourself up & start again, remorse & worry is the Devils strongest weapon & I'll have no truck with him … you can take all your worries to the Holy Communion & leave them with our Lord & draw fresh strength & courage from Him & start back into the World again feeling this strong within you.[47]

She also comments: 'I do so believe the moment we feel our cross if we call on Him & help us carry it, He does indeed carry it, and we soon after feel only joy, all the heaviness goes.'[48] The Smithson letters cover the period of the First World War, when the Vic was suffering badly from its proximity to Waterloo Station, a major and conspicuous target for German Zeppelin raids, and Baylis's absolute confidence in the power of prayer has to be seen as a practical resource for her in her struggle to keep her theatre going in desperate times.

The Smithson letters also provide an intensely private insight into Baylis's relationship with Father Andrew. On one occasion Baylis heard herself unexpectedly being praised from the pulpit by Father Andrew for her work at the Vic:

> I felt really ill, such praises from the Pulpit by a Saintly Priest made me hot and tingle all over and really I could not hear ½ he said, his voice sounded so far away as I became more and more overcome … I love F[ather] Andrew with all my heart & he is strong, bursting with life & the joy of living, yet he is so loving, so tender and beautiful, I believe I never realised God's love so much as when I make my confession to F[ather] Andrew, tho' I love

him, I'm afraid of his tenderness, I never knew loving words could hurt so much, I feel often I'd cry & whip myself for my rotten failings, but one feels aching from head to foot & just as if one had really been scourged all over after his words of loving encouragement. I've practised confession steadily for 19 years now & have had many dear helpful Priests but never one who makes me feel my sins as F[ather] Andrew does just because of his great loving heart, one realises a little God's love for us.49

The highly coloured language here has to be contextualised by Catholic traditions of confession and penitence, but there is certainly no doubt about the extent of Baylis's commitment, something which casts light on her similarly absolute commitment to the Vic and later the Wells.

Sybil Thorndike, who like Baylis took communion daily, admired and honoured Baylis's staunch Anglicanism, and insisted that 'Those who did not recognise the Religious in her – did not know Lilian Baylis.'50 One of Thorndike's favourite anecdotes about Baylis is the story of their very first encounter, when Baylis abruptly pronounced 'Your father's a priest, isn't he? Church and stage – same thing – should be!'51 Unfortunately, it was Sybil Thorndike who also, unintentionally, inspired something of a backlash against the spiritual Baylis. When she was preparing to play the leading role of the recalcitrant, inspirational, and infuriating Joan in the British premiere of George Bernard Shaw's *St Joan*, Thorndike was explicit about the fact that she was basing her characterisation on Baylis. Thorndike actually wrote to Baylis saying: 'I'm thinking such a lot about you – working on St Joan – she's so like you.'52 Thorndike went on to repeat this comparison between Baylis and St Joan many times during her long life, and this was something which infuriated some of Baylis's detractors.53

Perhaps the most important aspect of Baylis's religious practices was that in the regularity of her prayer and meditations, she created a space where she could get away from her theatre work. In so doing she was adopting a practice often recommended by management gurus nowadays: she was building herself up spiritually in order to be able to manage work effectively. Nowhere is this clearer than in her commitment to going on retreat – sometimes for just a day, sometimes for much longer periods – which must have helped her survive the manic pressures of the nine-month theatre seasons.

The retreat movement nowadays is big business, and some retreat venues offer to pamper the body as much as fortify the spirit, but for Baylis going on retreat would not have been a soft option. For the period of the retreat she would have lived alongside nuns, eating very plain food, possibly wearing a veil and, in some cases, vowed to silence. In one letter Henrietta Barnett wishes: 'I hope you will have a happy week in the "Retreat" and return strengthened for your work', and Baylis does seem to have found the escape such retreats provided from everyday rules of social behaviour truly liberating.[54] Retreats, even at convents, were then run by men such as Father Andrew, but the company Baylis would have kept whilst on retreat would largely have consisted of nuns, women who defied convention by refusing marriage and who were generally accustomed to managing their lives with very little reference to men.

Baylis enjoyed trying out new retreat centres, visiting different convents and establishing new contacts (although some convents she visited over and over again), and she built major friendships with many religious women.[55] When, in later life, Baylis hired Annette Prevost as a chauffeuse, part of Prevost's attraction for Baylis was that she was the niece of one of Baylis's conventual friends, Sister Edgytha of Malvern.[56] Baylis's retreats from her work life, however, did not mean respite for her employees: the Vic wardrobe master, Orlando Whitehead, remembers that, before departing for a retreat, Baylis 'would usually go round the departments and give them all a good blowing up, "To keep us quiet till she came back."'[57]

Many famous comic anecdotes about Baylis depend on her seemingly absurd religious enthusiasm, and people grew to expect some kind of ridiculous religious display. When Harcourt Williams joined the Vic, director Edy Craig warned him 'Wait until L.B. asks you to pray with her.' But Baylis 'never did' and Williams claims that never 'in the four years I worked with her, did she once question my faith or indulge in any of the legendary "kneelings in prayer" so often quoted'.[58] Indeed, Baylis could be hard-nosed in some areas of religion: for example, she insisted on producing concerts on Good Friday, which were technically unlicensed and which the London County Council tried several times to close down.[59] Baylis donated the proceeds of these performances to the St Giles home, but for some she was breaking quite a serious religious taboo by opening her theatre on Good Friday.

Generally the Baylis of the comic anecdotes is challenged, complicated, and sometimes even contradicted by the private lives that Baylis herself sought to record in her own writings: the niece mourning her aunt, the friend of Louie Davey, the avid traveller, the religious visionary. The job of running the Vic may have eventually turned Baylis into the grumpy caricature, or Baylis may have consciously used that caricature to protect what remained of the younger, more sensitive woman. However, the determination and commitment shown by the private Baylis – travelling all over the world, *demanding* help from God in a crisis, maintaining long-lasting and supportive friendships – were also characteristics that helped the public Baylis thrive. Certainly determination and commitment were very much on display in the first major solo career challenge that she set herself: to set up and run her own opera company.

NOTES

1   Lilian Baylis 'Reminiscences', typescript M&M, file labelled 'Talks by Lilian Baylis', 1924. A manuscript note indicates Greet was costumed 'as John of Gaunt'.
2   OVLB/000017.
3   OVLB/000017.
4   OVEC/000285/1, 2; OVEC/000285/3. The letters from Everest are all addressed to 'Miss Ellen', but Ellen was in such a state of collapse that Baylis dealt with Everest's demands, something indicated by the notes in Baylis's handwriting on OVEC/000285/5.
5   Harcourt Williams, *Old Vic Saga*, p. 93. OVEC/000285/5 raises

the question of the Hampstead shares.

6 I have edited the letter substantially and much of the detail of arranging the cremation and who attended the services is cut.

7 Baylis's brother Willie died in 1906.

8 Areas where Cons managed properties.

9 Auchmuty, 'By Their Friends We Shall Know Them', p. 94 points out how absurd it is that Davey's relationship with Baylis has been marginalised by biographers of Baylis and historians of the Vic. Findlater, *Lilian Baylis*, for example, makes only two references to Davey (pp. 98, 219). See the 1901 census for a record of Davey, aged twenty-one, as a 'student' at Oxford.

10 *OVM*, April–May 1938.

11 OVLB/000138/19, letter dated 19 August 1923.

12 The journal is OVLB/000158.

13 OVLB/000018/1.

14 These photographs appear in the album catalogued at OVLB/000400.

15 OVLB/000158/17.

16 See OVLB/000029/2, a letter from Newton Baylis written on 7 October 1900, which dates these holidays. For the Rhineland see OVLB/000406; for the Matterhorn see OVLB/000403. Findlater's statement (*Lilian Baylis*, p. 226) that Baylis 'seldom went abroad' is extraordinary and suggests the distorting influence of Annette Prevost's view of the post-1932 Baylis.

17 This travel journal is OVEC/000010/9. Only part of the journal is in Baylis's handwriting.

18 OVEC/000010/2, 3, 4, 7.

19 OVEC/000010/7.

20 Whoever paid for the holiday – Emma Cons is the obvious candidate – paid for a first-class ticket.

21 Baylis, 'Emma Cons', p. 285.

22 Kathleen Burne, *The Life and Letters of Father Andrew S.D.C.* (London, 1948), p. 54. This book includes several letters written to Baylis.

23 Baylis, 'Emma Cons', p. 263. May Hughes was the daughter of the author of *Tom Brown's Schooldays*.

24 Sophia Lonsdale in Violet Martineau, *Recollections of Sophia Lonsdale*, p. 165.

25 The claim to have God in her pocket is reported, for example, in Harcourt Williams, *Four Years at the Old Vic 1929–33* (London, 1935), p. 238.

26 Geoffrey Curtis, *William of Glasshampton: Friar: Monk: Solitary*

1862–1937 (London, 1947), p. 38; Stanley Browne, *Leprosy in England: Yesterday and Today*, pamphlet in East Hanningfield collection, 1977, p. 40. The Society of the Divine Compassion ran the home until 1924 and the tradition of caring for those ostracised by society because of what is seen to be handicap is still carried on at East Hanningfield today. Findlater, *Lilian Baylis*, p. 236 offers no supporting evidence for his breathtaking declaration that Baylis's 'sympathy' with the lepers at St Giles home 'may well … have been influenced by self-identification and perhaps masochism'.

27 OVLB/000154 is a set of notes by Baylis on the history of the home and although it is not clear if this item constitutes notes towards a publication or a speech, it is clear that in making them Baylis was doing something to try and raise awareness about the work at St Giles.

28 Burne, *The Life and Letters of Father Andrew*, pp. 152–3.

29 Jack Rosenthal's play about Baylis, *Auntie's Niece*, certainly suggests Baylis had a passion for Father Andrew, but their letters, although often frankly speaking of love and care for each other, consistently construct the relationship as that of 'pals'. See OVLB/000003.

30 Robert Atkins, 'The Lady of Waterloo Road', *The Times*, Saturday Review, 30 March 1974.

31 Edward Dent, *A Theatre For Everybody: The Story of the Old Vic and Sadler's Wells* (London, 1945), pp. 38–9.

32 OVLB/000003/4.

33 To be fair to Father Andrew, Baylis did encourage the staging of religious drama at the Vic – *Everyman* was frequently performed, especially at Easter, after Greet first introduced the play to the Vic, and Baylis produced a nativity play by Florence Buckton in 1913, as well as *The Child in Flanders* by Cicely Hamilton in the 1920s. In addition the *Era* (20 December 1919) reported it had been standing room only at a recent performance of Father Andrew's *Hope of the World*.

34 OVLB/000155. The document is not in Baylis's handwriting but *is* corrected and checked by her.

35 OVLB/000155 number 2. All quotations concerning this incident are taken from this document.

36 *OVM*, November 1921.

37 OVLB/000155 number 4. All quotations concerning this incident are taken from this document.

38 OVLB/000155 number 7.

39 OVLB/000155 number 5.

40 OVLB/000155 number 6.

41 Findlater, *Lilian Baylis*, p. 232.

42 *OVM*, November 1926.

43 OVLB/000139. This account was published in the All Saints parish magazine.

44 *OVM*, November 1926.

45 The letters to Ivy Smithson and to her sister, Laura Smithson, are held in the M&M Theatre Collection. Findlater, *Lilian Baylis*, p. 231 conflates the two sisters and describes Ivy as an actress, which she was not. It was Laura who wanted to be an actress and she asked for favours from Baylis, who provided her with opportunities to showcase her talents but did not offer her employment. Baylis did recommend Laura for the position of voice teacher at the Vic in 1924, but the majority of the committee were in favour of Dr Aikin, and Baylis accepted this decision. Laura was at first disappointed and eventually outraged that Baylis did not do more to provide her with a breakthrough, scrawling on one envelope 'This letter is the last straw', and fulminating that Baylis had promised more than she delivered. Laura also notes that in order to become successful she intends to learn to become ruthless; to break her word; and to identify with Freemasons.

46 Letter to Ivy Smithson, 2 March 1918, M&M. All quotations in this paragraph are from this letter.

47 Letter to Ivy Smithson, 28 January 1918.

48 Letter to Ivy Smithson, 2 March 1918, M&M.

49 Ibid. It is possible that Findlater, *Lilian Baylis*, p. 87 is inspired by such moments in the Smithson letters to make his otherwise completely unsubstantiated claim that Baylis had 'a perceptible tendency to masochism'. However, this makes no allowance for the prevalence of traditional Catholic iconography, and the customs of confession and penitence in the discussions between Smithson and Baylis.

50 *OVM*, December 1937.

51 Sybil Thorndike, 'Lilian Baylis', p. 29. Baylis's commitment to church and stage working together was long standing and she served on the Council of the Actors' Church Union.

52 OVLB/000307.

53 See Chapter 10. Although Sybil Thorndike was the major proponent of the St Joan comparison, it was made by others, for example *Country Life* (4 December 1937) and *Theatre Arts*

Monthly (February 1938). Those driven into a frenzy by this comparison include St John Ervine (*Observer*, 8 May 1938) and John Barber (*Daily Telegraph*, 22 April 1974).

54 OVLB/000013. The letter is dated 1920.
55 Correspondence in the Bristol archive includes letters from Sister Dorina (OVLB/053), Sister Laurence (OVLB/000090) and Sister Marion (OVLB/000092). OVLB/0000369 is a pressed rose flower on a card presented to Baylis in memory of her visit to the Dominican Convent, Dundee, in August 1924.
56 OV/M000041/1.
57 Harcourt Williams, *Vic-Wells*, p. 44.
58 Harcourt Williams, *Old Vic Saga*, p. 21.
59 *OVM*, April 1931. See also Executive Committee minutes of 8 January 1926.

[6]

Baylis's First Love: Opera

Most theatre and opera personnel who worked at the Vic under Baylis agreed on one thing: 'Opera was Lilian Baylis's *first love*', but Baylis herself always gave full credit to Emma Cons. Cons had pioneered concerts at the Vic, concerts by celebrated singers which often included opera arias.[1] These singers, who 'gave their services so generously to Emma Cons and laid the foundations' of the Vic, included Sims Reeves, Julius Benedict, Madame Sainton-Dolby and Antoinette Sterling.[2] Sterling was particularly loved by the Vic audiences – even though she astonished them by asking them to stop smoking so she could sing for them without damaging her throat (they obliged and her concerts continued).[3] From 1889 concert performances of operas were offered, and the repertoire was dominated by Michael William Balfe's phenomenally popular opera *The Bohemian Girl*, as well as *Maritana, Fra Diavolo, The Rose of Castile, La Sonnambula, Il Trovatore, Faust, The Lily of Killarney* and *The Daughter of the Regiment*.[4] The action of the operas, however, had to be interrupted and deliberately broken up, so that the Vic could not be accused of producing full, and thus illegal, theatrical performances. Mezzo Constance Willis recalls that 'in the middle of an aria a curtain would be dropped behind the singer, in order to break the show into so many acts, as required by a music-hall licence'.[5]

When she arrived back from South Africa Baylis had mixed feelings about the music at the Vic:

> I loved the Thursday Concerts, felt the Opera could grow into something worth while. I was interested in the lectures and tried to endure the Music Hall shows, introducing a

good Dramatic or Comedy Sketch as often as possible, and musical turns.[6]

Something of the Vic opera's gradual success in building an audience can be gauged from a patronising but impressed account quoted in the Annual Report for 1911–12:[7]

> The people in the stalls and balcony are mostly of the small shop-keeping and superior working classes; but it is the gallery that interests one most. One's first feeling is astonishment at finding these people present, as they mostly look like people to whom a serious work of art would not appeal. They are obviously poor, and very good-tempered to-night, taking in excellent part the discomforts incident to a crowded house … The bulk of the people come from the neighbourhood. They are thoroughly happy; and, in the matter of quiet attention, setting an example to some West-end audiences that I have known. Indeed, I have never seen a more attractive or appreciative lot of people.[7]

Under the music hall licence, of course, the audience was allowed to smoke, drink and eat in the theatre and breastfeeding babies accompanied their mothers.

In 1912, after the death of Emma Cons, Baylis applied for a new licence and, as she recalls, once 'the music-hall licence had been amended, whole operas two or three times a week' started appearing.[8] Singers and dancers were recruited from local church choirs and production values were erratic, but the performances started to build a local and loyal audience. Initially the opera company developed in tandem with drama at the Vic, and plays appeared at least as early as March 1913 when Queenie Fraser-Brunner's theatre company performed there. The operas and the melodramas favoured at the Vic early on had much in common, including heightened emotional states and convoluted, coincidence-riddled plot lines; indeed one of the Vic's most popular operas, *The Lily of Killarney*, was actually a version of Dion Boucicault's melodrama *The Colleen Bawn*.[9] However, drama was only provided intermittently, by visiting companies like Queenie

Fraser-Brunner's, and it was the opera company that really began to develop the local audience base. Crucially, the Vic company was also making opera newly accessible in two ways: operas were sung in English and they were offered at prices cheap enough for local waged people to be able to afford a ticket.

Of course, Baylis was not the first person to dream of running a company producing opera in English. The composer of the perennially successful *Bohemian Girl*, Balfe, attempted a similar project in 1841, and again ten years later.[10] Arthur Sullivan, working with W.S. Gilbert and producer Richard D'Oyly Carte, wanted specifically to promote English opera, although the D'Oyly Carte Company eventually started focusing on the lucrative works of Gilbert and Sullivan themselves; the Carl Rosa Opera Company toured England for decades from 1873 producing opera in English, and occasionally commissioning new English works; and the Moody-Manners Opera Company was founded in 1897 specifically 'with the aim of producing grand opera in English'.[11] Baylis, however, had an advantage in terms of balancing the books simply because all her musicians and singers were amateur and unpaid. Unlike other managers, Baylis expected all her singers and musicians to work for love – to be amateurs in the very real sense of the word – and she started building the Vic opera audience a long time before she started paying her performers.

The Vic opera repertoire initially remained very reliant on ballad operas and old favourites. The so-called English 'Ring' – *The Bohemian Girl*, *Maritana* and *The Lily of Killarney* – was still frequently played right up until the opening of Sadler's Wells in 1931.[12] W.R. Titterton, the Vic's press manager for two years during the mid 1920s, remembers that *The Bohemian Girl* 'saved the day' on many occasions: 'When there were sheaves of bills to pay and nothing to pay them with, Lilian used to say: "Put on the Old Girl." And the Old Girl did the trick.'[13] Baylis was also very good at working up a sense of occasion and soon established Vic rituals which helped the local, regular audiences feel part of a community. So, for example, *The Lily of Killarney* was always performed in the week containing St

Charles Corri. Courtesy of the Theatre Museum, V&A Picture Library

Patrick's Day, and in 1916 Baylis first began producing the dramatised version of Mendelssohn's *Elijah* on Sundays for charity, something which then became a regular Easter feature at the Vic for many years.[14] When she brought Verdi's *Otello* into the repertoire in 1929, of course Baylis launched it during Shakespeare's birthday week.

Baylis's right-hand man in this project of bringing opera to Lambeth was Charles Corri, who was already working for Emma Cons on the Vic concert series when Baylis came home from South Africa. Corri and Baylis worked very closely together and both believed that they were working on a 'crusade – the popularisation of opera in London'.[15] Corri, who, like Baylis, was not a conventional figure, became famous for reducing huge opera scores down to fit the tiny Vic orchestra: *Tristan and Isolde* was performed by an orchestra of twenty-eight.[16] He came from a long line of musicians and sang in music halls as a boy before joining the Carl Rosa Opera Company, which played at the Vic. Later,

> [w]hen he was in his thirties, Lilian Baylis made a lot of money – at least £2,000 – out of penny cinematograph entertainments. She asked Corri if, with the proceeds, he could arrange a series of symphony concerts. He could. When full-length operas were introduced into the music-hall programme, Corri conducted them.[17]

Singer Joan Cross paints a vivid portrait of Corri:[18]

> He enjoyed his beer with his cronies after rehearsals and performances in the adjacent pub, an enjoyment which was reflected in his eyes which were, alas! bloodshot and protuberant – not pretty. His daytime appearance suggested that he might be more at home behind one of the market stalls outside and all the time I knew him (about ten years) he wore, day in, day out, the same shabby old black suit, the same dusty bowler and smoked the same unwholesome pipe. His shirts were spotless – always! His evening wardrobe for performance dangled during the day from hooks on the walls of his room upstairs at the back of the stage. Here, dirty, untidy as everywhere else, was a confusion of manuscript paper, sheet music, old opera scores, blunt pencil stubs, pens and india rubbers. These littered the table where he worked, where he arranged music for every Shakespeare play currently in the repertoire and above all where he rescored his operas to accommodate his tiny band.[19]

Cross describes Corri's musical direction as 'totally inflexible': he apparently 'hated singers who paused or held a top note, often, if they did, proceeding without them to the general confusion of all concerned'.[20] On the occasion of 'a bad musical gaffe' on Cross's part 'a very audible remark from the conductor's desk must have been heard throughout the theatre, "She's a bar ahead, the bitch!"'[21] After his last performance in 1935, however, Corri became the very first person to retire from the Vic-Wells on a pension, which shows

Joan Cross. Photograph by Gordon Anthony. Courtesy of the Getty
Collection

how much his work meant to Baylis.

Corri and Baylis made a very successful team in producing
ramshackle but valiant 'opera from scratch' productions. Both
were passionate about spreading the enjoyment of opera to the
local Lambeth community, but a major change in direction
took place in 1918. Baylis was becoming more serious and
more ambitious about opera production and, in the Emma
Cons tradition of putting work in the way of women, she asked
singer Muriel Gough not only to star as Susanna in *The
Marriage of Figaro* but also to produce the work. Gough

declined but suggested Clive Carey as producer. Carey was willing to participate only if a new English translation of the libretto, that translated by Cambridge don Edward Dent, was used. Baylis agreed, and this initiated a series of Dent-translated and Carey-directed Mozart operas. The arrival of this team of outsiders led to some conflicts, as Carey demanded more rehearsals than was usual at the Vic, but the productions improved.[22]

Baylis always felt uncomfortable in the company of Edward Dent, who made her feel conscious of her lack of conventional education. Douglas Craig, the Sadler's Wells administrator, describes Baylis's relationship with Dent as 'love-hate', and conductor Adrian Boult states that Dent enjoyed 'the company of educated people who talked English well and accurately', which Baylis didn't, and that her 'Cockney mateyness' was not really his style.[23] Dent himself admitted that on first meeting Baylis:

> I at first formed the opinion that the only hope for a rational development of opera [at the Vic] lay in the removal of Miss Baylis; after a certain time, and after gaining a more intimate acquaintance with its workings, I gradually became converted to the view that whoever else might be recommended for removal, she was the one person whose presence was indispensable.[24]

Dent was also bound to be in conflict with Baylis because he wanted the cultured set to hear and see the productions he worked on, while Baylis 'often made it plain enough that she did not want the smart people to come inside at all'; 'She wanted money, but she did not want moneyed people inside her theatre.'[25]

Dent describes Baylis's voice as 'about the most disagreeable that I have ever heard issue from female lips'.[26] He also suggests that 'that repellent crust of hardness' which 'was a protective armour that she had either secreted subconsciously or deliberately assumed as a defence against all sorts of spiritual enemies' had actually

ossified all her innate musical sensibilities; during all the time that I knew her and worked on the outer fringe of the opera house I never once heard her say anything about music which would suggest that she was a trained musician, or indeed that she was particularly susceptible to music.[27]

And yet Dent also narrates how in 1921 during the first dress rehearsal for *Don Giovanni*, he wanted a mandolin to be played, and Charles Corri suggested he should ask Baylis:

> Considerably surprised, I asked her if she would play it. Still more to my surprise, a mandoline was suddenly produced from nowhere; Miss Baylis hurriedly tuned it, and, what is more, played the *obbligato* to the serenade from memory without a mistake, standing in the wings with the rapt expression of a seraph. She played it for the first performance and no more; she was a little nervous and timid – she had not touched the mandoline for years, she said – so that the instrument was barely audible in the front of the house, and for subsequent performances I am sorry to record that we relapsed once more into the traditional violin *pizzicato.*[28]

If Baylis really did say that she hadn't touched the mandolin 'for years', she was being economical with the truth. Indeed possession of Baylis's mandolin was hotly contested after her death, precisely because the instrument was so intimately associated with Baylis for those who knew her outside of the Vic.[29] And the Royal College of Music, which appointed Baylis as an external examiner in 1925, clearly thought more highly of Baylis's musical knowledge than Dent.[30]

Dent reports that Baylis announced to him 'I'm an ignorant woman.' He seems to have accepted this verdict, and from then on seen in her only a poorly educated, unmusical eccentric.[31] In fact, Baylis regularly stressed her lack of education when dealing with a certain class of person – the Dents rather than the Corris – and seems to have used this as a tactic for disarming people, securing their help and then delegating work to them. There is no doubt that in some company Baylis did feel poorly educated and defensive, but the Vic was a long way geographically and socially from the dreaming spires and vintage port of Cambridge and it was Baylis who was on home ground in south London and who had local knowledge, while Dent was the foreigner.

As the opera company grew and developed, conditions at the Vic remained a challenge. The *Old Vic Magazine* recounts that the orchestra sometimes went into the pit 'with two scores (uncertain until the last moment whether it would have to play the opera for which a cast could be acquired or the advertised one for which a cast could be materialised only by a miraculous chain of circumstances)'.[32] On one occasion Constance Willis, having generously agreed at the last minute to help out when a performer fell ill for a matinee performance of *Lohengrin*, stipulated that she had to leave for her evening engagement on the 4.30 p.m. train from Waterloo:

> Unfortunately, the curtain on the second act was a little late, owing to an orchestral light fusing at the end of the first act, and before its close, Miss Willis found she had only ten minutes in which to change and catch her train. She was forced to leave the stage – luckily there was only the final curse to act, and the Manager helped her change while the unfortunate understudy, still protesting that she was not due to appear until the fourth act, was hurled on to the stage, and told to hide her face as much as possible in her huge train while she pointed an avenging left hand at the bridal group. Most of the artists had been too busy singing to notice Miss Willis' departure, and consequently had the shock of their lives to see her transformed into somebody quite different.[33]

To be fair to the Vic, they were not the only company to suffer from such problems, and in 1934 the *Old Vic Magazine* reports rather shamefacedly, 'We can't help a sneaking satisfaction … at finding that even Covent Garden Gala seasons have difficulties from lack of understudies.'[34]

Quite apart from occasional shocks to the system like the disappearance of Constance Willis mid-scene, the Vic singers in the 1920s often worked in fairly grim conditions, some of which are detailed in singer Joan Cross's autobiography. Cross auditioned in 1923 and, like many actors and singers, found it difficult even to find the location of the audition.[35] After she had performed her piece, Cross began to leave when 'A harsh, abrasive voice came from the stalls of the darkened theatre' and Baylis shouted out 'Where's that girl gone? Fetch her back!' This was followed by an abrupt offer of work: 'I don't engage people to learn their job in my theatre. Sing in the chorus if you like. Shan't pay you.'[36] Cross's years at the Vic were 'blissfully happy' even while she was 'working in the roughest of conditions' and '[n]othing as business-like as a contract came my way' (although unpaid initially, she later received £3 a performance).[37] At this time the opera chorus were also expected to pay 10/6 refundable deposit on their scores and 10/6 for wear and tear.[38]

Cross describes the Vic as full of 'dirt and decay', with seats that 'were benches covered in worn and peeling American cloth' and dressing rooms that were 'whitewashed, uncarpeted and very cold'.[39] Cross is more enthusiastic about the eating house occupying the front part of the Vic, Pearce and Plenty, and remembers it as 'a commodious and far from elegant tea shop' which offered

> a large, high, steamy room, an arrangement of marble-topped tables and wooden forms, a counter with tea-urns constantly on the boil, a stack of large, thick cups and saucers, slabs of bread and butter, yellow cakes and bath buns, the whole presided over by a smiling family of genial Cockneys.[40]

Meanwhile, outside the theatre was a market, 'a struggling line of ancient stalls which sold meat, fish, vegetables and a strange delicacy, jellied eels', and rehearsals were held in the saloon,

> a purpose for which it was singularly ill-fitted. Since Miss Baylis was never known to say no to any kind of gift, it provided a resting place for couches, gothic chairs, glass-fronted cupboards and Victorian overmantels all unloaded by well-intentioned friends. It also included a piano of unbelievable antiquity. One side of this apartment had three floor-to-ceiling windows which offered a

comprehensive view of the activities in the Waterloo Road and the busy market in The Cut, a welcome distraction during the duller moments of rehearsals.[41]

This market also, along with the trams and buses, created a great many 'noises off' during matinees.

Cross felt that 'The Old Vic audience was special, with that same possessive attitude towards performance as that of today's Prom audience'; yet because the schedule was so hectic, performances 'must have been – they were – dreadful'.[42] The general schedule for the week that eventually evolved was that the Shakespeare Company performed on Mondays, Wednesdays and Fridays, the opera company performed on Thursdays and Saturdays, and the companies took turns to perform on Saturday matinees. Baylis claimed she couldn't afford to pay 'Union Terms' for the professional musicians in her orchestra to attend evening rehearsals, which were paid at a higher rate than daytime rehearsals.[43] But her amateur singers were unavailable during the day when they were at their paid work. This left very little time for joint rehearsals. As a result,

> on a Monday night the theatre was closed allowing time for a music rehearsal in the Saloon. Tuesday morning the single orchestral rehearsal took place with the principal singers only. Tuesday night was devoted to the one full rehearsal on stage for chorus and principals – no orchestra! On Thursday night, after these sketch preliminaries, the cast, chorus and orchestra were assembled on stage for the first time and the actual performance.[44]

As a performer, Cross also found it very distracting when onstage to be faced with the remains of a nineteenth-century theatre curtain, installed in 1835, which had been made up of massive mirrors and originally had great novelty value because it reflected an image of the audience back at themselves.[45] Eventually this mirror curtain had to be taken down as it was so heavy that it risked pulling down the roof of the building. Because Baylis couldn't bear to think of throwing the mirror curtain away, she cut it up and relocated the separate panels of mirrors. Some, appropriately, went to the cramped dressing room areas. Less appropriately, some went to the back of the stalls, where they were clearly visible to performers when they were onstage, which did not help concentration, especially in difficult moments when they could see how unconvincing they looked.

Cross's major source of grievance, however, was the costumes, which were shared, not always amicably, with the Shakespeare Company, and the appalling wigs. Edward Dent was less worried by the costumes, even if they were all multipurpose 'square-cut' (that is, vaguely eighteenth-century), and the ill-fitting wigs, but he was horrified by the stage furniture, which always suggested action onstage was taking place in a kitchen.[46] Cross, who actually had to wear the costumes, describes them as 'Much mended and none too clean'; in addition, 'We were left to provide our own shoes and stockings, gloves, fans and pieces of costume jewellery, appropriate or otherwise, all strictly vintage-Woolworth.'[47] Some costumes were 'old rags' and 'fit only for the totter's cart'.[48] One young prima donna attempted to compensate for her less than satisfactory costume for the role of Violetta in *La Traviata*. Edward Dent records that the singer 'said anxiously to Miss Baylis, "I hope you didn't think I overdid my make-up". "Ow now, dear," replied the great lady, "I always think Violetter ought to look a bit tarty."'[49]

The drawbacks – the worn-out costumes, the lack of rehearsal and the fact that the chorus were volunteers – all helped to keep ticket prices down; but to performers these were compensated for by the major benefit of working at the Vic, which was, as Cross states, the chance to sing roles 'which would never have come my way in another opera company.'[50] (These roles had to be learnt at home: 'there was no staff of expert coaches ... to spend hours and hours with singers and pass them into rehearsal as near perfect as makes no matter'.[51]) And 'It could only have happened at the Old Vic' that in Cross's second season she was invited while 'still in the chorus and with only one dubious success under my belt, to sing a major Wagnerian role' (Elisabeth in *Tannhäuser*), and, after singing the Priestess in the Vic premiere of *Aida*, to be asked only a fortnight later to sing Aida herself.[52] Baylis had first wanted to produce *Aida* in 1919 but had decided she could not afford the royalty fee, and so the *Aida* premiere marked an important step forward for the Vic.[53] The production featured members of the Shakespeare Company drafted in to swell the crowds as well as some of the Vic's office staff and a couple of galleryites. The set included an Egyptian god with 'trousers stuffed with sawdust, covered with tar, helped out with a little papier-mâché, and produced at a total cost of fifteen bob.'[54]

Vere Denning, writing in 1931, bears witness to Baylis as a hands-on, multi-tasking opera manager:

> Miss Baylis supervised the rehearsal of "Tales of Hoffman" which was in progress on the stage, calmed the more frenzied members of the cast, assured [a] worried girl that smaller breeches would be forthcoming, told the Stage Manager that the Old Vic did not possess £10 for a chandelier, ate bananas and talked to me, all at the same time.[55]

On a good day Baylis was offering the excitement of fringe opera, theatre on a shoestring – or, as she called it, 'potted opera' – long before the idea became fashionable.[56] However, even Baylis thought there was room for improvement, as she frankly informed the audience that attended the Sadler's Wells production of *The Mastersingers*: 'Of course, the company should have had another rehearsal, but I am afraid we could not afford it.'[57] But she certainly aspired to the best possible conditions for her opera company:

> My aim is to have a permanent orchestra, principals and chorus, no deputies, the chorus to rehearse daily studying the characters in addition to memorising their music till it is no effort to sing a full and beautiful tone, act and watch the [conductor's] stick at the same time.[58]

She wanted her opera singers and musicians to be on nine-month contracts like the Shakespeare Company, so they did not have to keep exhausting themselves by taking 'engagements in Aberdeen or Bristol before singing at the Vic';[59] as singer Herbert Simmonds ruefully reported, 'one of the greatest difficulties of a singer is to keep fit and not to catch cold with the continual travelling about in trains etc.'[60] Baylis also wanted her 'principals and choristers' to have time to 'get into the skin of each opera', and to avoid last-minute, panic-stricken measures such as those undertaken when the tenor in *Tannhäuser* lost his voice in the final rehearsal:[61]

> we had to start ringing up to try and find someone who would undertake this difficult part. All those who could save us were already engaged by others or out of town. We heard of one man travelling from the north of England due at the station just an hour before the curtain was to rise, we met him at King's Cross and simply listened to no excuses, kidnapped him one could almost say, bundled him into a taxi, took him to the Theatre where the conductor hummed his cues while he dressed.[62]

Another tenor, in *Lohengrin*, was 'visited by terrible pains', and with no understudy available Baylis:

> heated the electric iron at the nearest point and as soon as he came off the stage either prompt or O[pposite].P[rompt]. side we rushed to him and ironed him where the pain was – no hot-water bottles being available![63]

In such circumstances the opera performances were bound to vary in quality, but Baylis was always optimistic:

> I think an earnest performance of a great work, even if it falls short of the ideal is of more value to the theatre as a whole than an excellent performance of a trivial work. There can be no such thing, to my mind, as a completely worthless rendering of any great work, if it is undertaken with sincerity. And the remarkable thing is that if you work continually in an atmosphere of great thoughts, miracles do happen.[64]

Sometimes, however, the miracles did not occur. Joan Cross

remembers a performance of *La Bohème* when for Mimi's first entrance

> [a]n inexperienced stage hand was deputed to stand by, flapping a large newspaper to create the draught that would finally blow out the candle on cue. Alas! it was not only a situation audible in front of house but the over-eager newspaper flapper was too often visible.[65]

And when the company went on tour during renovations in the theatre, Cross recalls that 'Adrift from the loving and indulgent audience in the Waterloo Road we were totally unprepared for catcalls and pennies-on-the-stage from the gallery audience.'[66] Yet paradoxically for Cross, as production values improved at the Vic, the opera company lost 'just a little of the highly enjoyable, happy-go-lucky, all-right-on-the-night element'; and she heartily disliked what she calls 'the snob element from over the river', the West End audiences, who turned up when the Vic did Verdi's *The Force of Destiny* for the first time in London since 1867.[67] Baylis's response to the 'snob' element could be direct: Leo Kersley tells the story of Ralph Vaughan Williams's *Hugh the Drover*, which opened in April 1937, in tandem with *Job*, and filled the stalls but not the gallery. Baylis wanted to close the opera down, even though it was making money, because her precious galleryites weren't coming to see it.[68] And when it was proposed in 1932 that Sadler's Wells shows should start at eight o'clock, Baylis opposed this, as it 'would be most unpopular with the patrons of the cheaper seats' and only benefit the 'stalls patrons' who could have a more leisurely pre-show meal in a restaurant.[69] Baylis also argued that people who turned up to her theatres in a car ought to pay three times the normal price for a ticket.[70]

Although Joan Cross cites several examples of Baylis's obstinacy – such as ignoring all advice and giving the role of Venus in *Tannhäuser* to a completely unsuitable singer who then had to be dismissed after her first performance – overall she sees Baylis as a great enabler and someone who at the Vic 'tried to create circumstances under which I could develop'.[71] On the other hand, when Cross had the temerity to suggest that after singing Aida she might at last be allowed a salary,

Baylis immediately blacklisted her and Cross was without roles for a season.[72] Yet Cross's overall assessment of Baylis is unequivocally positive: 'she was hard-working, dedicated, indefatigable and, as far as the pioneering limitation of her time allowed, a highly professional manager'. Importantly, Cross also comments that the Baylis 'anecdotes diminish her. She was a very important person indeed. And she should not be remembered as the butt of a lot of funny stories' (although Cross herself fell victim to Baylis's fabled bluntness: 'You sing nicely dear – pity you can't act!').[73] Cross's subsequent career as the creator of many major roles in the operas of Benjamin Britten, and someone *admired* for her acting, owed much to her training via the ramshackle Vic productions of the 1920s and, for Cross, Baylis's belief in the 'right to fail' was crucial.

One of Baylis's biggest opera coups, given the underfunded, 'fringe' feel of the Vic, was Dame Nellie Melba's farewell appearance there in 1926. After the miracle (according to Baylis) which initially sent Melba to the Vic in 1914, thereby generating much-needed publicity for the theatre, it took twelve years before she honoured her promise to come and sing on the Vic stage, by which time the prima donna was sixty-seven.[74] Nevertheless the performance was a sellout. True to form, Melba was impossibly demanding during her visit; Baylis, however, struck back the minute the performance was safely over, when she hijacked Melba's bouquets of violets – the singer's favourite flowers – by suggesting very loudly and publicly that Melba didn't need so many flowers and that they should be sent straight on to local hospitals for the less fortunate to enjoy.[75]

Another feature of the Vic opera during the 1920s was its ongoing support for the composer Ethel Smyth. Smyth is known nowadays almost as much for her writing as for her music; in the former, Smyth constructs herself as ignored by the musical establishment and deprived of opportunities to produce her work. However, the Vic frequently staged *The Boatswain's Mate,* and the theatre's production of *Fête Galante* had scenery by Vanessa Bell;[76] Smyth conducted at several Vic performances; and revivals of her work were scheduled for special events such as her seventy-fifth birthday. Smyth was always forthright in her views: for example, she fulminates against orchestras such as the Hallé, which then excluded women, and argues that any orchestra should always include 'many women...because I think women more capable of devotion to an ideal than men'.[77] But she praises 'the simple, warm, human element you feel so strongly at the Old Vic', and indeed in 1921 laments on behalf of English opera that there cannot be another Old Vic because 'Probably there are not two Miss Lilian Baylis's in the world'.[78] Shortly after she was made a Dame in 1921, Smyth also wrote an article for the *Old Vic Magazine* – an issue advertising the forthcoming production of her opera *The Boatswain's Mate* in 1922 – which clearly demonstrates her allegiance to what was by then becoming classic Baylis rhetoric. Smyth declares the Vic audience is 'a real audience – an audience that goes to the theatre to hear the music, not in order to attend a social function.'[79]

The relationship between Baylis and Smyth was not always tranquil. In the words of Smyth's biographer Christopher St John (Christabel Marshal), 'Ethel and Miss Baylis had deep affection and respect for one another, but that did not prevent them from having rows which while they lasted were terrifying to the onlookers.'[80] The 'sketch' Ethel Smyth wrote of Baylis, in *Female Pipings in Eden*, compares her to Queen Elizabeth I and calls her a 'magician who in the Middle Ages would probably have been burnt as a witch like most other instinctive women'.[81] Smyth is fiercely supportive of Baylis's management, especially in view of the attempts by men (she is probably thinking of Edward Dent) who 'would rather like by degrees to hoist Miss Baylis out of her saddle'.[82] And in *A Final Burning of Boats* she celebrates

> Lilian Baylis – that very different and most amazing flower grown in the unpromising soil of the New Cut. She, a mere woman, consequently intensely practical and no megalomaniac, began by seeing, as in a vision, a great idea; she then set to work on quite humble lines, to realise it, and lo! by degrees she has done what no one else has done on any lines at all; she has created a dramatic tradition.[83]

Baylis, via the *Old Vic Magazine*, frequently returned the

compliment by celebrating Smyth's determination and her successes in the male-dominated world of music. For example, in 1922 an article enthuses over the pleasure of seeing 'a woman in the conductor's chair',[84] and later on the magazine rejoices at seeing 'an opera by a woman at a theatre created and managed by a woman',[85] In February 1934 the magazine marks Smyth's seventy-fifth birthday, proclaiming:

> Most musicians find one world quite enough for them to conquer; but Dame Ethel has not been satisfied with that. Her work for woman's suffrage and her delightful books would have entitled her to fame without the supreme distinction she has achieved as a composer in which field she has never been equalled by an Englishwoman or a woman of any nationality and few men.

It was during the 1930s, and especially after the opening of Baylis's new theatre, Sadler's Wells, in 1931, that the greatest changes in the opera company began to take place. With two theatres to fill, there were far more opera performances, and the move towards full professionalism became unstoppable. The stage at Sadler's Wells was also far better suited to opera (and dance) than to the spoken word; after a couple of years of playing drama, opera and ballet in repertory at both the Vic and the Wells, a basic pattern emerged of opera and dance at the Wells and drama at the Vic. However, this took the opera company away from its old traditional Lambeth audience, and its old traditional repertoire went too: by then even *The Bohemian Girl* was no longer the sure-fire success it used to be. In addition, in 1935 Charles Corri retired and Lawrance Collingwood took over as conductor. Collingwood

> [l]ived in Russia until the Revolution. He was actually in the Royal Opera House the night of Rasputin's murder, and he well remembers the tremor of excitement that ran through the audience and artists alike when the fateful news leaked out.[86]

Collingwood remained passionate about Russian music, and under his leadership the opera company performed works new to them, especially Russian operas such as *The Snow*

Maiden and *Boris Godunov*, modern British works such as Stanford's *The Travelling Companion*, Williams's *Hugh the Drover*, Nicholas Gatty's *Tempest* and *Prince Ferelon*, and Collingwood's own *Macbeth*, as well as the much-neglected English masterpiece *Dido and Aeneas* by Purcell. Edward Dent's opinion is that Collingwood 'was the one man whom Miss Baylis completely trusted, and she had need of him indeed, as she soon found that the operatic developments were soaring far beyond the ken of her somewhat limited experience'.[87] By contrast Joan Cross, while admitting that Baylis was 'frequently reactionary' and opera committee discussions 'stormy', still paints a picture of Baylis willing to stick her neck out and take a risk when she was convinced a project deserved a chance:

> we were summoned to [Lawrance] Collingwood's house in Willesden. Miss Baylis and a dozen or more singers plus Clive Carey. We all sat round and listened to Collingwood play through *Snegourochka – The Snow Maiden*. The Lady approved.[88]

Certainly the *Old Vic Magazine* was stating in 1933 that 'for many years Lilian Baylis has wanted to attempt a Russian opera', and the main obstacle seems to have been that Baylis thought that the potential cost in terms of costumes and décor would be prohibitive.[89] The decision to risk a Russian production, however, paid off in terms of box office and reviews, although Cross admits that '*The Snow Maiden*, perhaps because of the ballet, brought in a new audience, a snob element'.[90]

The 'snob' element's natural home was Covent Garden, and while she frequently lost singers to this establishment (which paid better wages than she did), Baylis remained on amicable terms with it, often taking advantage of free tickets when her favourite operas were staged there. A letter from Baylis to the managing director of Covent Garden, Colonel Blois, in 1931 offers a snapshot of the intertwined but slightly edgy relations between the two houses:

> I'm sorry that we can't help you with the loan of the Carmen dress, but as we are playing this opera at about the

same time it seems impossible. I am not dead certain which of the last act dresses Miss Cruickshank had in mind – the red and black one in which she looked so lovely has now been relegated to the chorus, and Mrs. Newman, my wardrobe mistress, refuses even to consider letting it out of the building it is so old and frail! The new one, which Miss Cruickshank would have worn had she been able to play for us this season, and which we are now using, was made from cheap cotton georgette bought at Barker's, and if Mrs. Tessell cared to come and see her sister, Mrs. Newman, she could, of course, copy it. In that case I would ask that acknowledgement be made of our designer, O.P. Smyth.[91]

Official relations sometimes became more complicated – Geoffrey Toye, for example, a governor of the Vic from 1926 onwards, resigned from the Vic-Wells governing board owing to increasing conflicts of interest once he became managing director at Covent Garden in 1933. This was a period in which suggestions of a merger between the two companies were frequently made, and Baylis also received overtures from Glyndebourne about collaborating.[92] But whereas the Vic-Wells had a ferociously protectionist stance in relation to its ballet work, good relations seem generally to have been maintained in the realm of opera.

One of Baylis's stated 'leading principles' was, and continued to be, that it was not possible to 'separate the Old Vic. from music'.[93] Joan Cross describes the Vic opera as Baylis's 'delicate sickly child to be cherished with the care and attention given by the head of the family to such a one'.[94] Baylis certainly cherished the sickly child that was the Vic-Wells opera in the early 1930s, when the film actor Charles Laughton obtained a grant from the Pilgrim Trust for the season in which he was to appear – with the idea that he would be able to wear smart costumes instead of worn-out Vic standbys. Laughton was then shocked to discover that the money generated by this very successful season had disappeared. When he demanded to know where all the box office takings had gone, he found that Baylis, who distrusted the 'West Endy' feel of this first year under Tyrone Guthrie, and was particularly unimpressed by the Hollywood star status of Laughton, had simply moved all the money into subsidising the temporarily more vulnerable opera company. For years during the First World War Baylis's beloved opera had subsidised Shakespeare, and now she was making Shakespeare return the favour.[95]

The debt that the Shakespeare Company owed to the opera company was something Baylis never allowed anyone to forget. In 1921 she is pontificating:

> It's the opera, in my opinion, which has created an audience for [Shakespeare]. There's nothing like music for the illiterate. It wakes their souls, when they are awake, there is something for the high thoughts and language of Shakespeare to appeal to.[96]

In 1923, in an article entitled 'Opera and the [Shakespeare] Tercentenary Festival', Baylis also reminds readers that she had to get people like Sir Frank Benson and Sir Herbert Beerbohm Tree 'to speak to the overflowing music-loving audience on Saturday nights, before the rise of the curtain' to encourage support for Shakespeare because the opera audiences were so plentiful and the Shakespeare audiences so sparse.[97] Charles Corri makes the point that opera 'played to capacity during the war, and kept the immortal Bard on his legs all through that trying period';[98] and Baylis even argued that the opera company could save the theatre because 'the Germans were an opera-loving people. They would surely respect the Vic.'[99] Baylis was still claiming that the opera had superior drawing power in an interview in *Theatre World* in 1931:

> Recruits to our audiences are generally attracted in the first place by opera, and it is only after they have been coming week after week to our performances of "Tannhauser", "Rigoletto", "Il Trovatore", "Faust", "Carmen", and so forth that they venture on plays.
>
> I don't pretend to understand why this should be so. One would imagine that the artificiality of the operatic tradition might prove a great difficulty, at first, to an

audience which is for the most part practically uneducated, but we have found over and over again that simply-produced opera will draw where Shakespeare is rather suspect. And the musical knowledge displayed by some of our regular patrons, especially at Sadlers Wells, would put many music critics to shame. One man, booking seats for a repeat performance of "Lohengrin", pointed out that last time the tenor had missed out two bars during a certain passage![100]

Just nine days before her death, Baylis published an article on the subject of 'The Romance of the Vic-Wells Opera' in the *Star*, which really spells out what she felt was important about the achievements of the opera company, and its offshoot, the ballet company:[101]

> I do not think it is an overweening claim if I say that the movement to provide opera and ballet in this country for the man in the street at prices he can pay, which began at the Vic and is now housed at Sadler's Wells, has played a very great part in building up the numbers and enthusiasm of the British musical audience.
>
> Week in, week out for nine months in the year four performances of opera and two of ballet are given at Sadler's Wells apart from the vacation tours of both companies to centres outside London.
>
> Last season's repertoire comprised seventeen different operas ranging from Mozart to the present-day and twenty-two different ballets. Both companies, apart from presenting popular classics, gave performances of new or unfamiliar works ... The prices at all performances range from sixpence to seven and six, so that for the price of one stall at a West End comedy, the keen music lover could hear from the Sadler's Wells gallery, twenty-five different operas lasting three hours each!
>
> The Vic-Wells opera organisation has shown in one generation what can be done to encourage and develop singing and acting talent ... Once the critics treated us with kindly but patronising approval as a "deserving effort". To-day we earn their genuine and enthusiastic praise by purely

critical standards, and at times they pay us the equal compliment of thinking us worthy of a good hard slam!

… Last season 300,000 people paid for admission at Sadler's Wells, but there is still room for more. May I suggest a trial trip to the rest of the city's music-loving millions?

It is typical of Baylis to end her article with what is in effect an advertisement, but her pride in her opera company is very clear.

Baylis boasted that the Vic-Wells opera had 'launched some of the world's finest singers'.[102] While performers such as Joan Cross and Arthur Carron (who started at the Vic as Arthur Cox) learnt their trade at the Vic, more established musical figures were also willing to be associated with the theatre – such as Edward Elgar, who conducted at the first performance of *Arthur*, and Thomas Beecham.[103] But it was the sheer audacity and the scale of Baylis's endeavours – under her the Vic company mounted at least fifty-two different operas – that made the company so many friends.[104]

When opera began at the Vic, the genre could still be counted as genuinely popular.[105] Opera was not seen to be the preserve of the rich, and a good proportion of the audience had enough musical knowledge to sing along with Mozart. But by the 1930s opera in England was threatening to become an elite art form patronised by the wealthy. The operas Baylis enjoyed – operas from which she had performed extracts during her professional career as a musician – were beginning to be seen as hopelessly out of date. Production values had improved, but the 'snobs' (to use Baylis's term) were taking over the audience, in spite of her attempts to repel them. In addition, despite her efforts to the contrary, the Vic-Wells opera was increasingly playing second fiddle to the playwright whose cause Baylis had adopted even though she herself considered him downright 'mucky':[106] William Shakespeare.

NOTES

1   Winifred Isaac, *Ben Greet and the Old Vic, A Biography of Sir Philip Ben Greet* (published by the author, 1964), p. 130.

2 *OVM*, November 1926. Booth, *The 'Old Vic'*, pp. 66–7 supplies another roll call of the singers who had contributed to the concert and opera performance of the Vic's early years under Cons and Baylis.

3 Harcourt Williams, *Four Years at the Old Vic*, p. 50.

4 Booth, *The 'Old Vic'*, p. 66 lists the repertoire up until 1916, the year of his book's publication. See also Dent, *A Theatre For Everybody*, pp. 30–1.

5 Constance Willis in Harcourt Williams, *Vic-Wells*, p. 88.

6 OVLB/000147/1.

7 The article is entitled 'Apollo in the New Cut' and originally appeared in *Musical Opinion*.

8 Lilian Baylis, '"The Old Vic" and "The Wells"', *Toc H*, March 1933, p. 109.

9 George Rowell, *The Old Vic Theatre* (Cambridge, 1993), p. 70 also points out many of the Vic operas 'began life as melodrama before becoming opera'.

10 Eric Walter White, *The Rise of English Opera* (London, 1951), pp. 99, 103.

11 Ibid., p. 123.

12 Edward Dent, *A Theatre For Everybody*, p. 71. White, *The Rise of English Opera*, p. 107 comments: 'During the first three decades of the twentieth century *The Bohemian Girl*, *Maritana* and *The Lily of Killarney* were still stock operas: but since about 1930 they have become so unfashionable that a new generation of opera-goers is growing up to whom these English romantic operas are completely unknown.'

13 *Daily Sketch*, 26 November 1937.

14 Dent, *A Theatre For Everybody*, p. 72.

15 *OVM*, September–October 1935.

16 Lawrance Collingwood in Harcourt Williams, *Vic-Wells*, p. 78. Collingwood puts the usual Vic orchestra at twenty strong. Four horns and three trombones would be brought in as extras on Wagner nights.

17 *OVM*, September–October 1935. In 1919 Baylis claimed the amount was only £1,000 – see Chapter 8.

18 Joan Cross's autobiography is deposited at the Britten-Pears Library at Aldeburgh. This is the main source for quotations from Cross in this chapter – however, Cross often went into print reminiscing about her early experiences at the Vic, and some of the material in such pieces as the Sadler's Wells Diamond Jubilee souvenir brochure overlaps with the autobiography.

19 Cross, autobiography, p. 11.

20 Ibid., p. 12.

21 Ibid., p. 13.

22 Dent, *A Theatre For Everybody*, p. 87.

23 Roberts, *Lilian Baylis*, p. 35.

24 Dent, *A Theatre For Everybody*, p. 39.

25 Ibid., pp. 20, 40.

26 Ibid., p. 40. The record that Baylis made in 1936 and the interview with Leslie Mitchell on television in 1937 do not seem to me to support this opinion of Baylis's voice, although she was probably speaking in her best voice for these occasions.

27 Ibid., p. 41.

28 Ibid., p. 42. See also the sketch illustrating this episode, p. 41. When this anecdote was related at *Tribute To The Lady*, a gala tribute performance in 1974, it produced gales of laughter in the audience of National Theatre celebrities.

29 See Chapter 11.

30 *OVM*, September–October 1925.

31 Dent, *A Theatre For Everybody*, p. 98.

32 *OVM*, April 1930.

33 *OVM*, March 1929.

34 *OVM*, September–October 1934.

35 Cross, autobiography, prologue p. 2.

36 Ibid., prologue p. 3.

37 Ibid., prologue pp. 2, 3. She is quoted by Bryan Crimp ('Opera at the Vic', Radio 4, 1985) as saying that a full house then brought in £150. Sarah Lenton (audiotape, 2001) recounts that on a contract signed by Cross, Baylis crossed out 6d of the agreed amount *after* Cross had signed it.

38 See letters to May Goring Thomas, M&M, 12 July 1923.

39 Cross, autobiography, p. 3.

40 Ibid., pp. 1–2.

41 Ibid., p. 2.

42 Ibid., pp. 6, 8.

43 See Lawrance Collingwood in Harcourt Williams, *Vic-Wells*, p. 77.

44 Cross, autobiography, p. 8. The *OVM* of April 1923 comments: 'The artistic success of some of the performances at the Vic. is miraculous when one realizes that principals, orchestra and chorus have never met together before the Thursday performance.'

45 Booth, *The 'Old Vic'*, p. 10 records 'The looking-glass curtain was

36 feet in height and 32 feet in breadth and consisted of sixty-three plates of looking-glass set in a massive gilt-carved frame.' It weighed five tons.

46 Dent, *A Theatre For Everybody*, p. 70.

47 Cross, autobiography, p. 15.

48 Ibid., p. 31. Many second-hand costumes were acquired at the auction of the Moody-Manners Opera Company's assets in 1920.

49 Dent, *A Theatre For Everybody*, p. 70. Dent disliked Baylis's voice intensely, and speaks of 'her harsh and almost offensive manner of speaking' (p. 40), hence, presumably, his stress on Baylis's, for him, comic accent.

50 Joan Cross in Roberts, *Lilian Baylis*, p. 33.

51 Cross, autobiography, p. 14.

52 Ibid., pp. 21, 24.

53 *OVM*, October 1919. The *OVM* of April 1923 reports the results of canvassing the Vic audience about what they would like to see. The same issue included an article by Harold Hodge arguing that the Vic should stop doing weak operas and only do the excellent ones, and an article by Nicholas Gatty on 'The Old Vic. Opera Repertoire'. For Baylis, the issue of royalties was always paramount as far as determining the repertoire was concerned.

54 *Sketch*, 9 February 1927.

55 *Theatre World*, December 1931.

56 Lilian Baylis, 'A Greatest Hour', *John Bull*, 10 February 1934.

57 *Star*, 25 November 1937.

58 Lilian Baylis, 'Aims and Ideals of the Theatre', 3 typescripts, M&M (broadcast 24 October 1928).

59 *OVM*, December 1930.

60 *OVM*, January 1926.

61 Baylis, 'Aims and Ideals of the Theatre'.

62 Baylis, 'Aims and Ideals of the Theatre'.

63 Lilian Baylis, 'Stories of the "Old Vic": A Chapter of Experiences', *Southwark Diocesan Gazetteer*, 31 December 1931.

64 Baylis, 'Aims and Ideals of the Theatre'.

65 Cross, autobiography, p. 49.

66 Ibid., p. 37.

67 Ibid., pp. 38, 66.

68 Private communication with the author.

69 Governors' minutes, 27 April 1932.

70 Anecdote recorded in Findlater, *Lilian Baylis*, p. 161.

71 Cross, autobiography, pp. 83, 101.

72 Ibid., pp. 3, 24. Cross also got blacklisted when she found she
    had double booked one night and could not afford to appear at
    the Vic (p. 17) when the other engagement paid so much
    better.

73 Joan Cross in Roberts, *Lilian Baylis*, p. 34; Cross, autobiography,
    p. 20.

74 For background to this event see the *OVM* of November 1926.
    Baylis's sense of Melba's visit as a miracle is discussed in Chapter
    5.

75 Findlater, *Lilian Baylis*, p. 180.

76 *OVM*, April–May 1939 comments that one of Baylis's 'ambitions'
    was to produce Smyth's *The Wreckers*, but this was only achieved
    after her death.

77 Ethel Smyth, *Streaks of Life* (London, 1921), p. 229.

78 Ibid., p. 228.

79 *OVM*, February 1922.

80 Christopher St John, *Ethel Smyth: A Biography* (London, 1959),
    p. 179.

81 Ethel Smyth, 'Lilian Baylis: a Sketch' in *Female Pipings in Eden*
    (London, 1933), pp. 177, 178. Virginia Woolf actually
    suggested Smyth omit the portrait of Baylis from *Female Pipings
    in Eden* as it seemed a 'tempting digression', but Smyth left it in.
    See letter dated 6 June 1933 in Virginia Woolf, *The Sickle Side of
    the Moon: The Letters of Virginia Woolf, Volume 5: 1932–1935*, ed.
    Nigel Nicolson (London, 1979).

82 Smyth, 'Lilian Baylis', p. 179.

83 Ethel Smyth, *A Final Burning of Boats* (London, 1928), p. 198.

84 *OVM*, January 1922.

85 *OVM*, March 1922.

86 *OVM*, September–October 1934.

87 Dent, *A Theatre For Everybody*, p. 156.

88 Cross, autobiography, pp. 83, 84. Lawrance Collingwood
    (Harcourt Williams, *Vic-Wells*, p. 80) states that it was not until
    1933 that Baylis brought in her conductors and directors 'to
    meet regularly to help her fix the repertoire and casts; until
    then she had been completely autocratic'.

89 *OVM*, February 1933.

90 Cross, autobiography, p. 84.

91 Letter dated 21 September 1931, Royal Opera House archive.
    Blois was managing director of Covent Garden from 1925 until
    his death in 1933.

92 The 'League of Opera' is discussed in the *OVM* of December
    1932. For Glyndebourne see OVLB 000042/2. John Christie,
    writing to Baylis on 12 July 1937, comments 'Covent Garden is
    hopeless to both of us while Beecham is there' and 'I should
    welcome a closer co-operation between your people and ours.'

93 *OVM*, March 1923.

94 Cross, autobiography, p. 4.

95 See Roberts, *Lilian Baylis*, p. 21.

96 *Time and Tide*, 15 July 1921, p. 673.

97 *OVM*, November 1923. Booth, *The 'Old Vic'*, p. 69 records that
    opera audiences at this time were often in excess of 2,000. He
    also lists theatre grandees who tried to rouse enthusiasm for
    Shakespeare: Lena Ashwell; Frank Benson; Hutin Britton;
    Constance Collier; Mrs Edward Compton; Philip Ben Greet; Mrs
    Kendal; Matheson Lang; Nancy Price; Herbert Beerbohm Tree;
    May Whitty.

98 *OVM*, February 1928.

99 Russell Thorndike, 'Lilian Baylis', p. 121. Baylis was proud of
    the fact that during the war Mozart and Wagner continued to be
    performed 'without a dissentient voice' (Baylis, '"The Old Vic"
    and "The Wells"', p. 111).

100 Vere Denning, 'Women who Count in the Theatre: The Power
    behind the "Old Vic": an Impression of Lilian Baylis', *Theatre
    World*, December 1931, p. 293. The year 1931 was a period
    when opera audiences were not doing so well as the
    Shakespeare audiences, and Baylis may have been trying to
    drum up support by complimenting her opera audience here.

101 For details on the growth of the ballet company under Ninette
    de Valois see Chapter 9. The *Star* article appeared on 16
    November 1937.

102 OVM, September–October 1936.

103 OVM, February 1934. Elgar composed incidental music for
    Arthur.

104 OVM, September–October 1936.

105 If nothing else the fights about copyright – both establishing it
    and then the infringements of it – make clear how much money
    could be involved when an opera became a big hit, or an opera
    melody became popular. See White, *The Rise of Opera*, p. 115:
    H.M.S. Pinafore was pirated over twenty times in New York
    shortly after its premiere in London.

106 See Thorndike, 'Lilian Baylis', pp. 119, 158 for 'mucky old
    Shakespeare'.

[7]

'I turned, in despair, to Shakespeare': Baylis and the Bard

While Baylis claimed that it was only 'in despair' that she 'turned to Shakespeare', under her management the Vic not only became acknowledged as the home of Shakespeare in London but also claimed to be the first theatre ever (apart, possibly, from the original Globe) to perform the complete works of Shakespeare: that goal was reached during the 1923–4 season with a performance of *Troilus and Cressida*, the final play in the Vic's march through the Shakespeare First Folio.[1] What is more, Baylis's management had a profound effect on the production of Shakespeare in the twentieth century, and although some of this was inadvertent it was none the less significant. Once she had decided that Shakespeare was going to be the Vic house dramatist, Baylis threw her very considerable energies into promoting his work, and the nine-month season of Shakespeare production which took place at the Vic each year significantly increased the amount of Shakespeare performed in the UK at the time. As certain plays inevitably came round season after season, the Vic audience became accustomed to comparing one actor's Hamlet or Petruchio with another. However, even more crucially, Baylis's tight-fisted approach to running a theatre and to staging productions meant that the house style had to be 'bare-boards' Shakespeare. In an interview many years later Baylis recalled:

> We hadn't a decent bit of scenery. We had to depend on the words. We had nothing else to depend on.[2]

This frugal style was, however, supported on aesthetic and intellectual grounds by most of the men Baylis hired to be the theatre's artistic directors.

The bare-boards aesthetic started gaining popularity at the

Baylis and her artistic directors. Taken from the programme for
Troilus and Cressida, 1923. Courtesy of the Theatre Museum, V&A
Picture Library

beginning of the twentieth century mainly because of the work of former Vic employee William Poel. After Poel left Emma Cons's Vic in 1883, he went on to develop and proselytise the theory that because Shakespeare and his contemporaries wrote plays very specifically with Elizabethan and Jacobean playhouse conditions in mind, these plays ought to continue to work best in similar conditions: on a thrust stage (that is, with an audience on at least three sides, possibly four); with very little scenery; with Elizabethan costumes; with lots of speeches directly addressed to an openly acknowledged audience; and with performers committed to ensemble playing. For Poel, the Shakespeare style that predominated at the end of the nineteenth century was anathema, with its end-on proscenium arch staging, its expensive, elaborate illusionistic scenery, its time-consuming scene changes (taking sometimes as much as a quarter of an hour), and its frequent cutting of the original text in order to exhibit the acting of the great stars. Poel put his ideas into practice in his own productions using mainly amateur performers, and the results were uneven, sometimes execrable. However, other theatre practitioners were inspired by his thinking, in particular the actor director Harley Granville-Barker, who started producing a 'user friendly' version of Poel's ideas in a short series of revolutionary, controversial, but in the end very successful, productions of Shakespeare. These influential productions took place during the period of 1912–14 – just as Baylis was turning in despair to Shakespeare.

Despite Baylis's initial reluctance to allow Shakespeare's plays onto her opera stage, she quickly learnt that there were major advantages to producing his works: there were no royalties to pay; the plays had such prestige that up-and-coming actors were willing to play the roles despite the dreadful pay she offered; and many of the plays were regularly studied on school syllabuses, creating the potential for very large if not always appreciative school audiences (detested by actors but excellent from the point of view of filling seats and outreach into the local community).

It was in February 1912 that Baylis first considered bringing 'Shakespeare to the people', in response to a proposal made by George Owen and W. Bridges-Adams, who had worked previously in Laurence Irving's Company.[3] The project did not work out, but by early 1914 Baylis had agreed to the first Shakespeare season at the Vic being directed by Rosina Filippi, an actress, director and teacher who claimed descent from the great actress Eleonora Duse.[4] Sybil Thorndike, whose brother Russell married Filippi's daughter, felt that this project was doomed from the start, because while Baylis and Filippi 'admired one another' they were 'perhaps both too domineering for a lasting partnership'.[5] Politically, the women were also very different, and the antipathy between Filippi and Baylis led to stories of Baylis attempting to sabotage the Shakespeare season by informing the opera audiences that they must not spend any of their opera money on Shakespeare.[6] Filippi's Shakespeare season certainly lost money, so her stay at the Vic was short-lived.

Baylis next engaged the auspiciously named Shakespeare Stewart to direct a season of plays, but again Shakespeare at the Vic met with little box-office success. Elisabethe Corathiel, first editor of the *Old Vic Magazine*, argues that Baylis persevered with Shakespeare because:

> Her only hope was to strike a "line" the public might be induced to want. She did this by modelling herself on Miss Horniman – and the idea literally ran away with her.[7]

But Annie Horniman was an heiress who dedicated much of her fortune to subsidising theatre firstly in Dublin and then in Manchester. When Baylis started her Shakespeare Company she had about sixty pounds in the bank.[8] However, the breakthrough for Baylis came during the first winter of the First World War, with a series of Shakespeare productions co-ordinated by husband-and-wife team Matheson Lang and Hutin Britton. At that stage Lang was best known for his success in the distinctly unclassical *Mr Wu*, yet in a period when received wisdom claimed that Shakespeare was box-office poison because the large casts and illusionistic settings were so prohibitively expensive, Lang and Britton achieved box office miracles at the Vic with cut-price Shakespeare. Baylis always gave Lang and Britton full credit here, but she did believe that

God had played his part as well: after all, she had been informed in a dream that she should take on the responsibility of running the Vic Shakespeare Company and not delegate this responsibility to anyone else.9 Baylis records that she was crying herself to sleep, 'soaking her pillow with her tears', and she 'cried out to God to help her in the work she had not chosen but had been thrust into'. Then a 'strong manly voice came out of the darkness' and asked her, 'Why have you allowed my beautiful words to be so murdered?' The 'strong calm male voice' told her to run the plays herself 'as you do the operas' and to get a company of actors together. 'I'm not an actress,' Baylis protested, 'I don't know enough about Shakespeare. I don't feel able to cast plays.' The voice simply instructed her: 'You are to choose your company of players and run the plays yourself.' And so the next day she started doing this with the help of Lang and Britton.[10]

For Baylis, Lang and Britton were quite simply the 'God-father and mother of Shakespeare at the "Old Vic."'[11] Their work could 'never be forgotten by the Vic's manager. Shoulder to shoulder with her they stood in the enormous difficulty encountered in starting the Old Vic. Shakespeare Company.'[12] Lang and Britton, however, were committed to a tour and could not stay at the Vic to build on their initial success. They departed in April 1915, leaving behind, as a loan, costumes and sets: some of these lent items, by then in a state of advanced dilapidation, were still being used in Vic productions in the mid 1920s. Lang left with the comment 'God alone knows how you will carry on.'[13] Baylis's reply was that God *did* know, and he would deliver. The way God delivered was by sending Baylis a new director, Philip Ben Greet; however, Estelle Stead, who had worked with Lang and Britton during the breakthrough season, also played a significant part here, as it was she who suggested Greet be approached.[14] Stead also helped by acting, directing, setting up a supporters' club and backing 'Miss Baylis tooth and nail, when the then Governors wanted to abandon the [Shakespeare] project owing to the outbreak of War'.[15]

At the beginning of the First World War, Greet wanted to volunteer but was too old for active service. At the Vic, by

Estelle Stead as Rosalind c. 1914. Courtesy of the Theatre Museum, V&A Picture Library

producing Shakespeare, he believed he could rally the hearts and minds of a nation at war. As Greet had been directing a touring company performing open-air Shakespeare for decades, performing extensively both in the UK and the US and often setting up in outside venues which had even less to offer than the impoverished Vic stage, the lack of scenery and the shabby costumes at the theatre were not a problem for him. Greet donated his services for the first year – that constituted his war effort – and in the following three years only took expenses.[16] He produced twenty-four Shakespeare plays for the Vic, as well as initiating several of what became well-loved rituals for the theatre: in a tribute written by Baylis on the occasion of Greet's death she reminded Vic audiences that he

> introduced "Hamlet" in its entirety to the Vic … We owe "Everyman" to him, and it was given here for fourteen years each Holy Week, and Mendelssohn's Oratorio "Elijah" in dramatic form.[17]

Greet also suggested the Vic hold its own Remembrance Day service and lay a wreath for its own fallen soldiers.

Greet helped further develop the Vic's tradition for outreach, and as early as 1915 the company was giving performances at the Excelsior Hall, Bethnal Green and the North London Polytechnic.[18] Greet also introduced the school matinees, an idea that had been canvassed for years by the Reverend Stewart Headlam, a theatre-loving cleric who had founded the Church and Stage Guild (Liebe Baylis was on the first council) to improve relations between the theatre and the church.[19] Although he had doubts over the liberties Greet took with Shakespeare's texts, Headlam convinced the London County Council they should support school matinees at the Vic.[20] In 1915, Baylis records visits by schoolchildren 'from Stepney and Woolwich, from Upper Tooting, Wimbledon, Putney, South Hackney, and Homerton'; in one week over 4,000 children saw *As You Like It*, which even at concessionary prices was good business.[21] The matinees were eventually stopped in 1921, when it was discovered that schoolchildren were not supposed to pay for theatre visits during school hours, and a subsequent grant made to cover this expense was also ruled illegal.[22] But the school matinees not only brought local children into the Vic, they also raised the profile of the theatre and increased the chances that the children's families would become interested in their local theatre and perhaps visit it some time.

Greet, like Baylis, combined a deeply religious sensibility with an explosive temper and over the years they worked together their rows became legendary. On one occasion Greet pulled Baylis's nose twice (hard), and Robert Atkins records a performance of *Macbeth* which was sabotaged by so bad an offstage quarrel between Greet and Baylis that even the habitually decorous Sybil Thorndike, the upstaged Lady Macbeth, swore in exasperation.[23] It was Greet who brought Sybil Thorndike to the Vic, and thus helped establish a pattern whereby rising stars joined the Vic to extend their range and to play roles they would not have access to elsewhere; they then moved on to become major stars. Thorndike came to the Vic after Greet sent her a letter stating: 'There's a strange woman running a theatre in the Waterloo Road, you'd find her exciting, Syb, because you're as mad as she is … you'll like Lilian Baylis, she's got ideals.'[24] Thorndike did like Baylis, and ended up working at the Vic throughout most of the First World War, even rushing into action straight from childbirth to meet Baylis's demands: for Baylis, whose mother had made such heroic efforts to combine childbirth and a career, a baby being born late was no excuse for Sybil Thorndike to turn down the role of Ophelia.[25]

The opportunities on offer at the Vic were like nothing else in London at the time: a London at war, when many theatres went dark and those that were playing offered escapist, light entertainment. Thorndike played a host of Shakespearian roles at the Vic, and this included many male parts, because the theatre was steadily losing men as they were called up to fight in the trenches. Thorndike records Baylis's attitude to cross-gender casting: 'after all, there should be no sex in acting – you ought to be able to understand men as well as women'.[26] When Thorndike was playing the role of the Fool to her brother Russell Thorndike's Lear, Baylis remarked during a rehearsal that Sybil looked like Russell's shadow. Thorndike then took this as the dominant motif for her entire performance, also incorporating Baylis's suggestion that 'It would be nice if you had a sort of face that might turn into Russell's if you put eyebrows and marks on it – a sort of blank Russell.'[27] In relation to Thorndike's playing of Lady Macbeth Baylis responded:

> I think Lady Macbeth is a very easy part for you – she loved her husband, and wanted him to get to the top of the tree,

and I expect you feel that way too, and if wasn't that you go to Communion I dare say you'd do all sorts of wicked things to help [Thorndike's husband] Lewis.[28]

Baylis's idea that Lady Macbeth should be treated as if she was a real person was not, when Thorndike first played the role for the Vic in 1914, the clichéd judgement it might seem today. Although the nineteenth century increasingly tended to *read* Shakespeare's characters as if they were real people, or at least the inhabitants of a triple-decker novel, the working practices of theatre in 1914 often still looked back to the heightened characterisation of melodrama. Lady Macbeth was frequently performed as an arch-villainess, and Stanislavskian ideas on complex character motivation in acting were relatively unfamiliar in England. Melodramatic acting styles prevailed in the cinema, and to see Lady Macbeth as understandably human was not the norm. In fact, seeing Shakespeare's characters as just human beings was precisely one of the subjects that Baylis rowed with Greet over; Greet felt that treating Shakespeare's characters as real people was new-fangled nonsense.[29]

For Thorndike the satisfaction of playing Shakespeare, despite the threadbare surroundings at the Vic, was accompanied by an opportunity to make a mark and, in effect, to audition for the West End. When Thorndike made this move to the commercial theatre, she was warmly encouraged to do so by Baylis, although in later years Baylis often professed astonishment that anyone could prefer success in the commercial West End over the family warmth available at the Vic.[30]

Shakespeare, Greet, Thorndike and the First World War together eventually brought great success to the Vic, but Baylis always remembered that 'we had a very hard struggle during those first years to get audiences'.[31] Indeed Sybil Thorndike recalled an early Shakespeare performance where the company played to 'about five people ... in the pit and three boys and an orange in the gallery'.[32] When Baylis asked the cast if they should cancel the show, they said they would play on and by the end of the performance the audience had swelled to twenty. Greet's productions were in many ways old-fashioned: heavily cut, full of traditional business and blocking. They borrowed candlesticks and coffins from the undertaker's shop opposite the theatre, and when the noise from air raids became deafening sent on Ernest Meads, an actor with a 'twenty horse power voice'.[33] Yet these wartime Shakespeares really put the Vic on the theatrical map, and audiences who would normally never go south of the river to the theatre had to visit the Vic if they wanted to see Shakespeare during this period.

The bard's patriotic kudos was also exploited by Baylis to the full. Once, during a performance of *King John*, a bombing raid took place and Falconbridge's lines created a great sensation:

> This England never did, nor never shall
> Lie at the proud foot of a conqueror

Baylis decided that these lines (although they ignore historical reality) should then be placed above the proscenium, and they remained there for the duration of the war.[34] Baylis herself certainly believed that the war years helped make the Vic, claiming that

> Colonial and foreign visitors seeing London for the first time, sometimes asked where they could hear Shakespeare in his own tongue in his own country; and our little efforts, in a theatre not a few hundred yards from the site of Shakespeare's own Globe Theatre, was the only answer London could provide.[35]

Baylis also believed that shell-shocked men coming back from the trenches could use Shakespeare at the Vic to help get their sanity back: 'by fixing their minds on the great lines of the plays, and working as we all worked in those days, they shut out their cruel memories and fought their way back to sanity'.[36] Soldiers and sailors were only charged half price for their tickets, while 'wounded soldiers and refugees from allied countries were invited free' to the Vic.[37] Baylis also cites the case of an actor who came back from the war 'nerve-wrecked' and unable to speak lines or even set foot on the stage: 'So …

we put on *Macbeth* again, and he played Scotch music off – and in a few weeks he was able to walk on'; he eventually returned to acting.[38]

Robert Atkins, who later in his career became artistic director at the Vic, records what conditions were like when he first joined the Shakespeare Company as an actor in 1914, while he was waiting for his call-up to the army.[39] The Vic was then a 'ramshackle, disinfectant-breathing fit-up' theatre which still had the grooves for old-fashioned scenery flats onstage, and it was a health and safety nightmare. Atkins remembers:

> The footlights were incandescent burners; number one and two battens were naked gas flames caged with wire. In the prompt corner the six brass handles that controlled this gas supply were badly worn, and often when "dimming" during a performance, both footlights and battens would pop-pop ominously and go out. The "perch limes" would then have to be used for the rest of the scene, and at the end old Bob would arrive with a taper to light up the burners. He was greeted with laughter and disappeared to applause.

Once a week 'a man with a cartload of sawdust arrived to scatter it through the auditorium', and the gin palace next door got so rowdy on a Saturday night that 'no women in the Vic company were allowed to leave without male escorts'. Meanwhile Baylis's office contained a

> large roll-up desk that occupied at least a quarter of the not over-spacious office. A Victorian sofa, a table, two or three chairs and, above the fireplace, a large corner cupboard added to the clutter.[40]

When the time for the evening performance came, however, Baylis would relocate to her box at the side of the stage, and would carry on with her office work during the performance.

The wartime Vic is also described by Winifred Isaac: like Joan Cross, she found the remains of the mirror theatre curtain a nuisance, as 'The reflections interfered with the stage lighting and distracted the actors' and it was a relief when eventually 'the glass was removed and the walls were afterwards covered with red paper'.[41] Meanwhile the audience sat on 'hard wooden benches' with a bar at the back, although in the gallery the benches were completely backless.[42] From Pearce and Plenty's refreshment bar in the front of the theatre 'The clatter of cups and the clink of pennies was only a minor disturbance compared with the noises which penetrated from the New Cut which was lined with the stalls of a very busy market.'[43] There was no box office, no dressing rooms, no wardrobes or scene docks, as all available backstage space was given over to Morley College. Actors had to dress in the circle saloon or in the tiny rooms, designed for quick-change music hall acts, on the sides of the stage. There was only one backstage water supply, on prompt side, and this water could only be heated on the famous gas ring on which Baylis also cooked steak, sausages and chops.

The experience of '[a]ppetising odours penetrat[ing] on to the stage and well into the stalls, during the last acts of matinees' became a notorious feature of the Vic and is often held up as a classic demonstration of Baylis's crazy style of management, distracting audiences from the plays they had come to see, and exhausted actors from the job they were trying to do.[44] Baylis's cooking also constituted a major fire hazard, but it enabled her to work long hours at the Vic without a break, and to feed her peaky-looking (perhaps because underpaid) performers. It also probably helped sustain the Vic's rat population, already flourishing because of the building's proximity to the river and the market. Theatre critic William Archer once looked down during a performance and discovered a rat was gnawing at his boot.[45]

Other smells, however, also permeated the Vic. Isaac comments on the strong smell '[o]wing to the theatre being lit by gas'.[46] Sybil Thorndike remembers the 'cheery smell of bloaters and bacon from "Pearce and Plenty's"'.[47] The smell of tobacco was also much in evidence. In trumpeting the improvements to the newly refurbished Vic in January 1927 the *Old Vic Magazine* points out:

One of the principal glories ... will be the 140 dozen

ashtrays affixed to the backs of seats; which will do away for ever with that embarrassing social exigency – what to do when one has extinguished the butt of one's cigarette on one's next door neighbour's hat.

Indeed during the early 1930s the artistic director, Harcourt Williams, was grateful when Baylis allowed him to insert a note in the programmes asking audiences not to strike matches during scenes. As he comments sadly, 'The striking of matches, of course, not only disturbs our neighbours, but the actors as well. The sudden flash of light in the middle of a long speech, or tense situation, is devastating to the player.'[48] By modern standards, even in the poverty-stricken, profit-share, fringe, conditions at the Vic when Baylis started producing Shakespeare were primitive, and they certainly contrast starkly with today's clean, hygienic, soundproofed, health-and-safety-checked, disability-access-available, subsidised theatres.

A glimpse of Baylis at work at the Vic during the war can be gained from some of Baylis's letters to her young friend Ivy Smithson.[49] Writing around Christmas 1917, Baylis confesses, 'I've had a very *bad* time with the Raids.' She retreats to the convent and leper colony at St Giles's, East Hanningfield, for a few days, although 'I hated leaving my family and the Vic but I felt if I didn't have a few days peace I'd never get to the end of this season.' Nevertheless, while supposedly resting at St Giles's, Baylis begins busying herself organising entertainments there. Back at the Vic in March 1918, Baylis is having to sell programmes alongside all her other jobs: she writes that *School for Scandal* is '*booked out*', but 'we are dreadfully short of stewards & programme sellers, so that job is added to the rest of our work'. She continues to worry about the air raids, tells the fervent Anglo-Catholic Smithson that there is great missionary potential in the Vic performances of *Everyman* and *Elijah*, and reports on the unveiling of the Vic's memorial to actors who had died in the war. She adds that nobody comes to the theatre on Mondays, but her beloved opera is packed to capacity on Saturday nights.

Because Shakespeare became established at the Vic during the First World War, a certain amount of hand-to-mouth staging was bound to be tolerated initially when so many energies were being diverted towards the war effort. After the war, however, the Vic house style continued to be bare boards. When Greet left the Vic in 1918, Baylis next employed George Foss to direct Shakespeare for her. Foss dedicated his 1932 book *What the Author Meant* to Baylis because 'Under [her] inspiring management I, with but ten actors and three stage hands, produced fifteen Shakespearian plays in the last years of the great war.'[50] Baylis thought Foss was 'potty' on account of his casting against type and expected him to 'cop it from the Press', but 'she loyally stuck by new ways'.[51]

In October 1918 the Vic received a huge boost in terms of publicity when Queen Mary attended a gala matinee celebrating the theatre's centenary. There was a wide range of theatrical fare on offer at the gala: Russell Thorndike impersonated the great clown of previous century, 'Joey' Grimaldi; C. Croker-King impersonated Paganini; Matheson Lang and Hutin Britton mounted a scene from *The Taming of the Shrew* as it would have been performed a hundred years previously; and a rather elderly Ellen Terry played the potion scene from *Romeo and Juliet*, culminating in what Elisabethe Corathiel remembers as 'a back-fall which was a miracle of acrobatics'.[52] Corathiel also remembers the planning process, with

> Ellen Terry perched on my table in Lilian's office while they discussed what her contribution should be. Ellen was already almost blind. Lilian didn't want to paint the picture too rosily. "I don't know where you'll dress," she was saying. "We are all crowded here, and no one has a proper dressing room." "Oh, don't let that worry you," said Ellen. "If it comes to the worst I'll nip over to the ladies' room at Waterloo Station and come back in a taxi."

Some time after this, the dreadful dressing rooms generated a very famous Baylis anecdote. Sybil Thorndike recalls that Baylis was arguing at a governors' meeting that money should be made available for improvements to the dressing rooms:[53]

> A very sympathetic Royal lady was there, and Lilian turned

to her in the midst of a burningly characteristic tirade and said: "Now, your Royal Highness, I just ask you, how would you like it, when you were dressing for a big function at the Palace like the Macbeth Banquet, to be so jammed and crowded, one person treading on your train and your crown getting knocked sideways, and everyone in a temper with hurry and no room. I just ask, how would you like it?" And her Royal Highness replied, laughing: "Miss Baylis, I shouldn't like it at all."

"Well, my girls don't like it either ... and they've got their livings to earn, you know."

Although they didn't manage to do anything about the dressing rooms, the duumvirate of Russell Thorndike and Charles Warburton, who succeeded George Foss as artistic director during 1920, did manage to pull off the coup of persuading Baylis to replace the Vic's scenery grooves, those outdated relics of Victorian staging practices. Russell Thorndike relates with glee the story of how he and Warburton, having secured Baylis's agreement to the modernisation, got the workmen to agree to start work at 6 a.m., because both the directors were worried that Baylis would change her mind overnight.54 When Baylis did duly arrive the next morning ready to countermand her previous decision, she found it was too late and the grooves system already demolished.

After Thorndike and Warburton, Baylis took on Robert Atkins as artistic director for the period of May 1921 to November 1925. Baylis had been waiting for Atkins to come back from army service so she could offer him the job, and his work ushered in a crucial period for the Vic Shakespeare Company, one in which it started to acquire a reputation for innovation and quality. In some ways Atkins was not the ideal man to work with Baylis as he was too fond of drink and womanising, and their rows became almost as legendary as Baylis's rows with Greet. However, Baylis's genius for picking the right person for the Vic's particular needs at a particular time is confirmed by her hiring of Atkins. Under Atkins, Shakespearian plays that were rarely performed were brought into the Vic repertory, experiments in staging were tried out, and generally the Vic's theatrical horizons expanded. Atkins was a disciple and friend of William Poel, and the two men had frequent discussions about the plays Atkins was producing at the Vic.55 In the Vic's theatre-on-a-shoestring laboratory, Atkins was testing out many of Poel's ideas about Elizabethan staging, one season even setting up a thrust stage by placing a platform across the orchestra in order to evoke a sense of the Elizabethan playhouse.56 The vital difference from Poel's own productions, however, was that the Vic provided professional performers and an audience that became increasingly accustomed to – and fond of – the bare-boards house style.57 Initially some resisted Atkins's daring

> in stripping the stage of all "scenery" in the old-fashioned sense of the word; [they] were not sure that they liked his use of curtains and of the "apron" stage, and his determination to give the play without "cuts".

Eventually, however, most of the audience were won over.

John Gielgud, who worked briefly as a spear-carrier at the Vic in 1921, remembers his time there under Atkins as 'thrilling', full of camaraderie, rushed – with productions often 'unfinished' – 'desperately cheap', and involving actors who were constantly heading for the bar and using 'terrible language'.58 Baylis's preference for hiring returned soldiers, like Atkins, who were still working through their experiences of the First World War trenches possibly contributed to the prevalence of swearing and drinking in the company. However, Gielgud, who appeared as a super in *Henry V, King Lear, Wat Tyler* and *Peer Gynt*, was 'enormously impressed' by some of the acting and indeed felt his own acting was dreadful. He also recalls the hazards attendant on the shortage of dressing rooms.59 One night while several actors were dressing in a stage box, the actor who was keeping check on the progress of the play so that they didn't miss their cues 'dragged the curtain roughly aside, and down it came, revealing us all, half naked, to the astonished and delighted gallery!'60

Atkins left the Vic when he was only one play (*Cymbeline*) short of having directed the complete works of Shakespeare, and he felt somewhat disgruntled as he thought that Baylis had deliberately stopped him from achieving this personal goal. Meanwhile the Vic itself made the most of the publicity coup of completing its own ten-year trawl through the Shakespeare canon just in time for the 1923 tercentenary celebrations of the publication of the First Folio.[61] The Vic had had to produce plays that were serious box-office risks in order to finish the canon; while five cases of fainting were reported on the opening night of *Titus Andronicus*, not even this level of sensationalism could manage to make such relatively unknown Shakespeare a financial success.[62] And despite Atkins's bravery in general in staging much more of Shakespeare's text than was usual, at least one of the lesser-known plays, *Henry the Sixth, Part One*, got severely edited. The Manager's Report for 1922–3 states:

> In marked contrast to the Vic.'s settled custom, many of the speeches of Joan of Arc which presented her in the light in which she was regarded in Elizabethan and pre-Elizabethan days were (rightly or wrongly) "cut" in order to avoid giving offence to any part of the audience.[63]

Baylis was not going to have the Vic stage presenting Shakespeare's cursing, diabolic version of Joan, a Joan who conjures up evil spirits, offers them her blood, body and soul, rejects her shepherd father, and claims she is with child in an attempt to escape death.

Despite the disagreements, Atkins in general had admiring memories of Baylis: 'Miss Baylis, for all her oddities, had planted a creative seed' at the Vic, and 'If she had faith in a person, she would fight, even if she did not quite understand the aim' – although she was also 'a queen as autocratic as Victoria'.[64] Very significantly, at the end of Atkins's artistic directorship, William Poel himself wrote to Baylis: 'I hope you will let me thank you and Mr. Robert Atkins – as I do sincerely and cordially – for all that you have done for Shakespeare which has been left *un*done by those who manage our theatre on the other side of the water' (that is, north of the Thames, in the commercial West End).[65] Such an acknowledgement from one of the theatrical pioneers of the early twentieth century says much for the impact that Baylis's management had in revolutionising Shakespeare production.

After Robert Atkins, Andrew Leigh (another disciple of Poel) succeeded as artistic director, and the West End influence at the Vic now began to grow. Edith Evans, who had actually started her acting career working with Poel, joined the Vic in order to stretch herself professionally. Evans had tried to join the Vic earlier in her career and had auditioned there: various outrageous responses by Baylis are recorded, including the story that she phoned up Sybil Thorndike and shouted, 'How dare you send me such an ugly woman.'[66] Later Baylis was said to have pronounced of Evans, 'I ought to have engaged her [earlier], but she didn't look the leading type'.[67] This of course was true. Leading ladies did tend to look alike, and they didn't tend to look like Evans (or indeed Baylis). But according to Sybil Thorndike, Baylis loved Evans's acting and personality: 'It's not only her lovely acting ... it's her herself; she's big, everything about her is big.'[68] While at the Vic, Evans rattled through a number of major Shakespeare roles and learnt a great deal, but both Evans and her co-star Balliol Holloway made 'considerable financial sacrifices in order to have the chance of playing the classic roles'.[69] Evans's time at the Vic, however, can also be seen as the beginning of the serious West End colonisation of the theatre, in terms both of the growing numbers of stars who worked there and of the social makeup of the audience.

After four years, in 1929, Andrew Leigh left to be succeeded by Harcourt Williams. For Baylis, part of Williams's attraction was the directing work he had done for his wife Jean Sterling Mackinlay in mounting children's plays for the Vic's Christmas matinees.[70] Williams was worried about working at the Vic: most particularly he was concerned that Baylis 'might interfere with my work', which she did not.[71] In fact she was extremely loyal, and when Williams was criticised for the speed of his productions, for jettisoning traditional business, and for directing a production of *A Midsummer Night's Dream* which completely dispensed with gauze, she backed him to the hilt, despite herself preferring her *Midsummer Night's Dream* to be gauzy.[72] Baylis pointed out that Williams must have taken far worse criticism for being a conscientious objector during the war and told him to ignore his detractors. In fact she was always willing to let her directors take risks in how they staged plays so long as they kept to their budgets. As the standard budget for set and costumes was 'under £15' during Robert Atkins's tenure, keeping to it was no mean achievement.[73] However, when Williams brokered a deal that was to secure both Martita Hunt and John Gielgud for the Vic, Baylis did haggle about salaries to such an extent that she jeopardised all Williams's plans. Gielgud was greeted by Baylis as a star member of the Terry clan: 'How nice to see you, dear … Of course, we'd love to have you here, your dear aunt, you know – but of course we can't afford stars.'[74] By the end of the interview Gielgud recalls he 'was begging her to let me join the company', and the 'question of salary' was settled by letter later on.[75] But Baylis then went on to offer ten shillings less to Martita Hunt than Williams had already promised; Hunt threatened to withdraw from the season and Williams had to work hard negotiating between his offended star actress and his manager, 'all for ten bob'.[76]

Despite Baylis's fabled meanness over money – Laurence Olivier maintained that her detested lapdogs were trained to go for the ankles of anyone requesting a pay rise[77] – under Harcourt Williams the attempt to harness up-and-coming stars like Gielgud became really established at the Vic. Williams knew that the Vic was offering something special, and at a time of economic depression 'the Old Vic engagement of nine months' assured income' was very attractive.[78] Williams's view was also that his contract with the Vic 'saved John Gielgud six years of toil, for it would certainly have taken him at least that time to put himself where two years at the Old Vic did'.[79] Before he went to the Vic Gielgud was a star, but he was known for lightweight, West End fare; at the Vic he established his credentials in Shakespeare, something which made a huge impact on his career as a classical actor and director.

Harcourt Williams always remained a loyal apologist for Baylis, although he was not uncritical: he regretted the parochialism of the Vic, and especially disliked the enforced attendance by actors at audience parties. He particularly criticises Baylis's unwillingness to praise artists, and comments of her behaviour during rehearsals:

> the effect can be startling at dress rehearsal (she seldom comes to an ordinary rehearsal) when some caustic comment drops from an apparently empty box. Do not jump to the conclusion that she interrupts the progress of the rehearsal. She is too good an artist to do that.[80]

Williams speaks of the 'classic yarns that showed up amusing idiosyncrasies' but believes they actually cloaked 'an intriguing personality and a lovable nature'.[81]

Baylis's next, and last, artistic director was Tyrone Guthrie, who, significantly, ran the Shakespeare Company in two separate instalments. Guthrie was a concept director who initially joined the Vic for one year in 1933 and then departed, ostensibly to retire to Ireland to regather his strength and creativity. Although Baylis maintains that 'Tyrone Guthrie endeared himself to us all behind the curtain' and that 'we parted with him with regret', it had become clear that in many ways he stood for the opposite of everything Baylis held dear:[82] Guthrie wanted production values, Baylis wanted social work; he wanted theatre, she wanted opera; he wanted stars, she wanted ensemble; he wanted the West End audiences to come, she wanted them to stay away. Harcourt Williams remembers that 'from what [Guthrie] once said to me I gathered that he had no great liking for Lilian Baylis', and she in turn disliked the 'West-Endy people' Guthrie wanted to court.[83] Williams evokes Guthrie's first season in vivid terms:

> Guthrie descended like a bomb. There was a crash and a great sheet of flame – [Charles] Laughton, [Flora] Robson, [Athene] Seyler, [Roger] Livesey, [Ursula] Jeans, new scenery, new costumes, all blazing to the stars![84]

This season

> shook the traditions and outlook of the theatre to its foundations. It brought down the hard light of the Press upon it and flooded the stalls with the Smart Set from the West End theatres. More money was spent on the

productions, higher salaries were paid to the players than ever before, and it was during this season that both theatres won exemption from the Entertainment Tax.[85]

The cost, in Williams's opinion, was that 'the worth of a repertory company' was lost. Certainly some Vic regulars were upset. John Gielgud tells how the famous (or notorious) Miss Pilgrim, a devoted member of the audience who saw every show at the Vic and who did not like innovation, responded to Guthrie's work by embarking on an energetic gathering of autographs at the stage door. The stars dutifully signed the piece of paper Miss Pilgrim offered them, whereupon she attached these autographs to a letter demanding Guthrie's resignation.[86] Baylis herself was certainly uneasy with this new-style Vic and not impressed by the stars who were suddenly invading her theatre. Margaret Webster records Baylis's own account of her interview with Charles Laughton:

> "Funny boy," [Baylis] said, "keeps on saying God this and God that ... didn't care for it. Told him, 'Well, dear boy, we don't care how much money you make in films – are you good in Shakespeare?' Said he'd slept with a copy of *Hamlet* under his pillow since he was seven. I said, 'That's not the point, dear boy. Can you say his lovely words?'[87]

Norman Marshall is even franker in his assessment of Guthrie's first season: 'Much of the acting ... was below the level which the Vic audience was used to in the leading parts'; he contends that 'Lilian Baylis herself quite frankly disliked many of the productions but she put up with them because they filled the Vic.'[88] Marshall is being political here, mourning the loss of the Vic as an exciting fringe theatre as it gave way to the forces of the West End: in letting Guthrie and the West End invade, Baylis had 'committed the fatal managerial mistake of not trusting her own tastes and opinions'.[89]

After Guthrie's departure, Henry Cass ran the Vic Shakespeare Company successfully for two years. When Guthrie returned to the Vic in 1936, Baylis's health was deteriorating and she was anxious about planning her succession; having cast around fairly desperately, she seems to have become resigned to the fact that Guthrie and his West End predilections were the best option available. From then on she gave Guthrie her loyalty and began ceding more and more power to him.

Guthrie brought great publicity to the Vic but jeopardised more than the traditional ensemble, anti-West End ethos. He was extremely keen to extend the company's repertoire, and while this in itself was not a huge problem it brought problems in its wake. The Vic had actually very rarely just done Shakespeare:[90] the Shakespeare Company performed other Renaissance plays, such as *The Shoemaker's Holiday*, or *The Knight of the Burning Pestle*. The theatre also produced plays by outspoken women such as Clemence Dane (*Adam's Opera*) and Cicely Hamilton (*The Child in Flanders*). For Baylis the crucial question in relation to any play was always: were the royalties manageable? A lesser-known Ibsen was manageable, and the company had a big success with the British premiere of *Peer Gynt* (directed by Robert Atkins with Russell Thorndike in the title role). The Vic produced Tom Robertson's *Caste* for the centenary of the author's birth, with Robertson family members such as Rachel Behrendt in the cast and taking part in the celebrations. When Baylis scheduled Sir Arthur Pinero's *Trelawney of the 'Wells'* as pre-publicity for her campaign to take on Trelawney's theatre, the Sadler's Wells, an important factor was the author's willingness to waive his fee. However, in 1936 Guthrie wanted to do William Wycherley's *The Country Wife*, and this production caused very specific problems. The racy Restoration comedy was a great fashionable success, but it produced a challenge to the Vic's newly won status as a charitable, educational and tax-exempt enterprise.

The long-serving and indefatigable governor of the Vic, Reginald Rowe, had been lobbying over the matter of tax exemption for nine years. Entertainment tax was then crippling many theatres and exemption would enable Baylis to keep ticket prices low, but this status had been extremely hard to secure. After many rulings against him and several appeals to the Chancellor of the Exchequer, Rowe finally secured the concession in 1934. Guthrie's production of *The Country Wife*, however, was palpably not educational, indeed it was nakedly commercial: a Broadway transfer was always envisaged, hence the importation of an American star, Ruth Gordon (who then insisted on the sacking of an actor she considered incompetent, Alec Guinness). A Mr Carroll wrote to the governors and told them in advance that he was going to attack them via the newspapers for doing the play:[91] he argued that the Vic was being given an unfair advantage if it could produce commercial material and not have to pay commercial theatre taxes like every other theatre. By contrast, Shakespeare – even mucky Shakespeare – was always educational because his plays were on so many examination syllabuses. Baylis herself had grave reservations about *The Country Wife*, but it is revealing that she did not oppose the production, and that at the very next executive meeting in 1936, Baylis is arguing that Guthrie should be given more executive power. She was clearly not only handing over the reins but also resigning herself to the fact that her ideals would not be cherished by her successor. Baylis the pragmatist presumably recognised that the Vic had to move on, had to develop, and that Guthrie was probably the most capable man around to take on her role.

Although many of the Shakespeare productions that appeared under Baylis's management of the Vic were significant and innovative, those from the early years have received comparatively little attention from theatre historians. This is partly because the Vic archive was destroyed in a bombing raid which hit the theatre in 1941, and many of the pre-Second World War productions are erratically documented. However, as early as 1935 Harcourt Williams suggested gender issues might be part of the equation and asked, while discussing critical neglect of the Vic, 'can the fact that a woman is at the head of it, still, in 1933, bring a slight stigma to the enterprise in the male mind?'[92] Another problem is the insistence of many raconteurs that Baylis's success with Shakespeare took place despite her complete ignorance of his work. Even one of the most energetic of the Baylis apologists, Sybil Thorndike, records that she 'was no scholar where Shakespeare was concerned; I doubt if she ever saw a play completely through.'[93] It is not really the job of a theatre manager to sit right through plays in her own theatre, but Baylis's lack of Shakespearian expertise is mentioned by many writers and used by some of them to demean Baylis's achievements, so it is worth pausing over.

Sybil Thorndike argues that despite her ignorance of Shakespeare Baylis had intuitive insight into the plays, and she quotes from one of the most influential theatre practitioners and theorists of the twentieth century, Harley Granville-Barker: 'Queer woman, Miss Baylis, I don't think she knows anything about these plays, but she's got something.'94 Thorndike then cites many examples of Baylis's reactions to Shakespeare's characters to confirm this view. In relation to Richard III Thorndike remembers Baylis saying, 'People don't realise how awful it must be to be deformed – even ever so slightly … we should have sympathy with people like hunchbacks, not drive them to lengths!'95 This comment perhaps carries all the more weight coming as it does from someone who felt she was disfigured because of her crooked mouth. On Edith Evans, as the Nurse in *Romeo and Juliet*, Baylis commented of the character: 'it's just a cosy mother, like earth, and cuddly too'.96 On the subject of the Vic performing in the Jewish area of Bethnal Green, Baylis stated 'I do like to see the Jews coming … Even if they aren't Christians, it must do them good, but I wish we didn't have to give them "Merchant of Venice", the Christians all behave so badly.'97 Of Thorndike's playing of the distraught and ranting Constance in *King John* Baylis said:

> That mad tearing-of-your-hair scene is just right for you – you can't cry and go on like that in real life. I wish I could play that scene and get rid of lots of chokes and tearing hair that I have inside *me*!98

The idea of using Constance for role-playing, and of abusing all and sundry with gusto, sounds like very imaginative therapy for exasperated theatre managers.

In fact it is clear that during her career Baylis acquired a good working knowledge of Shakespeare. Indeed she even identified the role she would like to play in *Macbeth*: 'the part of the messenger is the part I would like to play if I were a man' (unfortunately the newspaper report does not divulge her reasons for this choice).[99] While it is very unlikely that Baylis ever sat down and pored over a Shakespeare text, that she had some familiarity with Shakespeare is indisputable. In 1912 a letter from her father establishes that Baylis certainly owned a copy of Shakespeare as he comments that one copy 'is quite enough for the family'.[100] As early as the Vic company's pioneering visit to Stratford in 1916, to perform several plays there for the tercentenary of Shakespeare's death, she is reported as being present at several of the productions. Later in an article written in 1927 for the *Old Vic Magazine*, Baylis records non-Vic Shakespeare productions she has seen recently: Greet's *Twelfth Night*, John Laurie's Hamlet and Feste, Wilfrid Walter's Petruchio and Malvolio.[101] Baylis also sat through countless rehearsals during her lifetime, and she paid attention to what was going on. Laurence Olivier records that in a marathon rehearsal of *Hamlet*, as he uttered the line 'My thoughts be bloody or be nothing worth' for the 'umpteenth time', he heard 'a chuckling voice from Lilian's box' whispering 'I bet they couldn't be bloodier than they are, eh, dear boy?'[102] Before she employed Guthrie at the Vic, Baylis tested the director's credentials by going to the Westminster Theatre to see his production of *Love's Labours Lost*. In a typically loaded account, Guthrie claims Baylis 'talked throughout the performance to her pretty young lady-chauffeur in a tone almost as loud as the actors and in the unmistakable accent of South London suburbia'.[103] While Baylis made no secret of her liking for 'light music or drama', claiming such works help 'you to appreciate classical works', Guthrie also had a lot to gain from stressing Baylis's total ignorance, implicitly casting himself by contrast as her learned, insightful superior.[104]

In addition, the question of Baylis's familiarity (or lack of it) with Shakespeare also has to take into account that Baylis herself had something to gain by playing up her relative ignorance. Great delegator as she was, she knew the value of flattering the experts she hired, and stressing their superior knowledge. Harcourt Williams certainly thought that Baylis was disingenuous here: he asserts that Baylis definitely loved 'the sound of [Shakespeare's] verse, probably as a musician'.[105] A profile in *Everyman* similarly links Shakespeare and music and states that Baylis's 'first interest in Shakespeare had been raised by the music in his lines; they sang in her ears as sweetly as her violin'.[106] This was in an age when Shakespeare's verse was still sometimes almost sung on stage, as is clear from archival recordings of actors of the day.

Harcourt Williams also suggests that

> although [Baylis] may never have watched a single performance right through, or even read a play from beginning to end, she certainly acquired a very businesslike knowledge of [Shakespeare's] practicabilities as a playwright, and not a little rough commonsense insight into some of the characters.[107]

By the time of George Foss's directorship at the end of the First World War, Baylis 'and Shakespeare were becoming better acquainted', and in the end she acquired 'a very homely understanding of the plays and one that in some respects was no farther from the author's intentions than that of certain erudite professors'.[108]

Whatever her knowledge of Shakespeare, it is indisputable that under Baylis's management the reputation of the Vic Shakespeare Company steadily grew and top performers began queuing up to perform there. Of course some factors in Baylis's success in building her Shakespeare Company were not absolutely in her control: for example, it was good luck that the fashion for bare-boards Shakespeare at the beginning of the twentieth century coincided with Baylis setting up a poverty-stricken and therefore necessarily bare-boards theatre company. Another significant factor was the absence of an effective acting trades union: Equity was not fully established in the UK until the 1930s and closed shop only existed after 1933, so Baylis's appalling pay packages were not challenged during the formative years of the theatre company. But serendipitous factors contributing to the Shakespeare Company's success should not obscure the fact that once Baylis had decided Shakespeare was to be part of the Vic's profile, once she had taken on the mission to produce the plays, then she laboured mightily, in every way she knew how, to promote them at her theatre, so long as Shakespeare did not flourish at the expense of her beloved opera. The increasing success of the Shakespeare Company during the 1920s, however, was one of the major sources of strain and stress on the already over-stretched resources of the Vic theatre building: Baylis knew that her Shakespeare and opera companies were growing too big for one theatre to hold. So she began to look around for new premises. She found what she wanted in a derelict and abandoned theatre in Islington. Most people who knew about the scheme initially thought Baylis was crazy. Nevertheless, Baylis decided to take up the challenge of colonising, renovating and reopening the theatre at Sadler's Wells.

NOTES

1   Executive Committee minutes for 11 July 1924 record this
    performance took place on 5 November 1923 in the presence
    of Princess Mary Lascelles. Baylis made her statement about
    turning to Shakespeare in her gramophone recording, made in
    1936. She is often misquoted as saying 'In despair I turned to
    Shakespeare', for example, by Findlater, *Lilian Baylis*, p. 101,
    and this rather appealing misquotation is used as the title for
    Christopher Denys's play about Baylis.
2   Unidentified newspaper clipping from January 1924,
    OVLB/000366/1.
3   Booth, *The 'Old Vic'*, p. 70. Booth is clearly writing the latter part
    of his book with a great deal of help, and quotation, from Baylis.
    Bridges-Adams later went on to be artistic director at Stratford.
4   The idea of performing Shakespeare had been suggested
    before: Harcourt Williams, *Old Vic Saga*, pp. 23–4 speculates
    that the first Shakespeare at the Vic was a recital by Charles Fry.
    In the *Observer* (12 December 1937) F. Charlton Fry certainly
    wrote in to say his father did scenes from Shakespeare in the
    early 1900s at The Vic and the whole of *The Merchant of Venice*.
5   Elizabeth Sprigge, *Sybil Thorndike Casson* (London, 1971),
    p. 107.
6   Russell Thorndike, 'Lilian Baylis', p. 114.
7   Elisabethe H.C. Corathiel, 'Old Vic Memories', *The Stage*,
    9 November 1950.
8   *OVM*, September–October 1925.
9   OVLB/000155, number 3. All quotations relating to this story

are taken from this document.

10 Ibid. Later Baylis went on record stating that it was God talking to her and not Shakespeare: in the *Westminster Gazette* of 1 April 1928 she states this, adding 'I am a religious woman, but not a spiritualist, and I firmly believe the voice was Divine.' However, Beatrice Gordon Holmes's account of Baylis's story, *In Love With Life*, p.139, has the voice as Shakespeare's.

11 *OVM*, April 1920.

12 *OVM*, October 1921.

13 OVLB/000147/2.

14 Harcourt Williams, *Old Vic Saga*, p. 26.

15 Raymond P. Mander, 'Forty Years On, Part One', *The Vic-Wells Association Newsletter*, August 1954, based on the memories of Mrs Matheson Lang, Mrs Napper, Miss Estelle Stead, Mr Andrew Leigh.

16 Lilian Baylis, 'Busman's Holiday', *OVM*, September–October 1936.

17 Ibid. The 'entirety' meant the second Quarto and usually ran at around five hours. *Everyman* was performed on Tuesday evenings during Lent, introduced by a celebrity.

18 Booth, *The 'Old Vic'*, p. 72.

19 *OVM*, December 1924. Newton Baylis had sung in the choir at Headlam's wedding.

20 For Headlam's reservations about Greet's texts see F.G. Bettany, *Stewart Headlam: A Biography* (London, 1926), p. 199. Corathiel, 'Old Vic Memories' also plays tribute to the part played by Dr Robert Jones in getting the first school matinees going.

21 Lilian Baylis, 'The Royal Victoria Hall', *The Shakespeare League Journal*, July 1915.

22 *OVM*, May 1929. Rumours that the LCC was giving the theatre £1,100 for these performances were corrected in the *OVM* of February 1920, which reports the sum was actually £100.

23 Russell Thorndike, 'Lilian Baylis', pp. 144–5; *The Times*, 30 March 1974.

24 Sybil Thorndike, 'Lilian Baylis', p. 25.

25 Ibid., pp. 45–6.

26 Ibid., p. 56.

27 Ibid., pp. 56–7.

28 Ibid., pp. 33–4.

29 See Sprigge, *Sybil Thorndike Casson*, p. 110.

30 For example, *OVM*, February 1920.

31 Baylis, '"The Old Vic" and "The Wells"', p. 110.

32 Quoted in Isaac, *Ben Greet and the Old Vic*, p. 128.

33 Baylis, 'Reminiscences'. The undertaker, Tom Hurry, also lent his chapel for productions of *Much Ado About Nothing*.

34 Isaac, *Ben Greet and the Old Vic*, p. 128.

35 Baylis, '"The Old Vic" and "The Wells"', p. 110.

36 Ibid.

37 Russell Thorndike ('Lilian Baylis', p. 151), himself a wounded soldier, records this.

38 Naomi Royde-Smith, 'Lilian Baylis: An Impression', *The Weekly Westminster*, 12 January 1924.

39 Robert Atkins, 'The Lady of Waterloo Road', *The Times*, 30 March 1974.

40 At the time of writing, the Theatre Museum in London has a reconstruction of Baylis's office on display as a permanent exhibit.

41 Isaac, *Ben Greet and the Old Vic*, p. 126.

42 Ibid., p. 127.

43 Ibid. A governors' report of 1922–3 suggests erecting a screen to keep out chatter from J.P. Restaurants during performances.

44 Quotation from Isaac, *Ben Greet and the Old Vic*, p. 129.

45 Robert Speaight, *William Poel and the Elizabethan Revival* (London, 1954), pp. 108–9.

46 Isaac, *Ben Greet and the Old Vic*, pp. 126–7. Gas continued to be used for some time although electric lights on stage had been installed on the demand of Rosina Filippi.

47 *OVM*, September–October 1927.

48 Harcourt Williams, *Four Years at the Old Vic*, p. 91.

49 Letters in M&M.

50 Foss dedication. Although Baylis appreciated Foss's work, in later years, when Mrs Foss wrote to Baylis in 1925, asking if she would help find Foss a job, Baylis raised the subject at a board meeting, as she promised, but didn't press it when the governors voted in favour of a younger man (OVLB/000026).

51 Sybil Thorndike, 'Lilian Baylis', p. 89.

52 Details all taken from Corathiel, 'Old Vic Memories'. Terry also did the 'Quality of Mercy...' speech from *The Merchant of Venice*. Lang and Britton's reconstruction of *The Taming of the Shrew* was based on Cruikshank's illustrations to 'an old acting edition' (gala programme).

53 Sybil Thorndike, 'Lilian Baylis', p. 37.

54 Russell Thorndike, 'Lilian Baylis', pp. 159–64.

55 Speaight, *William Poel*, p. 234.

56 *OVM*, November 1929.

57 Harcourt Williams, *Old Vic Saga*, p. 51. One reason that Atkins's pioneering work has been largely unacknowledged is because his incomplete memoirs do not cover this period. An example of Atkins's ground-breaking work, the first restoration of the full framework of *The Taming of the Shrew* since the sixteenth century, is discussed in Elizabeth Schafer, *Shakespeare in Production: 'The Taming of the Shrew'* (Cambridge, 2002), pp. 26, 52, 54.

58 'Lilian Baylis – a Portrait of "The Lady"', radio programme 1997.

59 John Gielgud, *Early Stages*, 2nd revised edition (London, 1987, third impression 1988), p. 33.

60 Ibid., p. 32.

61 As mentioned earlier, the final play was *Troilus and Cressida* during the 1923–4 season. Baylis's line was that the Vic had started Shakespeare in 1914 and completed the canon in 1924.

62 *OVM*, November 1923.

63 Manager's Report, Annual Report 1922–3, p. 8. Lilian Baylis, 'What the Old Vic Stands For', typescript, M&M (broadcast 3 December 1924) confirms the cutting and explains that the Vic ran *1 Henry VI* and up to the death of Beaufort in *2 Henry VI* for two weeks, and then ran the second half of *2 Henry VI* and *3 Henry VI* for the next two weeks.

64 Atkins, 'The Lady of Waterloo Road'.

65 OVLB/000284.

66 Bryan Forbes, *Ned's Girl: the Authorised Biography of Dame Edith Evans* (London, 1977), p. 92.

67 Ibid.

68 Sybil Thorndike, 'Lilian Baylis', p. 88.

69 *OVM*, September–October 1925.

70 Jean Sterling Mackinlay was also the daughter of the Vic's favourite singer, Antoinette Sterling.

71 Harcourt Williams, *Four Years at the Old Vic*, p. 3.

72 Baylis's preference for gauzy fairies is recorded in Gielgud, *Early Stages*, p. 100.

73 Harcourt Williams, *Old Vic Saga*, p. 33.

74 Gielgud, *Early Stages*, p. 91.

75 Ibid.

76 Harcourt Williams, *Four Years at the Old Vic*, pp. 8–9.

77 Olivier relates this, for example, in a recording in 'Lilian Baylis – a Portrait of "The Lady"', radio broadcast, 1997.

78 Harcourt Williams, *Four Years at the Old Vic*, p. 7.

79 Ibid., p. 8.
80 Ibid., p. 115.
81 Ibid., p. 3.
82 Baylis's comments appear in 'The Manager's Foreword', *OVM*, September–October 1934.
83 Harcourt Williams, *Old Vic Saga*, p. 134.
84 Ibid., p. 126.
85 Ibid., p. 134.
86 1963 radio broadcast, 'Farewell to the Vic'.
87 Margaret Webster, *The Same Only Different: Five Generations of a Great Theatre Family* (New York, 1969), p. 339.
88 Marshall, *The Other Theatre*, p. 128.
89 Ibid., p. 127.
90 Booth, *The 'Old Vic'*, p. 70 provides a list of the plays done by 1916 – non-Shakespearian playwrights include Goldsmith, Hertz, Lytton, Sheridan, Russell Thorndike and Geoffrey Williamson.
91 Executive Committee minutes, 11 September 1936.
92 Harcourt Williams, *Four Years at the Old Vic*, p. 218.
93 Sybil Thorndike, 'Lilian Baylis', p. 60.
94 Ibid., p. 63.
95 Ibid., p. 62.
96 Ibid., p. 34.
97 Ibid., p. 73.
98 Ibid., p. 78.
99 Unidentified press clipping from January 1924, OVLB/000366/1.
100 OVLB/000029/1. Newton is writing on 3 December possibly about the disposal of Emma Cons's personal effects. See also details of Liebe Cons's performances alongside Clarance Holts's Shakespeare recitals in Chapter 2 which suggest the Baylis family could not be entirely unfamiliar with Shakespeare.
101 *OVM*, September–October 1927. It seems like overkill to assemble all the evidence that Baylis did go to the theatre and sit through plays but it is worth mentioning that there *is* plenty of such evidence, and it contradicts the dominant memory of Baylis as a theatre philistine: to take just two examples, Baylis recruited her theatre's cloakroom attendant, Mrs Morrill, from the Queen's Theatre, after Mrs Morrill 'used to give her tea when she came to the theatre' (Harcourt Williams, *Vic-Wells*, p. 71); and in a letter from Ernest Milton, dated 30 January 1935, the actor thanks Baylis for her useful criticism in relation

to a production he's appearing in, something which suggests at
least an alert and judicious response.

102 Harcourt Williams, *Vic-Wells*, p. 28.
103 Tyrone Guthrie, *A Life in the Theatre* (London, 1959, reprinted
1961), p. 76. Guthrie clearly could not pick up the South
African inflexion in Baylis's accent.
104 Lilian Baylis, '"Light" Shows and the Classics', unidentified
clipping, Vic-Wells Association Box 6, Theatre Museum, Blythe
House.
105 *The Listener*, 1 December 1937.
106 Profile by Louise Morgan, *Everyman*, 22 April 1933.
107 Harcourt Williams, *Old Vic Saga*, p. 26.
108 Ibid., p. 38.

[8]

The 1920s: Baylis Builds an Empire

The 1920s were an astonishing decade for Baylis. Her work began to receive recognition, but she was also energetically building her empire: she was not only taking on Sadler's Wells, she was at the same time having to rebuild the Vic Theatre, which was beginning to fall down in places. She was building up the persona of 'The Manager' and establishing a supportive network of professional women friends.

Recognition of Baylis's work started to appear in the form of a series of public honours. In 1921 the Vic company was invited to perform in Brussels at the Théâtre Royal du Parc, as representatives of English theatre, and Baylis declared this to be 'the first time in history that an English theatrical company has been officially invited to visit a foreign country'.[1] Baylis cherished 'delightful memories' of this visit, when the Belgian King and Queen

> asked that the Manager and Producer should be presented during an interval. Both were most charming and talked of the value of Shakespeare and the high standard of the Company. The King was especially delighted by the performance of Caliban; the name escaped his memory for a moment, and he copied the movements of the "Fish Man" – going round the large box almost on his hands and knees, as the Caliban had done on the stage.
>
> The Manager will always remember this noble-looking man in his military uniform acting Caliban.[2]

In 1924, another honour was conferred on Baylis when she received an honorary M.A. from Oxford University in recognition of the Vic's educational work with Shakespeare. The Oxford encomium (in Latin) commended the fact that

Sybil Thorndike, Lilian Baylis and Ethel Smyth in their degree
gowns. Courtesy of the Mander and Mitchenson Theatre Collection

Baylis 'has known how to draw the unlearned and ignorant to
the seats of her theatre' and thus saved 'the crowd of common
men, who but for this might be wholly given up to vulgar
pleasures'.[3] The Oxford address is patronising towards Baylis
and her 'unlearned and ignorant' audiences in almost equal
measure; yet not only was Baylis intensely proud of the M.A.,
claiming it as 'a great dignity conferred on the Old Vic. and all
it stands for', but from then on she wore her M.A. cap and
gown whenever she could, even though her begowned
appearance at the degree ceremony put one of her supporters
'in mind of the execution of the Duke of Buckingham'.[4] For
the rest of her life Baylis treasured a collection of eighty-four
letters congratulating her on receiving the M.A., and for a
woman always uncertain about her academic credibility, and

conscious that she had only been educated in music, the degree must have been a very significant boost.

Nineteen twenty-four was also important as the year that the Vic Shakespeare Company was invited to King's College, Cambridge, in whose chapel they presented the Mediaeval morality play *Everyman*; Baylis claimed it was 'the first play to be given there since the days of Queen Elizabeth'.[5] Other landmarks followed: in 1929 Baylis was made a Companion of Honour. Many were expecting her to be made Dame, but Baylis turned down the opportunity to become Dame Lilian, because, so the anecdote goes, she thought that if she became a Dame she would be charged double by everyone.[6] Companion of Honour has a limited membership of sixty-five and is therefore a more prestigious honour, and Baylis recalls:

> For weeks afterwards I thrilled with pride when I thought
> of the splendid dignity of the manhood and womanhood
> with whom I stood at the palace when the Prince of Wales
> (as the King was ill) conferred this honour on me![7]

Another account has Baylis in a rather more priggish mood, retorting to someone who had congratulated her on the Companion of Honour, 'I received a much greater honour this morning' that is, by taking communion.[8] More pragmatically, however, Baylis started praying, 'Oh God, no more honours. It's *money* I need.'[9]

Baylis certainly needed money for her building projects. Without wartime hardship as an excuse, it was no longer possible to deny the fact that the Vic building was unsafe: it was overcrowded and uncomfortable, and in certain seats in the gallery, when it was raining, 'it was necessary to put up umbrellas'.[10] Health and safety officers, considering the building to be dangerous, demanded that major sections of the theatre be remodelled, and in particular that the overly cosy arrangement whereby Morley College inhabited the Vic's backstage area should come to an end. Baylis managed these developments, as she managed people; in a slightly surreal style, staggering from crisis to crisis but always generating great team spirit. The terms of Morley College's occupation, however, meant that if the college agreed to move out the Vic was obliged to supply them with a new home. Consequently in the early 1920s Baylis plunged into a manic period where first one site for Morley College was found, then lost or found unsuitable, and then another. The biggest crisis of all, of course, was where the money to pay for a new building was going to come from.

The solution to this particular money problem was of the miraculous, *deus ex machina* variety. Suddenly, in 1922, apparently out of the blue, millionaire theatre entrepreneur George Dance donated £30,000, just when the money was most needed. Dance, a man who at one time ran twenty-four theatre companies, had led a rags-to-riches life, which included a period writing libretti for shows such as *The Nautch Girl* and *A Chinese Honeymoon*, as well as a song for Vesta Tilley entitled 'Girls are the ruin of men'.[11] Dance claimed that he had learnt 'the rudiments of dramatic construction' from attending the Vic when young;[12] however, he was in some ways an unlikely rescuer of the niece of suffrage worker Emma Cons, as early in his career he had written explicitly anti-suffrage drama.[13] In 1922, however, he had his eye on a knighthood, something he received shortly after his donation to the Vic as a result of the hard lobbying work of Lady Cunard.[14] Dance attached some provisos to his donation: he wanted the Shakespeare side of the Vic work to be strengthened, and the lecture series cut back (the lectures stopped in 1923). Because Dance was in theatre management himself, there was some speculation that he might start directly intervening in the running of the Vic, but the low profit margin would not have been to his taste. Dance later wrote to Baylis explaining that after the donation had been made, he actually made an effort to stay away from the Vic:

> when I did my little bit for the dear old place, the gossips at once started wagging their tongues as to my motives. They said I had some sinister designs on the place. They said I should soon be the manager.[15]

However, Dance's money really did rescue the Vic over the Morley College crisis, and in the aftermath of the donation Baylis loosened the purse strings, arranging extra rehearsals for the opera, and arguing that the women artists' salaries must be increased.[16]

With Dance's money the Vic governors were able to purchase the Yorkshire Society's Schools building, and to move Morley College in there. There was a last-minute panic over this scheme when the London Underground Railway attempted to enforce a compulsory purchase on a section of the grounds, which the Vic had just bought. The Underground wanted the land for a ventilation shaft, which would have ruined the site, but this idea was eventually aborted after a very astute campaign waged via *The Times* by the Vic governors, especially Reginald Rowe. After all the high-blood-pressure-inducing trials and tribulations, Morley College moved out in 1923, and in January 1925 the *Old Vic Magazine* was able to report, with an almost palpable sigh of relief, on the official opening of the new Morley College by the then Prince of Wales (later Edward VIII).

In her battles with officials Baylis was often aided and abetted by a strong team of philanthropic individuals who as governors of the Vic gave their services free, but no one was more important here than Reginald (from 1932 Sir Reginald) Rowe, whose business acumen and determination often proved critical. Rowe was a philanthropist, poet and novelist who also wrote about rowing (he was an Oxford blue in the 1890s).[17] He became a governor of the Vic in the early 1920s and his expertise in law and in finance were vital assets to the theatre for many years. He loved the theatre, he wrote plays, he fought many legal battles for the Vic and the Wells, but he also supported social housing projects, which, for Baylis, would have reassuringly looked back to the mission of Emma Cons.[18] Baylis's brilliance in delegating, and in finding people who would work effectively, strenuously and with dedication on behalf of the Vic, is nowhere better demonstrated than in her success in securing and retaining Rowe's services, and it is significant that Rowe himself identifies 'her power of making people work for her, slave for her when necessary' as 'the most remarkable of [Baylis's] gifts'.[19]

Once Morley College moved out, the Vic began to take repossession of its dressing rooms and backstage area.

Renovations were carried out throughout the building, with the aim of rendering it safe while at the same time preserving the distinctive horseshoe layout, which encouraged intimacy between performer and audience: indeed Ellen Terry so valued the dynamics of the space that she told Baylis, 'If you allow the circles to be altered, I'll haunt you, alive or dead!'[20] The planned reopening of the Vic in 1924, however, was threatened by a builders' strike. Baylis was overseas, in South Africa, having finally been persuaded to take a long overdue recuperative holiday, and Reginald Rowe was left to hold the fort. When the strike was called, the Vic had been partly demolished and much of the building lay open to the skies. Quite apart from potential damage to the stage, it looked as if there was no chance of the theatre reopening in September as planned, something which would have cost the Vic a huge amount in terms of lost income. Rowe managed to broker a deal whereby the Vic was classified in the same category as hospitals: as a high-priority institution and so eligible for exemption from the strike.[21] The building contractors handed their contract over to the Vic, which could then employ the builders since they would no longer be working for their normal employer. Consequently work on the Vic continued despite – and without technically breaking – the strike.[22]

Later in the 1920s Baylis was faced with yet more compulsory building work. Baylis's initial reaction to any safety inspection was always to say no, something which was very much an Emma Cons tactic. Sometimes such a knee-jerk reaction – as when Baylis vigorously protested at the cost of having to put an extra emergency exit from the circle – seems inappropriate.[23] (Of course, Baylis would have willingly put in such a safety feature had funding been forthcoming from the London County Council.) Compulsory work in 1927, however, gave Baylis a good opportunity to remodel the front of house, which was then occupied by J.P. Restaurants, or Pearce and Plenty, the refreshments company that did a roaring but often noisy trade in what is now the Vic box office area. The clientele for Pearce and Plenty was varied, and Sybil Thorndike tells the story of Baylis ejecting an indecently exposed drunk from the

Pearce and Plenty restaurant with the comment, 'I don't mind for myself, though you look disgraceful, but I won't have my boys and girls shocked.'[24] When the Pearce and Plenty lease expired in 1927, Baylis refused to renew it and had the entrance to the Vic converted into a conventional theatre foyer and box office. Initial building work, however, uncovered the fact that the basic fabric of the Vic was in a far worse condition than had been realised, and the bill for the renovations soared.

The minutes of the governors' meetings also document battles such as Baylis's attempts to get a local public house near the Vic closed on the grounds that drunks harassed theatre patrons, and her struggle to stop public meetings in the street, which could be heard in the theatre and were distracting audiences. Baylis spent time and energy fighting to get a urinal relocated from Webber Street, as the Vic gallery queue complained about it. She finally won through in 1926, commenting to Joan Cross, 'I never thought the time would come when I should jump for joy at the sight of a urinal.'[25] However, Baylis's most ambitious building project of the 1920s was undoubtedly the attempt to reopen the Sadler's Wells Theatre in Islington. She must have known that she was letting herself in for twice as many worries, twice as many battles and twice as many bills, but the Wells public appeal for funds began on 30 March 1925, with Baylis explaining that the expansion 'will lead to the natural growth of a National Theatre from the Old Vic'.[26]

The Vic as the National Theatre in all but name starts becoming a motif in Baylis's propaganda from this moment on: so, for example, in 1928 the *Old Vic Magazine*, reporting on plans to produce more plays by Ibsen, comments:

> it is surely only fitting that the Old Vic, which is the nearest approach at present to a National Theatre in England, should pay some tribute to a dramatist whose work had such a revolutionary effect on the theatre of his day.[27]

Whilst many were discussing the possibility of establishing a National Theatre during this period, Baylis's rhetoric consistently claims that the Vic-Wells was getting on and doing the job of a National Theatre anyway. Some outside the Vic were certainly willing to agree with her: in the year that Sadler's Wells reopened, Vere Denning, for example, writes of 'this extraordinary woman, who has succeeded, single-handed, in creating a National Theatre – a task that has baffled committees and commissions and drama leagues and divided families against themselves'.[28]

Baylis spelt out some of her thinking on the issue of the National Theatre in a radio broadcast to celebrate thirty years of her running the Vic. Prefacing her discussion with the remark that if, thirty years ago, 'you had told me I should still be here in 1928 I am afraid, as a girl of twenty-one, I should have been rather rude about it', Baylis continues:

> There is so much talk of a National Theatre nowadays that possibly some people may wonder if one of my ideals is not a state-endowed playhouse. I do indeed think there should be such a theatre; but I rather doubt whether it would really be any good to the workers; the tired people who find plays and music the easiest and most comfortable way of getting recreation to help them through their drab lives. I am inclined to think that a state theatre would be mainly supported by the intelligentsia. For the British public is very independent, and, I think, does not value very much what it gets for nothing, or what it is compelled to pay for through the rates and taxes. Perhaps the secret of the Vic's "wonderful audience" is that its members have, many of them, voluntarily given up so much to help us through our bad days …
>
> Years ago I did have a dream of one great building which could house all the greatest achievements in art; of drama, of music, of dancing and of painting. I have given that dream up now; from my experience of running opera and Shakespeare in the one theatre I have come to the conclusion that the idea wouldn't work, unless that one building were very ideal indeed.[29]

Baylis's scepticism about state subsidy (she probably didn't relish the idea of being accountable to government officials) is also evident in her claim that in running the Vic she 'wanted to prove that you could give great work at cheap prices and pay your way'.

The person who first suggested Baylis should take on the Wells was Estelle Stead, a remarkable woman who acted and directed for Baylis during the vital Matheson Lang/Hutin Britton Shakespeare season and who was also a writer and editor, following in the footsteps of her father, the social reformer, journalist and campaigning editor of the *Pall Mall Gazette* C.K. Stead.[30] Part of the appeal of Sadler's Wells for Baylis was undoubtedly its history. The wells underneath what became the theatre were originally associated with the Knights of St John, who had had a monastery at Clerkenwell. During the Reformation the wells were bricked up; they were rediscovered in 1683 by a Mr Sadler, who built up a music house with entertainment and spa waters on offer. During the nineteenth century, rather like the Vic, the Wells ricocheted from prestigious successes – such as appearances by Grimaldi and Edmund Kean, or actor-manager Samuel Phelps's Shakespeare seasons – to music hall. Like the Vic, the Wells was in an unfashionable district and even Phelps's highly acclaimed work sometimes struggled to get an audience so far from what was perceived as the theatrical centre of London, the West End. The fact that the Wells, like the Vic, was surrounded by working-class communities also appealed to Baylis's passion for social outreach. By the time Baylis became interested in the Wells, the theatre had been left derelict for some time. It had briefly been converted into a cinema, which closed in 1915, and it had recently been turned down as the possible site for a pickle factory. The nature of the terrain beneath the theatre building was suggested by the fact that marsh flowers were growing through the floorboards.[31]

While it was Estelle Stead who suggested the idea of taking on the Wells, in the long term the crucial figure was again Reginald Rowe. He convinced Baylis that the Wells project was feasible; he agreed to take on the inevitable legal and financial battles this project would entail for the Vic; and he took Baylis to see the Wells site. Rowe describes the theatre then as having 'huge rents' in the roof and 'crumbling' walls; 'None of the windows had a pane of glass' and the 'for sale' sign

'recommended it as suitable for "offices or a factory"'.[32] But
Baylis was being driven to despair by the large numbers of
opera fans routinely turned away from the Vic on Saturday
nights (those lucky enough to get into the performance with a
standing ticket often stood for hours with only one shoulder
against a wall for support) and she saw taking on the Wells as a
possible solution to this problem.[33]

Baylis sent out a signal to the Vic public that the Wells was
on the agenda by programming Pinero's *Trelawney of the 'Wells'*,
a romantic comedy set at the Sadler's Wells Theatre during the
period when Realism became established in British theatre.[34]
Meanwhile Rowe managed to get the price of the theatre down
to £14,200, but an appeal launched in March 1925 only raised
£2,200 during the six-month option period on that price.[35]
Lord Hambleden came to the rescue by taking on a bank
overdraft for the rest of the money, and two months later the
Carnegie Foundation donated the whole asking price. Baylis
and her team were then left fundraising for the money to
renovate and rebuild the theatre. Rebuilding actually began at
the end of 1928. The Shakespeare Company director
Harcourt Williams was unenthusiastic and claimed that at the
Vic 'All the departments were against it at heart, and the
difficulties really seemed insurmountable', but he had to
admit that everyone had underestimated Baylis's 'bulldog
tenacity' in relation to the project.[36] And in a brochure
celebrating the Wells's opening in 1931, Baylis placed it at the
centre of her great mission to provide top-quality live
entertainment for no more than the price of a cinema ticket:

> Great music and great drama at cheap prices are very real
> necessities in the life of the people …
>
> I have said often before, and I repeat, that nowadays we
> cultivate physical fitness in every possible way; and
> everybody knows that the full enjoyment of one's bodily
> faculties is only possible after exercise and effort. But what
> about the mental fitness of our younger generation? This,
> too, can only be acquired by exercise and effort; and it is
> toward this full realisation of the great kingdom in our
> minds that we shall labour at Sadler's Wells.[37]

The 1920s were also a period in which Baylis was embracing new technologies. She acquired a car in 1926 and learnt to drive after riding a bicycle for thirty years.[38] Her road sense was erratic: she felt free, for example, to disregard instructions by traffic police; her car, a Trojan, had a top speed of only 16 mph, but Baylis did not like stopping once she had got started, something which terrified some of her passengers. Russell Thorndike remembers Baylis's enthusiastic driving exploits 'on holidays with her great friend Miss Davey', but eventually the Vic governors insisted on Baylis hiring a chauffeuse.[39] Baylis also flew for the first time – in a twelve-seater Farman Goliath on 5 August 1925 – and regaled readers of the *Old Vic Magazine* with impressions of this journey, written down, she claimed, in mid-air:

> Someone handed me cotton-wool for my ears and I gave myself up to the delights of going through the air ... It felt to me that the earth had gently left us, and not we the earth ... I had a great thrill as we left the land and the blue sea was below us ... We flew inland over Abbeville and Amiens – the first year I worked at the Vic, my aunt Emma Cons took my sister and me abroad and we had a delightful week-end in Amiens. I never thought that 26 years later I should be looking down on the city from the sky.[40]

Baylis also brought in new technologies at work, a logical step for a woman who very early in her career had embraced the new medium of film. Baylis only abandoned film at the Vic once competition from purpose-built cinemas increased and, as she claimed, it became increasingly difficult to find what she considered to be decent films:[41]

> The French pictures were just then coming into England, and few of them were the sort of thing I would show at the Vic. I once spent eight hours watching a run-through to get one hour's performance.[42]

Nevertheless Baylis managed to make over £1,000 out of film showings, a great deal of money at that time.[43] Edwin Paterson remembers Baylis as a pioneer of early film shows at what was then known as the Old Vic Cinema. Queues of people waited for hours to get in to see the Vic's films, many of these films being of the thriller and cow-boy type just suitable for the type of film fan living within the vicinity of the Waterloo-road.[44]

In the 1920s, Baylis was quick to see the potential of radio and she started negotiating with the BBC about broadcasts in 1923.[45] Aspiring actress Doris Westwood remembers a broadcast of *A Christmas Carol* in that year but, as soon as she had checked there was no extra expense involved for the Vic, Baylis began broadcasting plays and operas on a regular basis, with the BBC funding extra pay for the artists, and paying an extra fee per station relaying the performances.[46] Baylis refused to let Vic artists go to the BBC studios, insisting that broadcasts should be from the Vic stage to ensure that the radio programmes functioned as an advertisement for the theatre. Later on Baylis secured lucrative deals from the BBC and a special grant of £5,000 towards Sadler's Wells in return for broadcasting rights.[47] She was constantly on the lookout for new opportunities and in 1929 was talking to British Illustrated Films about filming the Shakespeare Company during the season's summer break. With the arrival of ballet at the Vic, Baylis also started investigating the possibility of the Vic-Wells Ballet appearing on very early television. She was reportedly very unimpressed by the first broadcasts of the ballet: '"*That's* no good," she snorted. "*Much* too small. Those girls will never get married like that."'[48]

Baylis's own willingness to broadcast on radio attests to the other major area in which she was building during the 1920s: the public persona of 'The Manager'. What is most distinctive, indeed perhaps unique, about Baylis's management of her theatres was her deployment of this public persona. How close this character was to the real Baylis is open to question. Sybil Thorndike's view was that the Baylis speeches were made in the style 'of a Hyde Park Speaker'.[49] Cicely Hamilton, a close friend during the 1920s and 1930s, claims Baylis's performances were successful because they were unpremeditated, unselfconscious, almost 'animal': 'She never made speeches in the ordinary sense; she talked, she meandered, you might even say chattered – but always to the great joy of her listeners.'[50] Hamilton provides a detailed description of a last-night-of-the-season Baylis speech:

> Miss Baylis does not speak, as I understand speaking in public; she makes announcements, says good-byes, tells the people in front what they want to know about the programme and engagements for the autumn season – and all in an unceremonious manner, with the air of talking to a friend or two. She is curiously at home on the stage, Miss Baylis; unaffected, as few are unaffected, by the consciousness of being in full view of hundreds of eyes. Between her remarks, introductions and announcements, she settles herself down on a bench or the steps of a ducal throne, as if she were sitting by her own fireside and had forgotten the presence of the crowd.[51]

Hamilton's judgement is that of someone who knew Baylis intimately, but she does not acknowledge the skills, akin to those of a stand-up comedian, which Baylis would have honed over the years of her youthful career as a Gypsy Reveller.[52] And for formal occasions Baylis definitely did script her speeches; while she may have departed from her text in the delivery, she also had a 'phenomenal' memory, which would help her to appear impromptu when, in reality, she was well prepared.[53] Indeed, Hamilton actually quotes at length from the text of one such speech, which Baylis broadcast on radio:

> I so believe the theatre is our greatest power for good or evil, that I pray my earnestness may give me words in which to express this faith and to hold your attention ... I am cast to-night to speak on the Art of Living and the place of the Theatre in that life. The Theatre isn't an excuse for wonderful evening gowns and jewels; it isn't a fad of people with long hair and sandals or the perquisite of 'varsity men and women; good drama isn't only for the students of training colleges and boys and girls swotting for the Oxford and Cambridge Locals; it is a crying need of working men and women who need to see beyond the four walls of their

offices, workshops and homes into a world of awe and wonder.

Furthermore, all art is a bond between rich and poor; it allows of no class distinctions; more than that, it is a bond between nation and nation, and may do much to help widely differing peoples to understand the peculiar problems of life in each country. I think it was Dr. Dearmer who said: "Art is a spiritual necessity. Civilization cannot exist in its absence, for without it civilization is but organized savagery." The theatre is perhaps the most important and accessible and the most easily understood branch of art for the man and woman in the street.[54]

This is a carefully crafted speech, which clearly and deliberately promotes Baylis's view for the Vic.

Baylis also spelled out her vision of the function of theatre in a radio talk entitled 'Aims and Ideals of the Theatre':

People rest and refresh their bodies by using different muscles – they want to recreate their minds and feelings by becoming other people sometimes. The instinct to "pretend", to day-dream, is fundamental, and gives us most that is worth having from religion to the greatest art, and to many the art of the theatre, where the ear and eye combine to the same end, speaks most easily and directly.

People have the right to this re-creation – to this expansion of their own personality by the inclusion, however temporary, of that of others.[55]

Again, this is a considered and strategic speech.

Baylis seems to have promoted the idea of her speeches as spontaneous, off-the-cuff and responding to the moment, but when the *Old Vic Magazine* reports that Baylis is about to cut a record, and hopes that 'the ineffable charm of our manager's spontaneous and unpremeditated eloquence' will inspire donations to the Vic, the tone seems somewhat disingenuous, given the large number of typescripts of this extremely thoroughly drafted and redrafted speech in existence.[56] Among those who did question the degree of artifice even in Baylis's apparently most spontaneous public speeches were

Joan Cross and Harcourt Williams. Cross maintains that Baylis deliberately 'engaged in creating a personal image';[57] Harcourt Williams speaks of '[t]hat queer armour of gaucherie that she delighted to wear', adding:

> She will stoutly maintain that she knows nothing about art, that she is an ignoramus, but that is mere camouflage ... How far she is a conscious humorist I have never quite made up my mind. She is clever enough to leave it in doubt.[58]

In addition Williams comments that Baylis 'assumes' a 'character which is so utterly unlike her normal self that it must surely be a throw-back to some early stage experience'.[59] Norman Marshall is even more direct, suggesting that Baylis 'invented what was really an elaborate disguise. She became a "character", half comic, half frightening'.[60]

In this persona Baylis harangued, cajoled and flattered her audiences. Almost every speech ended with 'And look here, you bounders. Monday nights have got to be better.'[61] But Baylis also got to know her audiences: Adrian Boult recalls that 'She really did know more than half the people very well indeed' and personally greeted as many as possible.[62] Baylis also threw parties for her audiences, often on the stage of the theatre. Harcourt Williams makes an important point about the exploitation of actors that took place here:

> for the leading actors who have been rehearsing arduous parts all day, playing them all night, and must again rehearse arduous parts next morning, [an audience party] is an added burden, and I would gladly see the distribution of the cake and lemonade by the players abolished.[63]

However, such parties also built the partisan, community-spirited audiences that then paid for the actors' skimpy wages.

Several of the Vic parties evolved very elaborate rituals.[64] First and last nights for both the opera and the Shakespeare companies became great events and were often fully booked months in advance. First nights meant the director and Baylis taking a call, with Baylis, usually wearing her M.A. gown, making a speech.[65] Writer Dora Northcroft describes these occasions as 'Something like a Court, with Miss Baylis as chief actor', and issuing 'from the curtained recess, part queen, part showman.'[66] On last nights of the season, the audiences showered favourite personalities with gifts of bouquets, cigarettes, fountain pens and teddy bears, and presentations went on late into the night. On one occasion Baylis was presented with a bouquet of roses by her company only to respond with: 'Roses in winter! Roses! Don't you know we are hard up? ... This is extravagance. Now, dears, I don't want to be angry, but make it carnations next time.'[67]

The twenty-third of April, St George's Day and the day generally assumed to be Shakespeare's birthday, was one of the biggest Vic rituals of the year. The celebrations often involved cheerful chaos as large numbers of ex-Vic actors hurtled across London in taxis, dashing from the shows they were actually appearing in that night so that they could rush on at the Vic and deliver a scene from Shakespeare.[68] Successes of previous seasons were reprised, reminding the audience of how good Vic Shakespeare at its best could be but inevitably, given the makeshift nature of the night, under-rehearsal and improvisation predominated, making the occasion informal, prone to disasters and often hilarious. Even as early as 1915 a bewildering array of performances was on offer for a Shakespeare birthday matinee: scenes from the plays; songs from Shakespeare; Elizabethan music from the Dolmetsches; dances; recitations; slides of Stratford; and a finale described as 'The King's prayer' (a patriotic outburst from the play *Ralph Roister Doister*) followed by 'God Save the King'.[69] Audience members were sometimes allowed to walk on in crowd scenes: one such was an extract from *Julius Caesar* performed in 1915.[70] There were also sonnets, and burlesques (which often dealt in 'in' jokes that were understood completely only by the Vic cognoscenti, something which again helped generate a strong sense of an old friends' reunion in the audiences). Baylis herself occasionally took part in such burlesques: in one performance she

appeared as herself at an opera audition, and had to listen to Violet Butler girlishly singing Charles Corri's dreaded

"One fine day", which ninety-nine people out of a hundred
do choose for audition purposes.[71]

Later on she appeared as Elizabeth I 'in a huge ruff and horn-
rimmed spectacles'.[72] In 1925 a Shakespeare birthday sketch
included 'Ethel Harper, seated on a throne in the centre of the
room' impersonating 'Miss Baylis … talking to Shakespeare on
the telephone'.[73] In the 1930s 'gallery stools began to appear
in the New Cut before dawn on the morning of the Birthday
Festival' as the galleryites queued to secure a place.[74] Baylis
even turned the arduous task of queuing to secure a seat to
advantage, often going out to chat to those queuing, and
helping to make a chore into a social event.

Baylis always seized on any anniversary that looked as if it
might generate a party, publicity or money: in 1920, when she
celebrated twenty-one years of managing the Vic, the event was
used to launch the rebuilding fund.[75] She evolved several
festive Christmas rituals which included the Jabberwock
children's party around Christmas or New Year, with around
five or six hundred local children invited. Doris Westwood
describes one Christmas Jabberwock party in detail: the
theatre was transformed as 'long narrow boards were fixed
along the back of each row of seats to serve as tables', while
Father Christmas gave out presents assisted by helpers in
costumes from *As You Like It*.[76] Another great Vic ritual was
Twelfth Night. After claiming, via the *Old Vic Magazine* in 1920,
that on Twelfth Night 'the players in Shakespeare's day came
down from the stage at the end of their performance and
mingled with the audience', Baylis announces 'This old
custom will be revived at the Vic.'[77] The subsequent Twelfth
Night party included 'a grand march round the theatre by all
present, led in accordance with the ancient Twelfth Night
custom by the King and Queen of the Revels', and the cake was
cut 'by our genial Manager, Miss Baylis, who was the life and
soul of the party'.[78]

The biggest party of the Vic audience's social year was
undoubtedly the Fancy Dress Ball. Harcourt Williams states:
'Everybody goes, from the youngest galleryite to the oldest
member of the stage staff.'[79] This annual event started in 1921

and was held at the Lambeth Swimming Baths; later it moved to Covent Garden and in the last years before the Second World War to the Albert Hall. In 1938 4,500 people attended this ball.[80] Prizes were given in a large variety of categories, costumes were taken very seriously, and souvenir photographs and books on the Vic were sold.

While Baylis 'The Manager' appeared at all these grand social events, 'The Manager' also appeared, and became well known to the Vic audiences, by means of the *Old Vic Magazine*. This magazine was started in October 1919 by Elisabethe Corathiel, who had been hired as 'a very young girl' in 1915 as a press agent for the Vic when she was already editing the woman's page 'of a national Sunday newspaper'. She embarked on 'three years of heated argument and persuasion' before managing to convince Baylis that the *Old Vic Magazine* might be a good idea.[81] The magazine quickly became popular, and, in 1922, on the suggestion of Reginald Rowe, it was made available free of charge to members of the Old Vic Circle, an organisation which had its first social gathering after a performance on Twelfth Night 1920, and soon had 350 members.[82] As the magazine itself put it, it was founded to provide

> some tangible expression of the interest and affection felt
> by those before the curtain for those behind and vice
> versa.[83]

In reality, once she had realised its value, the magazine was dominated by Baylis. Although technically first Corathiel and later Irene Beeston edited the publication, Baylis the manager (never manageress) is constantly quoted, her views are referred (and deferred) to, news of her is reported. Baylis authored most of the early Editorial Notes and many of the regular 'Across the Footlights' pieces.[84] Given this personal contribution by Baylis, it is not surprising that the magazine is shamelessly biased, partisan and morale-boosting, but it is also a fund of very detailed information on Baylis and on Vic productions of both opera and Shakespeare.

The *Old Vic Magazine* format changed over the years, but generally the magazine opens with 'Across the Footlights', a chatty article which reports news, highlights fundraising activities, advertises forthcoming productions and introduces new cast members. 'Across the Footlights' often frankly discusses what has been good and bad box office: for example, it laments that *Henry VI* and *The Vikings*, which the Vic put on for the Ibsen centenary, did badly and tries to drum up support for such risk-taking ventures. Sometimes it instructs the audience on how to behave: for example, it tells them not to applaud first entrances of actors, not to applaud every song in an opera, and not to indulge in excessive autograph-hunting at Vic socials.[85]

'Across the Footlights' also articulates Baylis rhetoric, continually constructing the Vic as a plucky battler, the only alternative to decadent, commercial theatre: 'The West-end steals our stars: but all the lights of Piccadilly cannot offer them the human warmth of their old days at the "Vic."'[86] The Vic lost staff, especially tenors, and even more especially *slim* tenors who could transfer easily into musicals as well as opera, because 'the Old Vic. cannot give West-End salaries even to its most valuable servants'.[87] By contrast the Vic is 'democratic', the 'password' is 'Art for Art's sake', it is 'a great family' with a 'collective soul'.[88] Elsewhere, in signed articles, Baylis explicitly identifies these attitudes as hers:

> I am glad to know that our Companies are considered by some, "All Stars". We certainly don't want *one* Star. The beauty of the Heavens, in my humble opinion, would lose much of its restful charm if, instead of myriads of Stars, one alone shone brightly.
>
> It is the "ensemble" at the Vic. in which I delight.[89]

Sometimes, the rhetoric becomes tub-thumping. In 1923, an anonymous piece signed only 'NEMO', which prepares the audiences for the opening of the refurbished theatre, claims:

> everyone associated with the Old Vic. is chock full of enthusiasm and energy. All seem determined that each day shall be better than the last, each season an advance on its predecessor, each production more wonderful than any that have gone before it …

Beyond doubt, there is no Theatre in the world where such obstacles have been surmounted – such difficulties overcome and ditches crossed as at the Old Vic.[90]

But such propaganda was felt necessary to re-establish the distinctive sense of community in the audience after the disruptions of the building work and several months of the Vic theatre being closed.

The Vic audiences certainly did acquire a reputation for being extraordinary in all sorts of ways. Their partisan loyalty was extreme, and one 'galleryite', a porter, 'used to walk all the way from Hounslow twice a week to the "Old Vic" and then home'.[91] If performers dried, it was reputed that the audience would prompt actors and finish arias.[92] Indeed the *Old Vic Magazine* suggests that 'The Vic audience is perhaps more famous than the Vic productions; it has come to be reckoned as one of the "sights" of London.'[93] Baylis also enthuses:

> Our audience have been praised all over the world as perfect. I believe this is in a great measure due to the fact that many members feel actual rights of possession in the building; it is their theatre, built brick by brick by them with their love and self-sacrifice. It has actually cost them something to have an Old Vic at all; and therefore it has grown very dear to them.[94]

The 'friendliness of the audience' at the Vic was a friendliness that was 'occasionally disconcerting' for 'those bred up to the more controlled and chilly appreciation of the West End'.[95] Sometimes the anti-West End rhetoric becomes somewhat shrill, but a clear sense of 'them' and 'us' helped build the sense of identity and community, even if it did result in stark warnings to 'book your seats early' as 'outsiders roll up and oust our own folk'.[96] Geoffrey Whitworth, writing in *John O'London's Weekly* in 1922, describes the Vic audience thus:

> An Old Vic audience really "assists" as the French say, and this sense of active co-operation reacts most strongly both on the audience itself and on the actors. For together they become a single "group", and group-consciousness is one of the most important actors in dramatic representation.[97]

Whitworth then recounts the story of a performance of *The Merchant of Venice* where 'two well-dressed occupants of the stalls were roundly hissed for making their exit from the theatre at the conclusion of the trial scene instead of waiting for the fall of the curtain'. The fact that the offenders were 'well-dressed' is deemed worthy of comment, because the Vic, unlike West End theatres, did not expect patrons sitting in the stalls to wear evening dress. Whitworth then wonders, 'In what other London theatre would the public have shown the sensibility or the courage to resent such a peccadillo!'

While the *Old Vic Magazine* helped create a sense of identity and community and of community rules (which the 'two well-dressed' people broke), Baylis also used the magazine to spell out policies, and to justify artistic decisions. So in 1920 the magazine explains that because the Vic's central mission was that 'the People's Theatre and Opera House must always be within the reach of the poorest', Verdi and Puccini could not be performed when 'the royalties are beyond our finances'.[98] The magazine often defends Baylis's policy of parsimonious pay by maintaining that although working at the Vic for performers and backstage staff is very hard, and not well paid, it is very rewarding.[99] Compensation can be found in the fact that 'even the humblest assistants share in the glory of special occasions, such as last nights, etc.'[100] Nevertheless one ever-recurring theme is the desirability, sometimes the urgent necessity, of finding a philanthropic millionaire to help the theatre out of financial trouble.[101]

In its early years the *Old Vic Magazine* also disseminated the basic and vital information of what the Vic repertoire was for the coming month. For years Baylis refused either to pay for advertising in newspapers or to do the conventional thing and give free seats to newspaper reviewers, her argument being that 'The Dailies ought to advertise us for nothing if they really love Opera and Shakespeare' and 'If my gallery boys can save up and buy their seats, well then, so can your James Agates' – especially as critics 'criticise a first performance and have to form too quick an opinion on work that has taken my dear producer and boys and girls a whole week to perfect'.[102] And there was some logic to her refusal to advertise: the audience

Baylis was after – the Lambeth locals – probably did not read *The Times.*

The *Old Vic Magazine* also supplied background information about the theatre's forthcoming repertoire by means of personal essays by members of the company (who often begin by stating Baylis has demanded they write something). These essays range across topics as various as the performers' expectations of the roles they are to play, their theatre experiences so far, and sometimes even their adventures on recent holidays. Plays and operas new to the Vic repertory are often preceded by an introductory essay on the text, the author or composer. Births and marriages of the company and staff are announced, and obituaries are sometimes extended: the death of star actress Florence Saunders in 1926, then only recently married to actor John Laurie, inspired an outpouring of tributes. Social events are advertised, and the results of fancy-dress competitions and the 'guess the weight of the Twelfth Night cake' competition are published. Members of the backstage crew are occasionally profiled or prevailed upon to write about their work. Thanks are recorded for large cash donations and gifts of materials, costumes, furniture. The first magazine of the season (which ran from September to May) is usually a double issue for September and October and often includes a Who's Who of those new to the current company, a 'Letter from the Manager' outlining Baylis's hopes for the season, and an essay by the artistic director then in charge. The December issue includes a seasonal reflection from Father Andrew. The January issue wishes everyone a happy new year.

The *Old Vic Magazine* helps feed the perception that Baylis ran the Vic like a parish hall, complete with parish magazine, but the publication was clearly enjoyed by many, and helped to foster the community spirit that became so distinctive of the Vic audiences. While such magazines, and supporter groups, were not unknown elsewhere in theatre of the time, the one thing which really marks out the *Old Vic Magazine* as unique is that it seized every possible opportunity to celebrate women's pioneering successes in a male-dominated world. It also published essays on the history of the Vic, as well as essays on

Baylis's family history. A biography of Baylis appears in the very first issue, in October 1919. In March 1925 the *Old Vic Magazine* reports the death of Newton Baylis, aged seventy-eight, and looks back over his eventful career, stressing the important work he did for Emma Cons by singing in the very first of her Vic ballad concerts in 1881. The article pays tribute to Newton's 'tenderness to and affection for his invalid wife', to whom he had been married fifty-one years. An essay written by Baylis herself for the parish magazine of All Saints, the church where the newly married Newton and Liebe had worshipped for so many years, adds the information that Newton's death was sudden: he 'was clapping his hands and encouraging a little child to walk when he fell forward unconscious' and died shortly afterwards at St Thomas's Hospital.[103] Newton had continued to sing all his life – he 'sang in the choir at St. Paul's, Lorrimer Square, till the Sunday before his death' – and he carried on serving the Vic as best he could.[104] Even when he was elderly and frail Newton often cycled to the bank with the theatre's takings, and Baylis told a story against herself when she admitted that once, when Newton was knocked off his bike, her first thought was to worry about the money in his care and her second thought was to worry about her father.[105]

Later in the same year the *Old Vic Magazine* for December reports the death of Liebe Baylis, also aged seventy-eight. In an obituary for Liebe, Baylis pays tribute to her mother's artistic judgement and talent-spotting:[106] it was Liebe who recommended Russell Thorndike to Baylis, because Liebe had been impressed by Thorndike's acting when he came on as understudy to play Shylock in Johannesburg. Again it was Liebe who, in old age, battled on behalf of the Vic at bargain basement sales, obtaining 'the nucleus of the Vic Wardrobe, besides a number of stage-jewels that are still in use and the two positive organs that have been such a great acquisition to the theatre' at rock-bottom prices.[107] Despite the celebration of her mother's contribution to the Vic the bleak fact remains that in a very short space of time Baylis lost both her parents.

In 1928 Baylis was mourning another dear friend, Ellen

Terry. When Terry first took part in a Shakespeare birthday review at the Vic in 1916 she was generously lending her name, still a major draw card, to a struggling, if valiant enterprise. In an essay in the *Old Vic Magazine*, written to mark Terry's death, Baylis recalls how once it was confirmed that Terry was to perform, theatre staff went out and bought up all the red roses that were to be had locally so that the audience could shower Terry with them after her performance.[108] Baylis went on to argue for Terry's often unacknowledged but utterly crucial role at the Lyceum, when Terry and Henry Irving led the company there, and she also sadly remembers:

> On one occasion Ellen was sitting in our tiny office at the Vic on a crate of mineral waters. I urged her to take the only chair, and said, "I hate to see you on the stool of repentance." "My dear," she replied with a wistful smile, "the stool of repentance is where many people think I ought to sit until the crack of doom."

Terry's private life upset the moral sticklers but, to Baylis, Terry was always a gracious and generous friend to the Vic.

For Baylis, the *Old Vic Magazine* was a relatively easy arena in which she could build up her public persona, because she exerted ultimate editorial control over what was published. However, Baylis 'The Manager' also appeared increasingly in a range of external publications: Baylis wrote essays, she was interviewed and she was profiled.[109] One example in 1921, in the feminist magazine *Time and Tide*, is particularly revealing. Baylis is featured in an article under the heading of 'Personalities and Powers', and while the profile characterises her in lively terms – commenting on her 'racy, colloquial language' and her determination bordering on obstinacy – Baylis still managed to turn the interview around into a blatant request for donations to the Vic.[110] In 1924, in a rather differently flavoured interview bearing the headline 'How to be Fit at Fifty,' Baylis is claiming that her good state of health results from her fondness for cold baths and swimming, because of her efforts 'never to be idle', and because she has 'healthy parents'.[111]

Baylis 'The Manager' also became something of a visual

'The drawing of a great lady'. Portrait of Lilian Baylis by William
Rothenstein (1922). Courtesy of the Rothenstein Estate

icon during the 1920s. For someone so frequently categorised as 'ugly' – John Gielgud, for example, talks of 'drab looking girls like Lilian Baylis'[112] – Baylis was unabashed about using her appearance – if not beautiful, then certainly very memorable – to promote the Vic. She deployed publicity shots and formal poses to advertise her theatres, and soon an image of a dumpy woman with spectacles almost inevitably conjured up the Vic and the Wells in all their manifestations.

During the early 1920s the official postcard image was of Baylis leaning over her desk, pen poised and at the ready, looking kindly but efficient, the manager in action, in the middle of her paperwork. Later official photographs tend to feature the Oxford M.A. gown and the Companion of Honour medal. In the mid 1920s, stagily posed postcards were issued, showing Baylis and others gazing thoughtfully at the well at Sadler's Wells, presumably in order to fix the Wells in the public consciousness, and help raise the profile of the fundraising campaign. Generally, however, her later official images appear to be aiming at an impression of gravitas.

Portrait artist William Rothenstein offered a gentler view of Baylis in 1922, although he unequivocally entitled the drawing 'The drawing of a great lady' (see p. 185). In 1926 Baylis appeared in full formal regalia when Charles E. Butler was commissioned to paint her portrait. Sumner Austin records that Baylis wanted a warts-and-all image, and specifically asked Butler 'not [to] attempt to make her other than she was'.[113] She wears her Oxford M.A. cap and gown, and a hefty picture locket, containing a picture of Emma Cons.[114] She appears dignified, rather portly and impressive – as Harcourt Williams comments, when 'Miss Baylis would come swishing on to the stage in her cap and gown … she wore them well'.[115] Baylis chose to foreground her work with opera in this portrait and she is depicted holding a large embossed volume labelled *Lohengrin*. Indeed she may well have selected Butler as an artist because, as the *Old Vic Magazine* reported, his daughter Violet was then singing for the Vic opera company.[116] The portrait is full of dark and moody colours except for the flash of red in the lining of the degree gown hood. The twist in Baylis's mouth is very clearly shown and because of this she appears to be smiling wryly. She looks stocky, redoubtable and something of an immovable force.

Baylis 'The Manager' also supported and promoted books about the Vic, and her hand can very clearly be detected in the astonishing appeals for funds that appear in these works. Thus John Booth's history of the Vic up until 1916 includes a completely transparent discussion of what funds are needed at that time, how the interest on a deposit of £5,000 would help matters, and directs that 'Donations and subscriptions' should 'be forwarded to Lilian Baylis, who will gladly give further particulars'.[117] H. Chance Newton's 1923 book of reminiscences about the Victorian Vic, which was published with a foreword by George Dance, still includes a statement that, despite the recent windfall from Dance, more donations are needed. Doris Westwood's account of the year she spent at the Vic opens with a preface by Baylis, which unapologetically asks readers for money. All of Harcourt Williams's various books on the Vic were either sold in aid of the Vic Theatre or focused on advertising the theatre's achievements. Edwin Fagg's 1936 history, *The Old 'Old Vic'*, concludes with a very explicit call for donations for the current theatre, and the dustjacket supplies information on how to join the Vic-Wells association.

Whilst Baylis 'The Manager' thrived, the 1920s must have been a difficult period personally for her. In 1921 she had to go on a three-week convalescence trip to the Canary Islands after failing to recover properly from the accident in which she was knocked off her bicycle by a car.[118] As well as the deaths of her aunt Ellen in 1920 and both her parents in 1925, Baylis also had her sister Ethel's increasingly troubled marriage to worry about, and from the time of her visit to South Africa in 1924, she became more involved in this worsening domestic crisis.

Ethel had married Francis Johnston Dunning in 1908, and they lived in South Africa until the 1914–18 war. Then, whilst Dunning was on active service, Ethel and the couple's children, Gladys and Bobbie, lived in England. Ethel's 'graceful dancing' appeared at the Vic 'in both operas and plays when her military duties permitted'.[119] But by 1923 the marriage was in trouble, and Ethel's letters are documenting violence against her by her husband, while Ethel's daughter Gladys, who frequently reacted to these incidents by becoming hysterical, was emotionally damaged by her experiences.[120] Ethel eventually separated from Dunning, and wanted a divorce even though at that time the social disgrace would have cost Dunning his job with the South African civil service. Baylis was indignant that Dunning was hitting her sister, 'not even having the excuse of being drunk', as she puts it; and of a prospective visit by Dunning she states, 'I do not feel yet I could possibly have a husband who beats his wife under my roof', a man who was 'so cowardly and cruel and with a mind so mean'.[121] Dunning claimed that Ethel was selfish and flighty and that he was not to blame. Baylis was outraged that he 'feels you are so selfish that occasional wife beating is quite justifiable and in fact is quite proud of himself'.[122] The son of the marriage, Robert, seems to have emerged relatively unscathed from this domestic turmoil and remained with his father when his mother and sister left, although Dunning suggested that Gladys should stay and keep house for him. Baylis comments: 'I come so constantly across women who have kept home for Father or brother, with no profession to fall back on, Gladys unless her Father has a small fortune to leave her, must be a fool if she does it'.[123] Baylis advised Gladys to train as a nurse, secretary or teacher. In 1930 Baylis thought Gladys was 'making a good nurse', but eventually Baylis ended up supporting both Ethel and Gladys, in order to enable them to live independently of Dunning in England.[124]

There were several attempts at reconciliation to avoid the disgrace of divorce, but in some letters Ethel's anger is searing. She writes to Dunning: 'I don't think you realise that I have some pride and respect for myself, and that it is revolting for me to think that I must give my body to a man who has not kissed me for years.'[125] She concedes that 'I know my body is your right', but goes on to complain, 'for years past it has been hateful to be made a convenience of … about 3 years ago you ceased to respond when I kissed you goodnight'.[126] Ethel's descriptions of the kicks and blows she received from Dunning are interspersed with accounts of her retaliation, striking him back with any weapon that came to hand. One night Ethel attacked Dunning with a sjambok 'and gave him a cut across the face', before then cooking dinner for the family.[127] It is not surprising that young Gladys became subject to fits of nerves. By 1927 Dunning is writing letters complaining about Ethel's 'obsessions', her '*imaginary grievances*', '*fancied troubles*', and her association with 'tittle tattle women & flappers'; he orders her to come home and interest herself 'in the house & *garden*', exhorting her '*Be a woman & show your breeding*': Ethel responded to this comment by writing 'Bosh' in the margin of the letter.[128]

It is hard to feel sympathy with Dunning after reading Ethel's graphic accounts of the violence used against her, but while he managed to alienate his wife and daughter completely, he remained close to his son, Robert. Indeed, after Baylis's death, Robert Dunning 'was adamant' that her family in South Africa would not be interested in any of her effects, an attitude that may reflect the bad feeling generated by the Dunnings' years of marital dispute, in which Baylis would have been seen as aiding and abetting her sister Ethel.[129]

Baylis's 1924 visit to South Africa was not entirely focused on her family, and she was able to work hard at one of her favourite activities – networking. She combined her supposed holiday with outreach work, investigating the possibility of the Vic companies touring South Africa, and speaking on the radio about their work. She addressed various bodies such as the English Association at the University of the Witwatersrand, Johannesburg, and met up with old friends, with the Dr Campbell who saved her life when she was suffering from enteric flu at the age of seventeen, and with dignitaries such as Princess Alice and the Earl of Athlone.[130] She visited Cape Town, Johannesburg, Durban, Dundee, the Victoria Falls, the Motopas and Bulawayo, and while in Pretoria stayed with Bishop Nevill Talbot, whose family had always supported Emma Cons's work at the Vic.

Baylis also had her first chance to get to know her namesake, her eighteen-year-old niece Lilian. When Baylis's brother Willie died of consumption in 1906, he left a heavily pregnant wife, Katie, who shortly afterwards gave birth to

Lilian Baylis junior. Baylis had been hit hard emotionally by her brother's death but building relations with his daughter proved complex. In 1929 Lilian junior and her family visited England, and during this visit Baylis had to lend money to Roy Tremayne, Lilian's stepfather, to enable the family to return to South Africa. On arriving home the family found they would not be able to pay the money back straight away and Tremayne was then hounded by Baylis for the money. As Lilian junior's mother, Katie, had also voiced her suspicions that Lilian senior was trying to separate her from her daughter, relations reached an all-time low.[131] Lilian junior wrote: 'At first [Baylis] didn't like me and thought me dreadfully selfish', but later they learnt to 'love each other'; after the disagreements over the debts, however, she commented, 'I'm very unhappy that the question of money has interfered with our friendship, but I do feel you are not interested in me now we owe you money.'[132]

While her family were providing some uncomfortable challenges during the 1920s, Baylis was also building up a network of like-minded friends, women who were outspoken, professional career women like herself, whose friendship supported, invigorated and encouraged Baylis in her work as manager. One of Baylis's very closest friends from the mid 1920s was the writer, actress and political activist Cicely Hamilton. Baylis and Hamilton worked together on a project very close to Baylis's heart – a book detailing the history of the Old Vic and the work of Emma Cons – and the friendship really took off around 1925 when Hamilton invited Baylis down to her retreat at Betchworth Hill, Tadworth, Surrey, where a community of 'people with primitive dwellings on the hill' all chose to live 'the simple life at weekends'.[133] Hamilton herself camped out in an old tram carriage and on 28 April 1928 Baylis took possession of a 'tiny one-roomed hut, which stood 700ft. above sea level and had a small verandah overlooking the South Downs', which she had just purchased from Miss M.E. Sheppard.[134] From then on Baylis's diaries often record 'hut' at weekends, sometimes with a midweek visit on Wednesdays, and often the name of a guest, always a woman, whom she had invited along. In 1937 Hamilton reminisces:

Cicely Hamilton and Lilian Baylis c.1926. Courtesy of the Theatre Museum, V&A Picture Library

> My thoughts went back to a weekend – some twelve years ago, or it may be more – which I mark as the real beginning of our friendship. She came to my caravan for a Saturday to Monday holiday; arriving with a dog and a banjo and hoping I objected to neither. The dog, like all her dogs, was unruly, and I think there were moments when I wished it further; but when she took out her banjo and played, I knew it an instrument made for far better uses than twanging.[135]

Hamilton introduced Baylis to circles of professional women such as the Soroptimists; Baylis ensured that Hamilton's Nativity play was performed at the Old Vic, and insisted that Hamilton introduce some of the Vic *Everyman* performances at Easter.

Hamilton lived a very woman-centred life, and she was a close associate of a lesbian ménage à trois, who lived at Smallhythe in Kent, consisting of theatre director Edy Craig (the daughter of actress Ellen Terry), writer Christopher St John (Christabel Marshal) and painter Tony (Clare) Atwood. This group socialised with the woman who was the inspiration behind Virginia Woolf's hero/ine in *Orlando*, the bisexual aristocrat Vita Sackville-West, and their circle included high-profile and publicly 'out' lesbians such as Radclyffe Hall and Una Troubridge.[136] Another of Hamilton's close friends was suffragist Elizabeth Robins, who lived with Octavia Wilberforce, a medical doctor, for twenty years. Cicely Hamilton's friendship with Margaret Haig, Lady Rhondda (another celebrity commandeered by Baylis to introduce the Vic Easter performance of *Everyman*) links her, Baylis and the Vic with a prominent suffragette who divorced her husband, attempted unsuccessfully to enter the House of Lords (her title was inherited from her father), and lived for many years with Theodora Bosanquet while both women worked on and edited *Time and Tide*.[137] According to Hamilton, it was 'the proprietors' of *Time and Tide* who suggested Hamilton and Baylis produce their book on the Vic, and who subsequently published extracts from the book in their weekly paper.[138]

Lady Rhondda's *Time and Tide*, sometimes known as 'The Sapphic Graphic', was a paper established to provide feminist news and commentary on events.[139] The paper did include contributions from male writers, as well as sympathetic articles on male celebrities, but the writing for, and production of, *Time and Tide* certainly provided a meeting place for feminists, some of whom were lesbian. *Time and Tide* writers included, for example, Clemence Dane, who moved in lesbian and gay circles, whose *Adam's Opera* appeared at the Vic in 1928, who became involved in fundraising campaigns for the Vic, and who was another of the celebrities who introduced the Vic *Everyman*.[140] Baylis's association with *Time and Tide* and its writers brought her into contact with some of the most independent and feminist journalists of the day.

Publicly, of course, discretion was vital to such women. Hamilton's autobiography, *Life Errant*, gives little away about her sexuality and is in many ways a masterpiece of evasion: for example, she manages entirely to avoid explaining the mysterious, and scandalous, disappearance of her mother from the family home. She talks only very briefly about her friendship with Baylis and situates this primarily in terms of the

Vic: 'you can't know Lilian Baylis and be indifferent to her treasured theatre'.[141] Lis Whitelaw, Hamilton's biographer, who discusses Hamilton's relationship with Baylis in some detail, points out that Hamilton uses the word 'intimacy' to describe her relationship with 'the Vic and its manager', and that this is 'a stronger term than she uses for any of her other friends'.[142] Whitelaw chooses to identify Hamilton as lesbian, but she rightly cautions her readers that differing definitions of the word 'lesbian' in different periods can confuse a complex situation.[143]

What is indisputable here is that in being close friends with Hamilton, Baylis was associating herself with a woman very well known as a feminist. Hamilton wrote the words for the popular suffragette anthem 'The March of the Women' (Ethel Smyth wrote the music). Hamilton was also the author of the anti-marriage tract *Marriage as a Trade*, and the strongly feminist but also commercially very successful play *Diana of Dobsons*, which ventilates in dramatic form many of Hamilton's criticisms of the institution, and current practices, of marriage. *Marriage as a Trade* suggests several reasons why sensible women might choose not to marry. For example, Hamilton analyses the age of chivalry, claiming that the deference to women then arose because women had a viable alternative to marriage, in the convents. The end of chivalry, according to Hamilton, came about when the Reformation closed down conventual life, and thus closed down the readily available option for women to live with other women and without men. Although in the period after the First World War Hamilton was not so radical a feminist as she was before, she was still known as an activist when she and Baylis worked together to produce their history of the Vic. In a period that has been characterised as one of backlash against spinsters, this book was written by two remarkable spinsters partly to ensure that the work of another remarkable spinster, Emma Cons, was not forgotten.[144]

Baylis also worked alongside Hamilton when she joined the Women's Provisional Club, which first met on 8 February 1924: it brought women professionals together on a fortnightly basis and was based on the men-only organisation

Rotary International.[145] The first chair of the club was Lady Rhondda. Baylis was

> almost an original member, and was actually a member of the first Executive Committee. In those days they used to meet at Lady Rhondda's for dinner, and afterwards sit around and entertain each other. Miss Hamilton generally sat on the floor and kept the committee rocking with laughter while she, as Hon. Secretary, made periodic and quite unheeded pleas for the transaction of a little business.[146]

Baylis became senior vice president in 1928 when Cicely Hamilton was president, and several other committee members were women who were close friends, such as Beatrice Gordon Holmes and Cecil Leslie.[147] The Women's Provisional Club met on Thursdays for lunch when a guest speaker spoke on such topics as 'Awakening the interest of young women in Public Affairs', 'Laundry Management', 'Work of a Woman Magistrate', 'Part Played by Women in Political Organisations' and 'What is Orthophonics?'[148] Sometimes guest speakers were luminaries – Dame Millicent Fawcett spoke on 'The Appeal to Youth' – but often they were talking about their work, and the challenges they faced as professional working women.[149] Baylis's engagements diaries record her attending many of these lectures, but the Club also occasionally visited the Vic and minutes noting one such visit look forward to the Christmas play at the Vic, entitled *Christmas Eve*, where club members' talents were to be on display:[150] the libretto was written by Rose Fyleman, known for her authorship of fairy tales and rhymes; the music was by composer, pianist and professor of harmony and counterpoint at the Royal Academy of Music, Dorothy Howell; the production, or direction, of the play is credited as 'by Miss Baylis'.[151]

The 1920s for many meant the jazz age, the Charleston, and a great sense of release from the nightmare of the First World War. For Baylis the 1920s were a time when she was almost constantly working at full throttle, enjoying extraordinary success and overcoming the daunting obstacles in her path. In 1926, however, Baylis embarked on a new phase of empire-building in an area that was very dear to her heart. It was that year that Baylis first met Edris Stannus, better known to dance history by her professional name of Ninette de Valois. By dangling the prospect of the new Sadler's Wells Theatre in front of de Valois, Baylis was able to begin expanding her empire into the world of ballet and dance.

NOTES

1   *OVM*, Oct 1921. Harcourt Williams, *Old Vic Saga*, p. 50 also has details of this event.

2   *OVM*, March 1934.

3   OVLB/000168/4 and 5.

4   *OVM*, October–November 1924. See *Richard III*.

5   OVLB/000144/2. The performance took place on 15 March. Reginald Rowe's essay on the subject of performances at King's College appeared in the *OVM* for March 1924.

6   Sumner Austin, quoted in Roberts, *Lilian Baylis*, p. 53.

7   'Manager's Foreword', *OVM*, September–October 1934. The critic S.R. Littlewood of the *Referee*, writing to congratulate Baylis on the Companion of Honour, commented 'It should have been "Dame" long ago, but I expect this pleases you better.' Baylis wrote on the letter 'Yes it does much better' (OVLB/000254).

8   *Birmingham Post*, 2 December 1937.

9   Findlater, *Lilian Baylis*, p. 254, quoting Cecil Leslie, a fellow member of the Women's Provisional Club.

10 Mander, 'Forty Years On, Part One'.

11 Cross, autobiography, p. 35.

12 Edwin Fagg, *The Old 'Old Vic' or, From Barrymore to Baylis* (London, 1936), p. 121.

13 Susan Carlson, 'Comic Militancy: the Politics of Suffrage Drama' in Maggie B. Gale and Viv Gardner (eds.), *Women, Theatre and Performance: New Histories, New Historiographies* (Manchester, 2000), pp. 198–215, p. 207.

14 Findlater, *Lilian Baylis*, p. 170 passes on the story that when Lady Cunard asked Baylis for, in effect, commission on Dance's donation, Baylis angrily refused and 'The air was sulphurous at the Vic.' This seems extremely unlikely given OVLB/000049, marked 'very private', where Lady Cunard positions herself very much in the background and reminds Baylis that she had

introduced her to the man who 'is *really* the kind friend who found the donor', and asks her to convey this information in confidence to the Vic governors.

15 OVLB/000209.

16 Governors' minutes, 9 October 1922 and February 1923.

17 *Daily Mirror*, 2 May 1934. Chairman since 1900 of the Improved Tenements Association, Rowe was knighted in 1932, an event celebrated in *The Stage* (4 January).

18 *OVM*, February 1929 reports Robert Atkins's forthcoming production of Rowe's play *The Importance of Being William* at the Q Theatre.

19 *The Times*, 29 November 1937. Baylis's diaries (M&M Theatre Collection) are crammed with addresses of individuals she has met, with occasional notes about them, as if she is keeping a rather chaotic but effective record of people who might one day help her theatres.

20 Fagg, *The Old 'Old Vic'*, p. 5.

21 See Harcourt Williams, *Old Vic Saga*, p. 63.

22 The Vic's response later to the General Strike was that 'Several hundred seats were set apart each night for men and women who had been called out by their unions', while some in the Shakespeare Company volunteered 'for Government service'. See Annual Report 1925–6, pp. 4–5.

23 Executive Committee minutes of 17 October 1923. William Poel records (*OVM*, January 1935) a story about Emma Cons which shows a similar mentality: Cons demonstrated that by shouting 'Fire' she had two fire engines at the door in a minute and she argued that this was more effective than her wasting time on fire drills.

24 Sybil Thorndike, 'Lilian Baylis', p. 33.

25 Executive Committee minutes, 8 January 1926 record Baylis's success here. Joan Cross quotes this in 'The Bad Old Days' in Anthony Gishford (ed.), *Tribute to Benjamin Britten on his Fiftieth Birthday* (London, 1963), p. 180.

26 *OVM*, April 1925.

27 *OVM*, September–October 1928. The motif appears earlier: e.g. the minutes of the Vic Executive Committee for 1 August 1922 document Sir George Dance's view that the Vic was 'fulfilling the purpose of a national theatre'.

28 *Theatre World*, December 1931. See also John Elsom and Nicholas Tomalin, *The History of the National Theatre* (London, 1978), p. 57: 'Lilian Baylis seemed to be doing on a shoestring'

what the Shakespeare Memorial National Theatre committee
had been talking about for years. However, they also point out
(p. 65) that Baylis 'talked up' the Old Vic as the real National
Theatre because she hoped to get hold of some of the
committee's funds. See also the attack launched by Viola Tree
on Lord Lytton demanding that some of the National Theatre
fund (her father Herbert Beerbohm Tree was one of its
founders) be given to the Vic-Wells (*Evening Standard*, 22 July
1937).

29 Baylis, 'Aims and Ideals of the Theatre'. All subsequent
quotations in this paragraph are taken from this typescript.

30 Dennis Arundell, *The Story of Sadler's Wells 1683–1964* (London,
1965), p. 185. Stead's publishing house published John Booth's
1916 history of the Vic. For Baylis, C.K. Stead's links with South
Africa would also have been telling – he was a confidante of
Cecil Rhodes.

31 For the pickle factory see Mary Clarke, *The Sadler's Wells Ballet: A
History and Appreciation* (London, 1955), p. 42; for the marsh
flowers see Guthrie, *A Life in the Theatre* (London, 1959,
reprinted 1961), p. 102.

32 Reginald Rowe, 'Twin Theatres', *The Times*, 6 January 1931.
Clarke, *The Sadler's Wells Ballet*, p. 42 not only credits Rowe with
most of the fundraising for the Wells but also points out that he
gave six years of his free time to this project.

33 See e.g. the discussion in *OVM*, May 1925.

34 Appropriately *Trelawney* was again staged at the Vic for the
celebrations to mark the half century of Baylis's Sadler's Wells
(December–January 1980–1).

35 Rowe, 'Twin Theatres'.

36 Harcourt Williams, *Four Years at the Old Vic*, p. 81.

37 Lilian Baylis, 'Why We Wanted Sadler's Wells', *The Sadler's Wells
Book, A Souvenir of Sadler's Wells Theatre Past, Present and Future*
(London, 1931), pp. 9–10.

38 'The Manager's Letter', *OVM*, September 1926.

39 Russell Thorndike, 'Lilian Baylis', p. 187.

40 'The Manager's Letter', *OVM*, September–October 1925.

41 The Royal Victoria Hall Annual Report for 1909–10, p. 3
mentions that four years previously the Vic was the only large-
scale cinematograph in the neighbourhood but by 1909 it was
losing out to purpose-built 'Picture Palaces'. However, Baylis did
not abandon film entirely at this stage: for example, the
programme for Rosina Filippi's 1914 *Merchant of Venice* includes

a Bioscope section.

42 Baylis, 'Prayer – and One's Hour of Destiny'.

43 In the *Era* (14 May 1919) Baylis specifies she made £1,000 in two years with admission prices of 1d and 2d. She confirms the amount in Baylis, 'What the Old Vic Stands For', but later on she inflated her claim to £2,000 profit, e.g. *Westminster Gazette*, 28 April 1930 and *OVM*, September–October 1935.

44 *Southern Times* (Dorchester), 4 December 1937.

45 A letter from the BBC (11 September 1923) was discussed at the Executive Committee on 14 September 1923: 'As it was ascertained that this would cost no expense to the Vic (in the way of Royalties etc) and would afford useful publicity, the offer was accepted.' Notes concerning the broadcasting (p. 2 of notes) reveal that Baylis secured 15 guineas an opera or part thereof; and 10 guineas for a drama (14 December 1923). A note inserted into the Executive Committee minutes for 12 February 1926 explains Baylis was only willing to broadcast from the Vic and not send actors to the BBC.

46 Doris Westwood, *These Players: A Diary of the 'Old Vic'*, with a foreword by Lilian Baylis (London, 1926), p. 132.

47 *OVM*, February 1932.

48 Clarke, *The Sadler's Wells Ballet*, p. 126 records Baylis's initial interest in ballet appearing on television. See also Leshe Gordon's film of the ballet company's work 1936–8, discussed in the *Vic-Wells Association Newsletter*, February 1983.

49 Quoted in Roberts, *Lilian Baylis*, p. 17.

50 *Time and Tide*, 4 December 1937.

51 Hamilton and Baylis, *The Old Vic*, p. 243.

52 It is interesting that the first public performances of 'The Manager', in 1914, coincided with Baylis's reunion with her parents after over fifteen years apart: that is, Baylis began to perform again in public in the period when she was reunited with the people she had performed with in her youth – in the Gypsy Revellers as well as in other ensembles.

53 The *Evening Express*, 26 November 1937 attributes a 'phenomenal' memory to Baylis, but the numerous stories of her greeting galleryites by name and asking after their families also attest to this.

54 Reproduced in Hamilton and Baylis, *The Old Vic*, pp. 188–9.

55 Baylis, 'Aims and Ideals of the Theatre'. Baylis's diary, in the same collection, records her broadcasting on 24 October 1928 at 9.15 p.m.

56 *OVM*, April–May 1936.

57 Cross, autobiography, p. 7.

58 *The Listener*, 1 December 1937; Harcourt Williams, *Four Years at the Old Vic*, p. 115.

59 Harcourt Williams, *Four Years at the Old Vic*, p. 217.

60 Marshall, *The Other Theatre*, p. 126.

61 Russell Thorndike, 'Lilian Baylis', p. 180.

62 Quoted in Roberts, *Lilian Baylis*, p. 35.

63 Harcourt Williams, *Four Years at the Old Vic*, p. 215. Baylis also tried to foster good relations between the opera and Shakespeare companies by giving an annual party for them both at her home in Stockwell Park Road. Generally, however, what happened was that opera guests socialised with other opera personnel and the Shakespeare Company did likewise.

64 Dent, *A Theatre For Everybody*, p. 93 stresses a link with church here – 'Miss Baylis, accustomed as she was to the observance of Saints' days in church, always liked to have something of a calendar of anniversaries in the theatre.'

65 Harcourt Williams, *Four Years at the Old Vic*, p. 34.

66 Northcroft, *Girls of Adventure*, p. 114.

67 *Public Opinion*, 3 December 1937.

68 Audrey Williamson, *Old Vic Drama: A Twelve Years' Study of Plays and Players* (London, 1948), pp. 144–5. The Vic wasn't original in celebrating this date. Quite apart from David Garrick's jubilee celebrations, Herbert Beerbohm Tree celebrated Shakespeare's birthday for many years.

69 Isaac, *Ben Greet*, pp. 133–5.

70 Findlater, *Lilian Baylis*, pp. 137–8.

71 *OVM*, September–October 1927.

72 Williamson, *Old Vic Drama*, pp. 95, 94. Williamson adds a jibe about Baylis and Elizabeth I being equally famous for their parsimony.

73 Westwood, *These Players*, p. 246.

74 Williamson, *Old Vic Drama*, p. 144.

75 *OVM*, February 1920. The *OVM* for May 1921 looks forward to Baylis's 'Silver Wedding' as manager of the Vic, a celebration that will provide a high-profile occasion for raising funds.

76 Westwood, *These Players*, pp. 137, 139.

77 *OVM*, December 1920.

78 *OVM*, February 1920. The Vic-Wells Association still today celebrates Twelfth Night.

79 Harcourt Williams, *Four Years at the Old Vic*, p. 58.

80 Reported in the *Sketch*, 3 March 1938.

81 Corathiel, 'Old Vic Memories'. Corathiel remained press agent until 1936. Executive Committee minutes of 12 June 1936 record the 'termination' of her engagement.

82 *OVM*, February 1920. Non-circle members could buy the magazine for 2d, occasionally 3d. Other Vic social groups include the Old Vic Club, consisting of a group of actors and actresses who had appeared at the Vic since 1914 (and who were often prevailed upon to come back and perform something on Shakespeare's birthday); the Victorians, a group of teachers in the London area interested in the work of the Vic; and the Vic-Wells Society.

83 *OVM*, September–October 1927.

84 *OVM*, May 1921. In 1925–6 the Vic Annual Report (6) records that 'Miss Baylis is the Editor of the Magazine' although helped by Irene Beeston. The refusal to use the word 'manageress' complements the mindset noted by Harcourt Williams (*Vic-Wells*, p. 46) when he states that after Emma Cons's death Baylis soon dropped 'Miss' as a title, stating 'We don't care about the 'Miss' down here.'

85 The *OVM* of February 1931 reports that the opera audience were 'drilled in the unwritten rules governing applause by the "regulars"', indicating how wedded to a specific code of behaviour Vic audiences became.

86 *OVM*, February 1920.

87 *OVM*, May 1922.

88 *OVM*, April 1920

89 Lilian Baylis, 'Things Near my Heart', *OVM*, May 1921. By 1937, however, Baylis was modifying her message: team work was best, but 'I strongly believe, from the box-office point of view, in the value of having one big star' like Olivier (Lilian Baylis, 'The Home of Repertory: Old Vic's Policy: Team Work and the Star System: Art and the Box Office', *Glasgow Herald*, 1 April 1937.

90 *OVM*, March 1923.

91 Baylis, 'A Greatest Hour'.

92 Early opera programmes at the Vic actually included the lyrics to the major songs, so this was not necessarily an indication of the audience's prodigious memory.

93 *OVM*, February 1931. For the audience finishing speeches and arias see Findlater, *Lilian Baylis*, p. 135.

94 Baylis, '"The Old Vic" and "The Wells"', pp. 110–11.

95 *OVM*, May 1930.

96 *OVM*, April 1920.

97 Geoffrey Whitworth, *John O'London's Weekly*, 18 February 1922.

98 *OVM*, May 1920. At the time this meant a top price of 3/-. Cheapest seats were 3d. The first issue of the *OVM* (October 1919) put the case even more bluntly, quoting a letter from the publishers of *Aida* refusing any concession whatsoever over royalties.

99 For example, *OVM*, May 1920.

100 *OVM*, March 1920.

101 For example, December 1921, May 1922.

102 Russell Thorndike, 'Lilian Baylis', p. 169; Sybil and Russell Thorndike, 'Preface' to *Lilian Baylis*, p. 8. 'Producer' refers to what in the UK would now be called 'director'.

103 OVLB/000139.

104 *OVM*, February 1925.

105 Findlater, *Lilian Baylis*, p. 213.

106 The article is unsigned but, given the familiarity with the subject, must have been written by Baylis.

107 *OVM*, December 1925.

108 Lilian Baylis, 'At "the Old Vic"', *Home Chat*, 14 June 1924.

109 For some of Baylis's essays see the bibliography. Irene Beeston, in Harcourt Williams, *Vic-Wells*, p. 49, claims she helped Baylis write books and prefaces, and was paid extra for these.

110 *Time and Tide*, 15 July 1921.

111 'How to be Fit at Fifty', *Daily Chronicle*, 30 May 1925. Baylis was fifty in 1924 and the irony is that her 'healthy' parents both died in the following year.

112 Richard Mangan (ed.), *Gielgud's Letters* (London, 2004), p. 61.

113 Sumner Austin in Harcourt Williams, *Vic-Wells*, p. 85. The portrait was bought for the Vic by public subscription. Executive Committee minutes of 10 February 1928 record Baylis being presented with the portrait. The portrait currently hangs in the Coliseum Theatre, home of the ENO. It is reproduced in e.g. Harcourt Williams, *Old Vic Saga*, frontispiece.

114 The locket is now in the London Theatre Museum.

115 Harcourt Williams, *Old Vic Saga*, p. 66.

116 *OVM*, November 1926.

117 Booth, *The 'Old Vic'*, p. 69.

118 *OVM*, November 1921. For this accident and Baylis's spiritual response to it see Chapter 5.

119 *OVM*, November 1919. See also *OVM*, October–November 1924.

120 OVLB/000019 (no date) confirms 'Bad news about Gladys. She is to see a big brain specialist on Fri I hope.' The letters detailing the domestic violence in the Dunning household are written in the mid 1920s.

121 OVLB/000021/2, 2–3.

122 OVLB/000021/3.

123 Ibid.

124 Letter to 'Chris', 6 October 1930, Roy Waters collection. This letter records that Frank Dunning was then lecturing at Stellenbosch University.

125 OVLB/000055/5–6.

126 OVLB/000055/6.

127 OVLB/000056/2–3, letter dated 1 December 1926. In this letter Ethel also states she is keeping a revolver in her room.

128 OVLB/000058/2.

129 OV/M/000088/6.

130 'The Manager's Letter', *OVM*, October–November 1924.

131 OVLB/000027/5.

132 OVLB/000027/4, 27/10.

133 Lis Whitelaw, *The Life and Rebellious Times of Cicely Hamilton: Actress, Writer, Suffragist* (London, 1990), p. 212. Findlater's neglect of the Baylis/Hamilton relationship is one of the real weaknesses of his book.

134 Description is quoted from a letter by 'N.S.', a 'fellow-camper' at Betchworth, who also reports on how much Baylis 'looked forward to the peace and simplicity' of her Betchworth hut (*The Times*, 30 November 1937). The record of Baylis's purchase appears in her diary (M&M Theatre Collection).

135 *Time and Tide*, 4 December 1937.

136 See Auchmuty, 'By Their Friends We Shall Know Them' for more detail on these lesbian networks. It has been questioned, notably by Julie Holledge, *Innocent Flowers: Women in the Edwardian Theatre* (London, 1981), p. 155, why Baylis never gave any work to Edy Craig, who as the daughter of Baylis's beloved Ellen Terry would have seemed to be in a strong position. However, Craig was a perfectionist and didn't suffer fools gladly, and it is likely that Baylis had not forgotten the arguments she had with Rosina Filippi.

137 Lady Rhondda's contribution to an *Everyman* performance is noted, for example, in the Executive Committee minutes of 11 September 1925. For her relationship with Bosanquet see Whitelaw, *The Life and Rebellious Times of Cicely Hamilton*, p. 113.

See Margaret Haig, Viscountess Rhondda, *This Was My World* (London, 1933), p. 298 for her attempt to enter the House of Lords.

138 *OVM*, September–October 1925.

139 For 'The Sapphic Graphic' see Hallett, *Lesbian Lives*, p. 17. Ethel Smyth, for example, was famous for her passionate attachments to women, including Emmeline Pankhurst and Virginia Woolf, although her best-documented affair was with a man, Harry Brewer.

140 Maggie Gale, 'From Fame to Obscurity: in Search of Clemence Dane' in Maggie B. Gale and Viv Gardner (eds.), *Women, Theatre and Performance: New Histories, New Historiographies* (Manchester, 2000), pp. 121–41, especially pp. 132–5. For Dane's contribution to the Vic see e.g. Executive Committee minutes, 11 September 1925.

141 Cicely Hamilton, *Life Errant* (London, [1935]), p. 207.

142 Ibid.; see also Whitelaw, *The Life and Rebellious Times of Cicely Hamilton*, p. 212.

143 Whitelaw, *The Life and Rebellious Times of Cicely Hamilton*, pp. 109–10.

144 See Sheila Jeffreys, *The Spinster and her Enemies: Feminism and Sexuality 1880–1930* (London, 1985) for this period as one of backlash against spinsters.

145 All information taken from the Records of the Women's Provisional Club (1924–84), Women's Library.

146 Minutes of the AGM, 10 March 1938 – noting the death of Baylis.

147 For Cecil Leslie's portrait of Baylis see Chapter 10, p. 227.

148 Diary for 1928, 26 January, 19 April, 29 November, 13 December; Diary for 1930, 23 January (M&M).

149 Fawcett's lecture took place on 1 November 1928. When men were allowed to the luncheons this was signalled as an unusual event – Baylis's diary for 26 June 1930 has the phrase 'men guests welcomed' underlined (M&M).

150 For example, the Club visited the Vic on 17 May 1925.

151 Minutes of the AGM, 31 March 1927. For details on Howell see Sadie (ed.), *The New Grove Dictionary of Music and Musicians*. Elsewhere the producer is identified as Andrew Leigh (Shakespeare Birthday programme 1926). Dances were by Ninette de Valois.

[9]

Baylis and the Ballet

It was Emma Cons who first kindled Baylis's passion for dance:

> I particularly remember my aunt returning from one of
> these [a country house] weekend party & describing a
> wonderful American dancer who had been there and had
> amazed them by the ethereal quality of her dancing – she
> seemed almost to float through space as in a trance, so
> enrapt did she become in the spiritual beauty of her work.
> This left a lasting impression on me and gave me a great
> interest in dancing.[1]

In South Africa, Baylis both worked as a dancer and taught
dance, and her secretary, Evelyn Williams, claims she 'wanted a
ballet company ever since she had run a dancing school of her
own on the Rand in the gay '90s'.[2] Meanwhile, Baylis winced
over the awkwardness of some singers and actors appearing on
the Vic stage, and their lack of grace in dance sequences in
both operas and plays.

During the 1920s Baylis made several attempts to address
this problem: for example, Phyllis Cornish is credited with
training the dancers in *Carmen* in 1922.[3] Then Baylis realised
that she could make money out of people's desire to work in
theatre, and started charging 'students' for training at the Vic.
Initially this was little more than the opportunity to walk on as
part of a crowd and learn by observing, but by 1923 the Old
Vic Dramatic School, which then had forty students, had a
teaching staff consisting of the dancer Rupert Doone, the
actress and director Beatrice Wilson, and Cyril Shields, a
conjurer. Dr Aikin taught voice production.[4] Flora Fairbairn
also taught dance at the Vic, but as she was busy fulminating in
print about the need for a British Ballet Company, it is not

surprising that she was not satisfied for long with an arrangement whereby she had to take her dance classes 'in the small gap at the back of the Circle', and she soon left.[5] By 1925 Martha Mayall, the wife of conductor Charles Corri, and a former dancer with the Carl Rosa Opera, was responsible for choreographing and rehearsing dance at the Vic.[6] In the same year Jean Anderton was also working on dance sequences for the operas.[7]

These rather piecemeal attempts to improve the standard of dancing in Vic productions to some extent reflect the state of British dance at that time. While dancers could make a living if they worked as chorus girls or in the less respectable end of the market – music hall, vaudeville – there were few sustained work opportunities for British dancers in classical or modern ballet. Individuals were doing important work – Marie Rambert, for example – but the expected career trajectory for a serious and talented British dancer in this period was to work in Europe under a Russian- or French-sounding stage name. Nevertheless, during the 1920s there were several attempts to build British ballet up into a significant force. Initiatives included the publication of the magazine *The Dancing Times*, which advertised, critiqued and encouraged British work, and the foundation of the Camargo Society, in 1929, which was established specifically in order to support and promote British dance.[8]

A catalyst for real change appeared in the summer of 1926, when Baylis first met Ninette de Valois. De Valois was twenty-eight years old and had already enjoyed a long and varied career in dancing which included professional engagements as a child dancer at what seemed like 'every old pier theatre in England.'[9] De Valois had then gone on to dance in pantomime, revues, musical comedy, opera ballet and music hall, followed by a period dancing for Diaghilev's Ballets Russes in Monte Carlo and elsewhere in Europe. In 1926 she opened her own Academy of Choreographic (sic) Art in South Kensington, but she wanted to expand her horizons: her ambition was to found a serious ballet company in Britain.[10] De Valois thought she should begin by creating a small dance company within a repertory theatre, because she did not

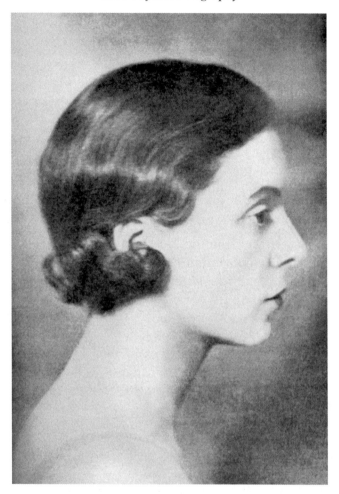

Ninette de Valois. Photograph by Mesdames Morter.
Reproduced in *Dancing Times* (March 1932)

believe that a significant enough audience base then existed to
support a full-time ballet company. She argued that if ballets
could be introduced as part of a theatre repertory season,
support might gradually build until a ballet company could
realistically begin to operate independently. She had already
approached Barry Jackson, a wealthy and often adventurous
theatrical impresario in Birmingham, about this project, but
starting a ballet company was far too risky a proposition for his
liking.

De Valois records that after meeting her Baylis stated:

> that she liked my face; she then added that she thought I
> was practical and appeared to have had a great deal of
> professional experience. She next went on to tell me that
> she had no money and no second theatre as yet; there were
> no rehearsal rooms and there was nothing to be done.[11]

Baylis had received many applications from dancers and dance
teachers wanting to work at the Vic, and she proceeded
cautiously; according to de Valois, Baylis offered to come 'with
her producer (Andrew Leigh) to my private studio to see me
give my students a lesson', because, as she pointed out, the fact
that de Valois could dance did not mean she could teach.[12]
Baylis decided that de Valois's pedagogic skills were of an
acceptable standard and hired her specifically

> to teach the drama students how to move. She said that
> they all had dreadful hands, and that most actors and
> actresses had dreadful hands, and as they did not know
> what to do with their hands, they appeared in the end to be
> even more dreadful; she added that she preferred
> beautiful hands to beautiful faces.[13]

De Valois always stressed to Baylis that a ballet company was
never likely to be a money-making concern, but Baylis decided
she was willing to take the risk. Like many before her, de Valois
took a cut in salary to join the Vic: she was offered £1 a week
for teaching the Vic students and £2 for arranging
choreography for Shakespeare productions, and from this she
earned on average £40 a season. De Valois also trained the
audience members and Vic office workers who volunteered to
dance in the operas; although one had a wooden hand, she
remembers that 'Miss Baylis informed me that an excellent kid
glove was preserved for her special use.'[14] The general
standard, in de Valois's opinion, was 'terrible'.[15]

De Valois started by arranging dances for *A Midsummer
Night's Dream* in 1926 and progressed to opera ballets. Her
hope was that a full ballet company might become a possibility
in the future, if Baylis's plan to open Sadler's Wells became a

reality. For Baylis herself, there was no question but that the Wells *would* open; in her opinion the 'most far-reaching and important events' at the Vic in the 1928-9 season were

> the Old Vic's first tentative efforts at founding a school of English Ballet. Such a development of the operatic side of the work has always been an ideal that the Manager has set in front of her; and in the indomitable hands of Ninette de Valois this idea has been translated into an achievement.[16]

Baylis and de Valois were from such different backgrounds, and had such different world views, that their successful partnership is a real tribute to both women's commitment and determination. De Valois was from a semi-aristocratic, military and Anglo-Irish background. While she was based at the Vic-Wells she often choreographed for her pioneering cousin Terence Gray, who was running an experimental theatre in Cambridge. Gray founded the Cambridge Festival Theatre specifically in order to experiment with and test out his theories on theatre, and he was wealthy enough not to have to worry too much about whether this theatre made a profit. De Valois also moved in experimental theatrical circles: she worked with W.B. Yeats in staging his poetic dance dramas at the Abbey Theatre, Dublin, theatrical events that were almost the antithesis of most of what was on offer at the Vic.

Where de Valois and Baylis connected was in their total, almost ferocious dedication to the job in hand, their willingness to attempt what others assured them was impossible, and their pragmatic, strategic thinking. Both women were also capable of volcanic rage, particularly when faced with what they felt was laziness or sloppiness. Furthermore there was a slightly bizarre connection between them in that, when she was aged eleven, de Valois had briefly been taught by Mrs Wordsworth, an old-fashioned teacher of what was called 'fancy' dancing. Mrs Wordsworth had arranged dances for the early Shakespeare productions at the Vic and it was her dance methods that Baylis had taught to her pupils in South Africa.[17] For de Valois, Baylis was always somewhat limited in her appreciation of dance, seeing everything in terms of 'pretty', which was good, or 'ugly', which was bad, but this may well have been a legacy from Baylis's period of teaching 'fancy' dancing.[18] Baylis also expressed her appreciation for '[t]he perfect dancing of the Astaires', which she thought 'as necessary a contribution to theatrical art as any classical play',[19]

For several years de Valois and her dancers put up with working on opera ballets, interludes and curtain raisers for short operas, plus occasional dances for the drama company, in the hope that Sadler's Wells would give them the chance they needed to grow. The opera ballets, an odd, hybrid form derived from court masques and entertainments, were the focus of de Valois's early work at the Vic.[20] Later on de Valois claimed that, if nothing else, her experience of the form as she encountered it at the Vic kept her sense of self-importance at bay. The opera ballets

> taught me a great deal; the give and take between dancer, producer, choreographer and conductor. I feel the opera ballet work is good for aspiring choreographers – even the ensuing disillusionments! To see your little ensemble smothered by corpulent singers in the background and to realise that the conductor has it all his own way – time after time.[21]

The embryonic ballet company also had to make room for itself in the crowded Vic building, which had only just ejected Morley College from the premises.

Short ballets really started appearing at the Vic in the 1928–9 season, beginning with *Les Petits Riens*, which appeared as a curtain-raiser to the Vic Christmas show *Hansel and Gretel*.[22] By the time of the opening of the Wells in January 1931 the ballet company had grown to seven permanent female dancers, with men engaged as required. This was the year that de Valois agreed to the 'removal of my own private school from South Kensington and its re-erection as the property of the theatre in the famous "Wells Room"' in return for the chance to establish a permanent presence for the school at the Wells.[23] It was also the year that Baylis agreed to produce the first Vic-Wells gala night for the ballet on 5 May. This included guest appearances by Anton Dolin, Stanley

Judson (a fine dancer soon to become lead dancer at the Wells) and Leslie French. All choreography was by de Valois, and music included Mozart's *Les Petits Riens*, Williams's *The Faun*, a ballet sequence from Gounod's *Faust*, Debussy's *Danse Sacrée et Danse Profane*, selections from Schubert and Bach respectively entitled *Hommage aux belles Viennoises* and *Suite of Dances*, and Hugh Bradford's *The Jackdaw and the Pigeons*. As the show was a sellout, with hundreds making do with standing room only, Baylis immediately scheduled a repeat for the following week at the Wells and started programming 'Nights of Ballet' once a fortnight for the following season.

Although the ballet school was initially only for girls, Baylis had plans to increase the number of male dancers; as she cheerfully informed dancer Sheila McCarthy, 'Now dear, I want all you girls to marry all those boys and breed me a nice strong race of male dancers.'[24] While Baylis was always ready and willing to point out the attractions of a male dancer's beautiful behind, she did prefer relationships between theatre personnel to be blessed by marriage: she is reputed to have declared, 'I won't have my students mating in the wings.'[25] She also once stated disapprovingly that de Valois's equanimity on the subject of Vic-Wells love affairs was a result of her spending 'too long in the Russian Ballet'.[26] But Margot Fonteyn remembers Baylis as 'not in the least strait-laced', and given the numbers of young, sometimes underage, girls dancing at the Vic-Wells and its school, Baylis's concern about backstage sexual adventures can be understood.[27]

As with the Vic drama and opera companies, the Vic-Wells ballet could only offer token wages but it did give dancers the chance to work in London for nearly nine months of the year, something no other British classical dance company of the time could rival, and a range of roles that no other company could compete with. The company tended to focus on new ballets – often choreographed by de Valois – which had obvious advantages: the ballets were specifically designed for the small Vic-Wells company, de Valois did not demand royalties, and this in turn kept costs down. Baylis also wanted to promote the work of British artists. Writing in 1934, she claims:

It has been a great source of pleasure to me that British composers, as well as British dancers, have had a chance under the new scheme [at the Wells]. Vaughan Williams's "Job"... is agreed to be a milestone in the history of ballet; Elgar's "Nursery Suite", Gavin Gordon's "Regatta" and "Scorpions of Ysit"; Bliss's "Rout", Lambert's "Pomona"; Toye's "Douanes" and "The Haunted Ballroom" have proved that native dancers need never lack inspiration from native composers. Nor is there a lack of English designers and choreographers – MacKnight Kauffer, Duncan Grant, Vanessa Bell, William Chappell, Frederick Ashton, Hedley Briggs, to name a few at random.

Yes, I believe British ballet to-day has a better chance of survival than it has had throughout the ages.[28]

What this emphasis on new work also meant was that the ballet company acquired a cutting-edge modernity, which played alongside tradition in its classical work.

In 1931, Anton Dolin was warning the Vic-Wells that

[t]o give a performance of "Les Sylphides" with only eight girls, perhaps, instead of the original eighteen or twenty-four, and to cut this or that little dance, alter this particular group because of the inadequate number of dancers to compose it, is to spoil a precious memory for those who saw it many years ago, and give them a justification for saying "Ballet is not what it was".[29]

Eventually, however, de Valois felt confident enough to mount *The Nutcracker, Swan Lake, Coppelia, Les Sylphides, Carnaval* and *Spectre de la Rose*; some of these productions were the first by a British company. Of *Giselle*, with Alicia Markova in the lead, Baylis is recorded as stating

that, in spite of the most wonderful Shakespeare company the Vic and the Wells have yet known, and in spite of what she believes to be the tremendous strides made by the opera, yet [the Vic-Wells *Giselle*] is, in her opinion, the most epoch-making production of the season.[30]

Despite her excitement over the developments in dance, Baylis still expected established ballet stars such as Markova and Dolin to subsidise the Vic-Wells and dance for a token fee. Meanwhile rising stars such as Margot Fonteyn and Robert Helpmann were expected to work for almost nothing, as their work was part of their training. Some of the productions were very cut-price: Pamela May, one of a chorus of only six girls in *Coppelia*, with de Valois as Swanilda, remembers an alarming number of quick changes, in which the chorus had repeatedly to rush offstage, put on different costumes and also change shoes (from point to character shoes, and then back again).[31]

Alicia Markova's subsidy of the Vic-Wells company was particularly generous, and it was critical in helping to build up the company's audience. Baylis began by offering Markova £5 a performance, later adding, 'I want you to do lots of well-paid work but hope you'll manage to come to us in between the good engagements.'[32] But when Markova did do 'well-paid work', Baylis asked that the advertisements identify Markova as a Vic-Wells performer, thus securing useful free advertising.[33] Markova herself was very clear that her relationship with the Vic-Wells was mutually beneficial:

> We served each other. Ninette gave me the classics. She knew I wanted to dance them. She also knew that if she wanted to establish a company she had to do it with the classics. They are the training ground for dancers, just as Shakespeare is for actors.[34]

And in Baylis Markova had a manager who also wrote her fan letters: 'I hope you enjoyed dancing last night. You were in perfect form, and I loved every minute of you'; 'I *loved* your work on Monday. It made me very proud and happy … I am glad that the press was so good – you deserved every word they said.'[35]

The Vic-Wells ballet continued to grow, establishing the Wells as its primary home during the 1935–6 season. For some time Baylis tried to carry on with a true repertory system, with different productions on every night in her two different theatres, but everyone got confused – actors and directors as well as audiences. Theatre reviewer James Agate, dropping in at the Vic to catch the second half of *The Taming of the Shrew*, and expecting to 'snooze out' what he considered a dreadful play, was surprised to hear 'so much music', and very startled to wake up and witness a duel between 'two ruffians' taking place 'in a snowscape'.[36] In fact Agate had picked the wrong theatre: the Wells was showing *The Taming of the Shrew*, but the Vic was playing Tchaikovsky's *Eugene Onegin*. The repertory system also caused extra wear and tear on scenery and costumes, which were repeatedly transported backwards and forwards from the Wells to the Vic, and on one occasion the entire scenery for *La Traviata* got blown off Blackfriars Bridge.[37] Crucially for the ballet company, however, at the Wells there was more space offstage so that exits could be made on the move without the risk of crashing into a wall; the stage itself was far better suited to dance than the Vic stage, which was rough and full of nails; and the acoustic at the Wells was better suited to music, whereas the spoken voice sometimes got lost. Eventually the Vic focused on drama and the Wells on opera and ballet when the terms of their Trusts, which could only be cancelled by the Charity Commissioners, were changed during the 1935–6 season.[38]

The relationship between Baylis and de Valois was critical in the development of the ballet company. De Valois's extensive memoirs are full of respect for Baylis, who receives credit for giving 'London a permanent ballet company'.[39] De Valois also consistently resists seeing Baylis as a joke figure. One of her anecdotes concerns her own production of Constant Lambert's *The Rio Grande*, which originally had a backcloth containing the figure of a distorted nude female statue. The ballet company returned from lunch one day to find that Baylis 'had had the offending nude figure painted out'.[40] De Valois stresses that it was because the 'body beautiful' had been distorted that Baylis acted in this way, although elsewhere she comments: 'It was the action of somebody who thought along the lines of a nineteenth-century member of the Salvation Army and was meant for the best.'[41] The Salvation Army also came to mind for de Valois in remembering the way Baylis took a hand in drumming up audiences:

> [Baylis] was possessed with the fervour of a Salvation Lass
> of her period. Her banner took the form of the famous

green leaflets that we were asked to "mislay" in buses and
tubes. At one time she marched through the streets of
Lambeth and Islington distributing the leaflets at various
houses. She would tell the occupants that she had
something both beautiful and respectable to give to the
general public, and that she had the support and approval
of the Lord.[42]

De Valois not only consistently refuses the easy laugh at Baylis's
expense, she is deeply irritated by the comic anecdotes that
demean her:

> I have no wish to join the ranks of those who succeed only
> in stressing her as a quaint character. In my opinion this is
> to underestimate her wholly. Above all, she was a very real
> person, and it was from this quality that she derived her
> strength of purpose. Mentally, she was not unlike a sincere,
> shrewd, devout peasant.[43]

Overall, de Valois's real appreciation of Baylis is very clear:

> She inspired affection and loyalty from those who worked
> with her. She informed me once that she was very ignorant,
> but she always knew who knew. What she did not know, in
> her great and fearless simplicity, was that she possessed
> something greater than knowledge – a natural wisdom; this
> wisdom sprang from experience, piety and kindliness, the
> paths that lead to human understanding.[44]

De Valois's generosity in her memoirs is particularly striking
given that she frequently suffered from Baylis's legendary
parsimony. Even here she defends Baylis:

> People have called Miss Baylis mean, but I emphatically
> refute this accusation. She thought about money as a
> peasant thinks about it – safer in the stocking than in the
> bank. She thought banks were clever robbers, and
> regarded with suspicion business transactions concerned
> with "loans". She considered any debt as a matter of
> honour eventually requiring honourable discharge: but
> she could not see, if your intentions were honourable, why
> you should be robbed (her views on interest) during your
> struggle to repay.[45]

De Valois suggests that Baylis had a 'housekeeper's mind'; and the association between women and housekeeping led her on to assert that 'Women, therefore, really are best at getting things going.'[46] But there were times when de Valois caught the full blast of Baylis's lack of tact on the subject of money:

> One matinée, I came off the Old Vic stage where I had just danced *Spectre de la Rose* with Dolin. I had an urgent message to go to Miss Baylis at once. I found her sitting at her desk, with the box office returns in her hands. The command was: "Sit down, dear," and wearily I sank into a chair, still clad in poke bonnet and crinoline. "We are losing money on these matinées. What are you going to do about it, dear?" For one fleeting moment the inopportunity of asking a breathless Victorian maiden to consider financial matters must have flashed across my face, for I was told not to worry, but instead, to have a cup of tea.[47]

On another occasion:

> It was a "last night" of the season and ballet night at the Old Vic. I was sitting in [Baylis's] office when she came in to join me. We could hear the shouts that greeted the finish of the ballet. "Hark at them, my dear, shouting away – and you and I have lost £1,000." I personally felt that I had dropped my £500 over Waterloo Bridge. But that was her genius; her personal staff were always kept within the limits of any feelings of extreme optimism or pessimism.[48]

And so in the face of any 'really bad financial setback' Baylis would take it 'entirely upon her shoulders', saying 'never mind, at least everyone is giving of their best – thank God'.[49]

De Valois's various portraits of Baylis are positive and admiring; they are also particularly telling in that they are the assessment of one successful professional woman by another. De Valois resists the Baylis of dance folklore, the Baylis who on seeing a famous leading lady dressed for her role immediately expostulated 'That wig must go back to Gustave' and then when someone explained that the 'wig' was the dancer's own hair retorted 'I don't care what it is, it must go back to

Gustave.'[50] De Valois's appreciative portraits of Baylis also downplay the Baylis who was willing to fight hard, and dirty, in her campaign to establish the Vic-Wells ballet as a serious force. In an attempt to secure better facilities at the Wells, for example, the Vic-Wells governors started buying up local houses, something which was not always popular with the theatre's neighbours, who felt intimidated and under pressure to leave their homes.[51] In a move that presumably would have astonished housing reformer Emma Cons, the governors started hounding recalcitrant house owners to sell out to the Vic-Wells, and the minutes of governors' meetings at this time have very little interest in what the residents' rights or feelings might be. The governors' focus instead is on not letting greedy home owners force up the price of property so that the Vic-Wells might have to pay more than they absolutely had to for the houses they wanted to purchase.[52]

The Vic-Wells also fought a series of very hard-hitting campaigns against any foreign dance companies wanting to visit London during the October to April season that the Vic-Wells operated, arguing that these companies should be denied work permits as they might take away the hard-won Vic-Wells audiences.[53] The Vic-Wells claimed that it was unfair that commercial managers should try to take advantage of their hard work in building an audience for ballet, and they wanted to block such managers from making an easy profit, now the ballet audience existed, by bringing in touring companies from abroad. The commercial managers objected, with reason, that such a ban would effectively grant the Vic-Wells a monopoly for most of the year, and would deprive British ballet-lovers of the chance to see the work of world-class foreign companies. They particularly complained in a 'rather stormy meeting' in 1936 when the Vic-Wells went so far as to prevent the René Blum Ballets Russes de Monte Carlo from visiting Glasgow in order to safeguard the interests of the Vic-Wells ballet in London.[54]

Another area where Baylis was hard-headed and protective of her ballet company was in her increasingly frequent dealings with the leading economist of his generation, John Maynard Keynes.[55] Keynes, a member of the Bloomsbury

Group and intimate of Lytton Strachey, had deeply shocked his peers when he unexpectedly married a woman whom the Bloomsbury set considered to be intellectually beneath him: the Russian dancer Lydia Lopokova. By the time the Wells opened, Lopokova was past her prime as a top dancer, but her name was still enough to guarantee good audiences, and she would occasionally dance for de Valois in order to help the new dance company.[56] Keynes provided further support both by financial contributions from his own pocket and by keeping relations with the Camargo Society amicable.

The Camargo Society had sponsored several major dance productions since its foundation, and one of these was Ninette de Valois's ballet *Job*, based on a scenario by Keynes's surgeon brother Geoffrey. Because of the original sponsorship, the Camargo Society was entitled to a fee when de Valois wanted *Job* performed at the Wells. This situation resulted in protracted negotiations between Keynes and Baylis over prices, with Baylis using all her usual tricks, constantly pleading poverty and trying to chip away at the cost. Keynes might know about economic policy, but what mattered to Baylis was that the Vic should balance its books. She argued over the cost of everything: for example, in 1936 she is writing to Keynes, very pragmatically criticising Cecil Beaton's exquisite costume designs for the next ballet:

> I hate making any suggestion about designs which have given me the very greatest pleasure, but I do, unfortunately, know that the point I make is a practical one, and I feel it is fairer to draw [Beaton's] attention to it immediately. I know that the Camargo hopes, as we do, that *Apparitions* will appear regularly in the programmes for a long time to come, and I feel that the bead flowers will risk shortening, by a very considerable period, the lives of dresses which, in any case, being made of tarleton, are frail.[57]

Baylis is quite right here: the bead flowers would have increased wear and tear on the costumes. She then adds: 'the tassels [Beaton] wanted for the funeral scene would cost too much, would not looped ribbons serve the purpose?' Baylis also importuned Keynes over writing for the *Old Vic Magazine*, and Keynes had to refuse politely, but firmly:

> Lydia has shown me your letter about a contribution to your [*Old Vic Magazine*]. But, I must ask you to let us off this effort. I am too busy to manage it.[58]

Although he died in 1946, Keynes was one of the architects of government subsidy of the arts in the post-Second World War period, and it is tempting to speculate that his thinking must have drawn on – and indeed reacted to – his extensive experience of dealing with the entirely unsubsidised Vic-Wells theatres and their begging, wheedling, persistent and extremely canny manager.

What Baylis had to offer in return for Keynes's and Lopokova's generosity to the Vic-Wells ballet was an opportunity for Lopokova to act. Baylis allowed the Vic-Wells's 1933 production of *Twelfth Night* to be, in effect, sabotaged by Lopokova's appearance in the role of Olivia. Lopokova's pronounced Russian accent was incomprehensible to most people and was much ridiculed by reviewers. Virginia Woolf, embarrassed at being asked by Lopokova to review the production, occupied as many column inches as she could with a general meditation on the difference between reading and seeing a play by Shakespeare, thus delaying the moment when she would actually have to pass comment on Lopokova's performance.[59]

Not all of Baylis's support for crossovers from ballet to acting were this disastrous: she personally encouraged one of her male dancers, Robert Helpmann, to move into acting, and he had a long and very successful career as a Shakespearian and later a film actor. But while Baylis's support for Lopokova upset the Shakespeare reviewers, there is no question that it paid long-term dividends for the ballet: in 1934 Keynes announced that the Camargo Society's rights to ballets, and its existing resources including scenery and costumes, would be divided between the Vic-Wells ballet company and Rambert.[60]

Ballet, like opera, is hard to produce on a shoestring. Baylis might have enjoyed telling first-night ballet critics who 'went into raptures about the lovely head-dresses … [that] they had all been made from "a few pennorth of pipe-cleaner and ping pong balls"' but, besides Keynes, many other generous supporters were needed to provide subsidy for dance at the Vic-Wells.[61] Dance bills for quite enormous amounts were picked up by Mrs Sebag Montefiore, and a very generous and ongoing donor to the Wells Theatre was Harry Lloyd.[62] Mrs Laura Henderson, more famous now for her Windmill Theatre than for her sponsorship of the ballet, also arranged via Vivian Van Damm to sponsor a tour of the Vic-Wells ballet headed by Alicia Markova. Henderson knew that this philanthropic venture was going to cost her a vast amount of money, and Baylis made sure it generated much valuable, and free, publicity for the Vic-Wells. And when Baylis outrageously said she couldn't afford a wooden floor for the 'Wells Room', even though the concrete floor risked damaging the dancers' knees, Lady Moyne came to the rescue and paid for a wooden floor to be laid over the concrete floor.[63]

There was some controversy about who was actually going to see the ballet and whether it was elitist or popular in its appeal. Musicologist Edward Dent writes:

> It is amusing to see how the proletarian theatre which Miss Cons and Miss Baylis thought they were creating has brought forth a type of ballet which is anything but proletarian in its appeal – not indeed a ballet for the aristocracy of imperial Moscow, but certainly for the intellectuals of Bloomsbury.[64]

But Baylis never gave up on the 'proletarian' audience, and it was only after her death that seat prices for her dance companies were allowed to soar. Dent's view is also challenged by an article in 1931, in the *Era*, which claims Baylis is

> making ballet come to life in London, on the sixpences and the two-and-fourpences of Rosebery-avenue; not on the subsidies of the green beer snobs of Chelsea.
>
> She is making her own school of ballet, where working-girls can go in the evenings to learn the gracious art.[65]

The *Daily Express* concurs, maintaining that Baylis 'created an English ballet with a working-class audience', while Alicia

Markova certainly remembers very unBloomsbury behaviour from audiences who, at the end of a ballet, would throw pennies on the stage to contribute to Vic-Wells funds.[66] And one Islington working-class boy, Leo Kersley, certainly spent many nights at the Wells:

> Sixpenny stools hired in the morning on the way to work (or school) were occupied by 6.30: one sat on one's stool for half an hour and what more natural than to chat to one's neighbours? Then after a shortish run up the stairs one put one's coat on the preferred seat and hey! for another hour of serious discussion in the bar, over tea and a sandwich.[67]

The ballet gallery crowd at the Vic-Wells occupied the cheapest seats in the house, and became famous, even notorious, for their enthusiasm and rapturous applause, which certainly upset some commentators. Actor, composer and theatre historian Dennis Arundell fulminates about the galleryites' lack of discrimination and their 'unbalanced loyalty', and claims that 'the sex-frustrated clapping by hearty females at the Wells' encouraged 'among the less dedicated dancers a dangerous complacency'.[68] More reasonably, de Valois, who actually agreed that the effect of excessive applause on dancers was bad, suggested that while 'Upon such occasions one has often heard the audience blamed for the ensuing hold-up ... it would be fairer to censure the artist.'[69]

Other crucial supporters of the Vic-Wells ballet included conductor, composer and musical director Constant Lambert, whom de Valois describes as 'entirely responsible for the musical evolution of British ballet'.[70] As musical director, Lambert would suggest composers and scores to fit ideas and scenarios for new ballets and thus he had a crucial input into the development process. Lambert's driven lifestyle, his heavy drinking and his affairs (such as his relationship with the young Margot Fonteyn) did not distract him from unstinting, energetic and inspirational service to the young Vic-Wells ballet.[71] Arnold Haskell describes Baylis's motto as:

> "If you want anything done, always go to the very best

person. The best people understand." Since she was always in debt she added "and they usually are prepared to do the work for its own sake." They were *for her*.[72]

Lambert was one of the best, and he gave generously and recklessly to the Vic-Wells ballet. And yet Baylis never asked more of others than she asked of herself.

By the time of Baylis's death, the Vic-Wells ballet company consisted of twenty women dancers and twelve men, two resident choreographers, a resident conductor and a ballet school of around forty pupils.[73] A special issue of *Dancing Times* focusing on Baylis's work claims she was

> one of the first to visualize the establishment for the first time in English theatrical history of a permanent ballet in a repertory theatre, and ... actually the very first to give practical expression to this ambition.[74]

A less grand but equally appreciative perspective is provided by Joy Newton, one of the original seven permanent dancers in the 1931 company. She remembers Baylis as

> that unforgettable lady, who, among many other activities, would play the piano inexhaustibly while the members of her companies danced "Sir Roger de Coverley" at her annual Christmas parties, and through whom, and with whom N[inette] de V[alois] was able to realise her great ambition to establish her Ballet Company and School.[75]

Newton's memory offers a connection all the way back to Baylis's career in South Africa, when she taught the 'Sir Roger de Coverley' and other dances in conditions as pioneering, in their own way, as those encountered thirty years later by Ninette de Valois in London. And for Baylis her love of dance always did connect back to South Africa. As she herself said in a speech given at a dinner held in her honour just before her death,

> I am an ancient person in my 40th year at the Vic, but I used to be a great person in the dancing world in the goldfields of South Africa.[76]

NOTES

1 Lilian Baylis, 'Myself When Young'.

2 Evelyn Williams, 'How They Began: I: The Sadler's Wells Ballet', *The Dancing Times*, July 1950.

3 *OVM*, November 1922.

4 *OVM*, October–November 1924 mentions Aikin's voice production classes. Letters to Miss (that is Laura) Smithson (M&M) show that Baylis put her friend Ivy Smithson's sister forward for the job but the Vic committee preferred Aikin.

5 Clarke, *The Sadler's Wells Ballet*, p. 36. See also *OVM*, October–November 1924.

6 Clarke, *The Sadler's Wells Ballet*, p. 50.

7 *OVM*, September–October 1925 and the Executive Committee minutes of 8 May 1925.

8 The Camargo Society was founded by Arnold Haskell, Philip Richardson, Edwin Evans, John Maynard Keynes and Lydia Lopokova.

9 De Valois, *Come Dance With Me*, p. 31.

10 Kathrine Sorley Walker, *Ninette de Valois: Idealist Without Illusions* (London, 1987), p. 61; Clarke, *The Sadler's Wells Ballet*, p. 37. The academy was initially funded by de Valois's stepfather.

11 De Valois, *Come Dance With Me*, p. 79.

12 The other applicants are mentioned by de Valois in interview in 'Lilian Baylis – a Portrait of "The Lady"', radio broadcast, 1997; the quotation is from Ninette de Valois, *Step by Step: The Formation of an Establishment* (London, 1977), p. 32.

13 De Valois, *Come Dance With Me*, p. 79. Baylis kept a print of Dürer's 'Praying Hands' on her desk.

14 Ibid., p. 80.

15 De Valois interviewed in 'The Lady', 1974 radio broadcast.

16 Quoted in Clarke, *The Sadler's Wells Ballet*, p. 51. See the Old Vic's Annual Report for 1928–9.

17 Harcourt Williams, *Old Vic Saga*, p. 26. The Annual Report for 1914–15 records that Mrs Wordsworth's dancers appeared in *The Tempest*, *A Midsummer Night's Dream* and *Macbeth*.

18 De Valois interviewed in 'The Lady', 1974 radio broadcast.

19 Baylis, '"Light" Shows and the Classics'.

20 Ninette de Valois, 'The Opera Ballet' in Kathrine Sorley Walker, *Ninette de Valois*, pp. 148–51.

21 Ibid., p. 151.

22 Clarke, *The Sadler's Wells Ballet*, p. 50.

23 De Valois, *Step by Step*, p. 27.

24 Of course a significant number of the Wells male ballet stars were gay.

25 Eric Phillips, 'Memories of the Old Vic', *The Listener*, 14 February 1957. Baylis may also have encouraged marriages amongst Vic personnel, as she followed nineteenth-century practice in paying married couples less on the assumption that they would pay less rent once they could share lodgings.

26 De Valois, *Come Dance With Me*, p. 81. For Baylis's appreciation of Robert Helpmann's 'nice little bottom' see Elizabeth Salter, *Helpmann* (London, 1978), p. 53.

27 Margot Fonteyn, *Margot Fonteyn: Autobiography* (London, 1975), p. 42. See Meredith Daneman, *Margot Fonteyn* (London, 2004) for an account of some of the affairs being conducted backstage at the ballet.

28 Lilian Baylis, 'Preface' to Kate Neatby, *Ninette de Valois and the Vic-Wells Ballet*, ed. Edwin Evans (London, 1934), pp. 8–9.

29 *OVM*, December 1931.

30 *OVM*, February 1934. De Valois, *Step by Step*, p. 29 records that the steps were taught by Nicolai Sergueeff, with the help of Lydia Lopokova, who translated his Russian into English. This was the first time Markova danced Giselle. The Vic-Wells also gave Markova her first opportunity to dance the leads in *Swan Lake* and *The Nutcracker* (see Ninette de Valois in Harcourt Williams, *Vic-Wells*, p. 97).

31 Sarah Lenton, audiotape, 2001.

32 Quoted in Anton Dolin, *Markova: Her Life and Art* (London, 1953), p. 158.

33 Ibid., p. 165.

34 Maurice Leonard, *Markova: The Legend* (London, 1990), p. 129.

35 Letters quoted in Dolin, *Markova*, pp. 165, 177. See also Baylis's letter of gratitude for Markova's 'lovely work' and generous help dated 5 May 1934 (ibid., p. 179).

36 James Agate, *Ego 2: Being More of the Autobiography of James Agate* (London, 1936), p. 60.

37 Tyrone Guthrie interviewed in 'Lilian Baylis – a Portrait of "The Lady"', radio broadcast, 1997.

38 Arundell, *The Story of Sadler's Wells*, pp. 194, 209. Speaight, *William Poel*, pp. 62–3 comments acidly on the Wells, 'it is difficult to understand how the governors of the Old Vic, not to mention Miss Baylis herself, who had imbibed, mainly through Robert Atkins, the essentials of Poel's teaching, could have

sanctioned a building so inimical to speech of any kind whatsoever'. Like the Vic, the theatre allowed smoking (Arundell, *The Story of Sadler's Wells*, p. 188).

39 De Valois, *Step by Step*, p. 33.

40 De Valois, *Come Dance With Me*, pp. 81–2.

41 Ninette de Valois in Roberts, *Lilian Baylis*, pp. 41–2.

42 De Valois, *Step by Step*, p. 35.

43 De Valois, *Come Dance With Me*, p. 80. This again points to the class chasm between the two women.

44 Ibid., p. 84.

45 Ibid., pp. 80–1. Roy Tremayne, who was hounded by Baylis when he owed her money (see Chapter 10), would probably take a different view.

46 Ninette de Valois in Roberts, *Lilian Baylis*, p. 42. Astoundingly, de Valois then avers 'Then the men do have to take over.'

47 De Valois, *Come Dance With Me*, p. 83.

48 De Valois, *Step by Step*, p. 33.

49 De Valois, *Come Dance With Me*, p. 33.

50 *Dancing Times*, July 1974.

51 Executive minutes, 1937, e.g. 7 May, 10 September, 8 October; in the 8 October minutes it is actually suggested that since an inhabitant named Mr Siani has no right to be in his house owing to a mistake made by his solicitors, 'the roofs be removed from the houses', presumably in order to drive him out.

52 Arundell, *The Story of Sadler's Wells*, p. 186 also records that there was some general opposition to the Wells and quotes an irate tax payer who didn't want their taxes spent on the theatre. However, Baylis did support the work of housing associations in Islington and Finsbury (see photograph on p. 245 and the obituary in *The Islington Gazette* for 29 November 1937).

53 See Executive Committee minutes for 25 October 1933; the minutes for 8 March 1934 announce the intention to fight the proposal that the Ballets Russes visit Covent Garden; on 11 October 1935 the Executive was discussing the threat posed by the Woizikowsky Ballet, who wanted to appear at the Coliseum, produced by Oswald Stoll; the minutes for 8 May 1936 report that the Fokine Ballet has been denied permission to perform at the Alhambra until 15 May so that competition with the Vic-Wells would be less of an issue.

54 Executive Committee minutes, 13 November 1936, plus separate sheet offering an account of the meeting.

55 The Royal Ballet School archive includes several items relating

to Baylis and Keynes – contracts, terms and conditions and a series of letters – which are the primary source of information for this paragraph.

56 Milo Keynes (ed.), *Lydia Lopokova* (London, 1983), p. 23 discusses a television recording of Lopokova rehearsing with the Vic-Wells Ballet in June 1933.

57 Letter dated 11 January 1936, Royal Ballet School archive.

58 Letter dated 10 December 1935, Royal Ballet School archive.

59 *New Statesman and Nation*, 30 September 1933.

60 Clarke, *The Sadler's Wells Ballet*, p. 93.

61 *Birmingham Daily Mail*, 2 December 1937.

62 Gratitude to Mrs Sebag Montefiore was recorded in the Executive Committee minutes of 11 September 1936. Thanks to Harry Lloyd appear in the minutes of 16 July 1930. De Valois, *Come Dance With Me*, p. 113 pays tribute to an anonymous benefactress who backed the ballet company's provincial tours for two years. At this time Mrs Amy Sebag Montefiore was also giving money to Morley College, as the Principal, Eva Hubbock, was writing to her (as 'Aunt Amy') to thank her for her donation (Morley College archive box 15, letter dated 7 October 1935).

63 De Valois, *Come Dance With Me*, p. 101.

64 Dent, *A Theatre For Everybody*, p. 113.

65 *Era*, 27 May 1931. The ballet school charged, according to one undated prospectus in the Royal Ballet School archive, £13 6s 8d per term for 12–14 weeks, while private lessons were 7s 6d each.

66 *Daily Express*, 26 November 1937. Alicia Markova interviewed in 'Lilian Baylis – a Portrait of "The Lady"', radio broadcast, 1997.

67 Leo Kersley, 'A Reminder of the Past', *Dancing Times*, January 1998. Kersley first visited the Wells at the age of eleven, when Baylis was up with the 'hoi polloi in her gallery'. He became a Wells devotee, trained as a dancer and later led the Sadler's Wells Theatre Ballet, 1945–50.

68 Arundell, *The Story of Sadler's Wells*, p. 207.

69 Ninette de Valois, Invitation to the Ballet (London, 1937, reprinted 1953), pp. 108, 109.

70 Ninette de Valois in Roberts, *Lilian Baylis*, p. 41.

71 See Daneman, *Margot Fonteyn*.

72 Arnold Haskell, *Ballet Since 1939* (London, 1946), p. 11.

73 Ninette de Valois in Harcourt Williams, *Vic-Wells*, p. 97.

74 *Dancing Times*, March 1932, p. 659.

75 Letter from Joy Newton in the Royal Ballet School archive.

76 *Star*, 25 November 1937.

[10]

The 1930s

The 1930s brought new triumphs for Baylis, but her health was beginning to suffer: constant stress and decades of crisis management were taking their toll, and Baylis had to cut back on the explosive, stand-up rows that had been such a feature of her dealings with her Shakespeare directors Philip Ben Greet and Robert Atkins. Despite being interviewed in 1925 as an example of 'How to be Fit at Fifty', by the early 1930s Baylis (who at 5 feet 5 inches tall weighed 14½ stone) had diabetes, high blood pressure and angina.[1] On 30 January 1932 she had a hysterectomy and was still haemorrhaging heavily a month later.[2] Instead of resting, she carried on with work, and then in June embarked on a touring holiday which took her down through France to Biarritz (although the itinerary did include Lourdes, where she went into the bath with the rest of the pilgrims).[3] It is not surprising that Baylis suffered from ongoing attacks of exhaustion and when she saw her friend Ramsay MacDonald only a few days before his death, Baylis commented: 'He looked so tired, my dear. And, my dear, when you're as old as I am, you will know what tiredness means.'[4]

Despite her health problems, however, Baylis was planning positively for her retirement, and with this in mind she bought property in Hastings: 10 Rotherfield Avenue, a terraced house with a glorious view across the cliffs to the sea. Baylis still loved swimming in all conditions; in 1934 she enjoyed a holiday where

> I was standing on the edge of a derelict pier in a remote corner of Ireland wondering whether to dive or to jump into a rather unpleasant-looking sea, when suddenly a huge wave settled the question for me decisively by pulling me in, head over heels.[5]

Portrait of Lilian Baylis by Cecil Leslie (1931), National Portrait Gallery, London

Baylis continued to seek out chances to swim at every opportunity – often insisting on being driven through the night so that she could enjoy an early-morning bathe, and making a note in her diary in 1930 that Lambeth baths were now offering an experience advertised as 'Musical Bathing'.[6] On holidays she continued to enjoy scenery – her diary for the touring holiday to Biarritz is full of appreciation of woodlands, the Pyrenees and the silver sands as well as beautiful churches, religious statues and the cathedrals at Orleans and Chartres.[7]

Although Baylis enjoyed taking holidays in Wales, she also often combined these holidays with forays to local Eisteddfodau in the hope of talent-spotting a star tenor in the making.[8] However, she particularly fell in love with Oxwich, near Swansea, and paid for Leslie Gomay, one of the Vic-Wells scenery painters, to decorate the ceiling of St Illtyd's Church with a painting of the rainbow from the book of Genesis (symbolising God's covenant after the Flood).

As Baylis had finally begun to acknowledge that she should rest and recuperate properly, her diaries also begin to record regular appointments for massage, alongside the more frantic round of rehearsals, auditions, dress fittings with a couturier called Felicia, and power lunches with the Women's Provisional Club. It is likely that this Club is where Baylis met the woman, Cecil Leslie, who painted Baylis's portrait in 1931 (see p. 227). Leslie was an etcher, an illustrator of children's books, a still-life, flower and portrait painter, and a woman who became Vice President and later President of the Women's Provisional Club.[9] Minutes of the club meetings are full of compliments to Leslie on her ability, as secretary, to secure lively and entertaining speakers for the meetings. In the autumn of 1930 Baylis sat several times for Leslie, and the resulting portrait was exhibited in early 1931.[10] Although this was a difficult, stressful time for Baylis, she appears comfortable and relaxed, and she has her favourite ornament – an acrobat – by her side. The overall image is informal and not at all the classic Baylis of the anecdotes. While Leslie does not go as far as Ann Dalston, who in 1930 found a much gentler image than usual to portray and painted Baylis in profile so softening the visual impact of the paralysis around her mouth, what is really striking about Leslie's portrait of Baylis is the complete absence of references to the Vic-Wells.

Baylis was beginning to face the fact she would have to leave her theatres behind at some stage. In 1928 she announced on radio that 'before long' she would like 'to hand over my managership secure in the faith that the work would go on'.[11] There were, however, no obvious candidates. Baylis explored the possibility of following Emma Cons's example in passing on her theatrical empire to her niece, and Lilian Baylis junior was seriously considered by Baylis as a potential heir before family disagreements put an end to this idea.[12] By the mid 1930s Baylis was ceding more and more power to Tyrone Guthrie in running the Vic-Wells Theatre Company, and to Ninette de Valois in running the ballet.

Before this, however, Baylis had to weather one of the biggest challenges of her management career. She reopened Sadler's Wells Theatre on 6 January 1931 with a huge gala celebration, and a speech from Sir Johnston Forbes-Robertson. The elderly Dame Madge Kendal, who had worked with Samuel Phelps, was present in the audience as a link back to Sadler's Wells's fame in the nineteenth century under Phelps's management. The play being performed was *Twelfth Night* (on Twelfth Night), whose very first line – 'If music be the food of love, play on' – reminded the Shakespeare audience that music and opera were also going to be a force to be reckoned with at the Wells. John Gielgud, who was playing Malvolio, vividly remembers Baylis's speech on that grand occasion:

> Lilian carried a huge basket of fruit in her right hand, and when she began her oration her gestures were somewhat hampered by her burden. However, she ploughed bravely on until, enthralled by the force of her own argument, she swept her right arm out impulsively. An enormous apple fell from the basket with a thud. There was a slight titter from the audience. Lilian looked at the basket, and then, edging towards the truant apple, tried to hide it with her robes. She went on with her speech, but soon sincerity overcame technique, and the basket shot out to the right to accentuate another point. This time a pear fell on to the stage. I gave one look at it and burst out laughing. The audience followed suit, and the solemnity of the occasion was irrevocably shattered.[13]

Unfortunately, there was less to laugh about in terms of finances. The western world had plunged into massive economic depression, and January 1931 was a time when the last thing many people could afford was to go to the theatre.

Only three months after the opening it became 'an open secret that during the past few weeks the management has been forced seriously to contemplate the closing-down of Sadler's Wells, temporarily at all events.'[14] It was only the ballet which in 'a year of bad fortune' had been able to carry on being 'almost uniformly successful and self-supporting'.[15]

Around this time Baylis was also involved in a car accident. Although her own driving was reckless and terrified her passengers, Baylis had always managed to avoid serious traffic accidents, but her chauffeuse Frances Edith Mary Clarke was not so lucky. During the drive home after a banquet to celebrate the reopening of the Wells, Clarke overtook a taxi and crashed into a motor coach in Portman Square. She was later summoned for driving without due care and attention, and Baylis had to appear in court as a witness. This accident was the occasion on which, having been identified as 'Miss Baylis of the Old Vic', Baylis surfaced, uttered the famous line '...*and* Sadler's Wells' and then collapsed. She was able to laugh about the incident but later insisted that, on a night given over to celebrating the opening of the Wells, 'I could not bear to have my new acquisition ignored.'[16]

Baylis needed an operation to aid her recovery, and the Vic Executive insisted that she take a holiday to recuperate.[17] She went through a real personal crisis, suffering severe depression that stemmed mainly from the huge – and increasing – financial burden posed by Sadler's Wells.[18] The initial launch of the fundraising drive had been immediately hit by competition:

> Unfortunately for our Appeal the Festival Theatre at Stratford-on-Avon was burnt down at this juncture, an event which naturally caused almost world-wide concern and interest. Thousands of pounds were soon subscribed for its rebuilding and we meanwhile had to struggle on as best we could with our Appeal somewhat overshadowed by this other catastrophe. Then came the worst financial crises in the history of our Land. The Theatre was ready, but there was a debt of £27,000 on the building. The fact that we could give work to more than two hundred families – at

a time when unemployment was so terrible – was weighed against the burden of the debt.[19]

Baylis 'plumbed depths of despair', but an unexpected and anonymous cheque for £1,000 in US dollars enabled her to avoid the heartbreaking decision of closing Sadler's Wells; this donation, as she put it, 'saved my life's work'.[20] As always, however, Baylis kept her eyes on the pennies as well as the thousands of pounds, and when, in 1934, she applied for an alcohol licence for Sadler's Wells, she put in for a bar backstage as well as front of house, arguing that there was no reason why her backstage crews should spend money in a nearby pub when they could be spending it at the Wells. And even local children at Queens Head School were subjected to the full force of Baylis's fundraising rhetoric when she implored them to donate pennies and halfpennies to the Wells, impressing on the young girls that they would benefit from their donations when they grew up and went to the theatre, and that the Wells would belong to them in a very real sense because of their contributions.[21]

Ironically, given her ongoing financial crises, Baylis was increasingly being seen by her contemporaries as an extremely successful theatre manager, and in 1934, in recognition of her outstanding work in music and theatre, Birmingham University awarded her an honorary doctorate. The degree ceremony was very different from the M.A. at Oxford. Baylis relates:

> I had expected the ceremony at Birmingham would be very much like the impressive, almost religious atmosphere of the Sheldonian. I had not realised, however, the established precedent of "ragging" by the students at Birmingham. They let me off comparatively lightly, except that they very audibly counted my steps up to the platform (there were nine) ...
>
> The Public Orator ... made his speech in English and not in Latin as the Vice Chancellor did at Oxford, so that I did not miss any of his charming and heart-warming compliments on our work, and was very happy that the honour was for Music as well as Drama.[22]

Baylis was also increasingly seen as a celebrity to be interviewed and feted. For example, in 1930, *Queen* magazine headlined a feature on Baylis with the panegyric: 'The Soul of the Old Vic: An Interview with the Creator of England's National Theatre, Miss Lilian Baylis, whose Indomitable Enthusiasm, Energy and Courage have made Stage History in this Country.'[23] Two years later *Queen* revisited Baylis, and bestowed a similarly rapturous headline upon her: 'The Woman Who Has Made Stage History: Miss Lilian Baylis Talks About the Theatre of Yesterday and To-day.'[24] Finally, in 1937, Baylis was interviewed for *Queen* by Elizabeth, Lady Kilbracken, who finds 'greatness' in her and describes her as running the *de facto* National Theatre.[25]

Baylis also disseminated her ideas, and publicity for the Vic-Wells, by means of the articles she wrote. In 1933, in the *Toc H* journal, Baylis took the opportunity to spell out again her favourite sense of mission in relation to the theatre, arguing, as she had on previous occasions, that the goal of acquiring a cheerful outlook on life despite 'distress and trade depression' could be achieved by

> keeping our minds fit as we keep our bodies fit, by exercise; by escaping, now and again, from this painfully real world into the great countries of the imagination, with the thinkers of the ages as our guides. We may find this way of escape in books, in paintings, in music; but the easiest, most accessible way is still by means of the drama; the theatre and all it comprehends. As a vehicle for broadening people's minds, as a means of teaching, the theatre is still what the mediaeval church recognized it to be – the greatest weapon they possessed.[26]

But Baylis, of course, had very definite ideas on how people's minds were to be broadened, something highlighted by her contribution to a debate, hosted by the theatrical newspaper, the *Era*, in 1936, on Illusion versus Reality. Here she states:

> If by "illusion" you mean unreality, then I am all in favour of "realism" ...
>
> Briefly, I believe that the function of the stage is to help

the audience by translating them into a more intense emotional atmosphere, thereby extending their sympathy, and helping them to lose themselves for the time being.

It seems to me that this can most easily be done by the representation of Life; whether the actual life of to-day or yesterday, or the ideal life of a wished-for to-morrow, does not seem to me to matter.

The main thing is that the emotional appeal of the play should be something real, and should be founded on something which can awaken a response in the hearts of the various members of the audience.[27]

It would appear that, under Baylis, the Vic-Wells would be in no hurry to stage the work of Bertolt Brecht.

By the mid 1930s Baylis was much in demand as a public speaker; for example, in 1936, she gave a 'charming speech' containing 'just that element of humour and human interest which we would expect' to the Electrical Association for Women.[28] Speeches usually included a fundraising dimension: at one luncheon 'adulatory speeches were poured forth so gushingly that one expected her to be in tears', but Baylis got up 'and almost brusquely suggest[ed] that if they thought so much of her they had better help her theatres'.[29] Baylis also now routinely attended high-profile events – the unveiling of the memorial to Emmeline Pankhurst in 1930; Royal Ascot with Alicia Markova as a guest of the Sainsburys; the Malvern Theatre Festival, where she socialised with George Bernard Shaw (whose plays were now appearing at the Vic, and who often attended rehearsals).[30] Baylis also cut a record in March 1936, to accompany the release of a collection of recordings of operatic 'Stars of the Old Vic and Sadler's Wells'; here she recounts the history of her work at the Vic, before launching, predictably, into an appeal for funds.[31] Her voice is clear, precise and rather formal. The following year Baylis appeared on television, in a programme entitled 'Picture Page' (see p. 234). She was interviewed by Leslie Mitchell, and spoke about her (nearly) forty years at the Vic before introducing three current Vic-Wells stars: Joan Cross, Marie Ney and Pearl Argyle, representing respectively opera, drama and ballet. The women then took questions from the audience. Subsequently

Lilian Baylis being filmed for BBC television 'Picture Page', 29 September 1937 (standing figure is Pearl Argyle). Courtesy of the Mander and Mitchenson Theatre Collection

Baylis was disappointed to find out that after she had taken a great deal of trouble to dress up in her best clothes, she was only visible on the screen from the waist up.[32]

Baylis sat for another formal portrait when Ethel Gabain, a lithographer, painter and etcher whose son Peter Copley joined the Vic Company in 1932, painted her in 1936 (see front cover illustration).[33] Baylis is holding one of her famous green leaflets, her preferred means of disseminating information about the Vic-Wells repertoire; the image is dignified, centred and peaceful. This, however, provides something of a stark contrast with the reality of her life in 1936, when, amongst all her other commitments, she made one of the most prestigious of all her public appearances, addressing the 1936 International Federation of Business and Professional Women in Paris.

Baylis took for her subject 'Women in Theatre Management' and, rather modestly, claims that 'pressure was brought to bear upon' her 'to accept' the invitation to speak.[34] She had spent a weekend holiday in Paris with Beatrice Gordon Holmes before the conference, and after the conference finished Holmes took on the financial management of the Federation: Baylis is among the people Holmes identifies as supporting her in networking on behalf of the Federation, and helping her to set up a UK branch.[35]

The 1936 Paris conference brought together an impressive assembly of women who were successful in a wide range of fields: barristers, politicians, academics, stockbrokers. Baylis socialised enthusiastically and was entertained by the British Ambassador, Sir George Clerk, who gave a luncheon in her honour: guests included Harley Granville-Barker and the Duchesse de la Rochefoucauld.[36] At the conference she met Lena Madesin Phillips, who was president of the Federation, and Senator Franciska Plaminkova, the Czech campaigner for women's rights, who was vice-president; she rubbed shoulders with Dean Leonard of the University of Illinois, and with Madame Elsa Schiaparelli; she encountered the then still disenfranchised Frenchwomen who were staging suffrage protests, particularly during the radio broadcast of a speech given by Frances Perkins, US Minister of Labour and the first woman to serve in the US cabinet.[37] Baylis kept in touch with several delegates and also carried on speaking to gatherings of career women after this event: in 1937, for example, just days before her death, Baylis addressed the Birmingham and Midlands Association of University Women, an audience of around eighty.[38]

In her speech at the 1936 conference Baylis constructed a history of the impressive achievements of women who had, like her, managed theatres.[39] While most of these women, unlike Baylis herself, were also professional actors and were operating within the actor-manager tradition, Baylis's stress is always on these women's business acumen, their successes and their pioneering spirit. Baylis argues that many women have run theatres 'indirectly' as 'the wise and untiring helpers of their husbands' and cites Ellen Terry as an example of a woman who, while working in an intimate relationship with a man who was not her husband, Henry Irving, was crucial in always 'keeping the peace at rehearsals and performances'.[40] Baylis's sisterhood of women theatre managers is wide-ranging and goes far beyond the legitimate theatre, but she is particularly intrigued by her own theatre's record in this area:

> At my Vic, in 1820, Mrs. Henry Beverley was managing, and Eliza Vincent from 1851 to 1856. At Sadler's Wells, our second theatre, Alice Marriott was manager from 1869 for five years.[41]

In her notes Baylis also implies that inspiration for the subject of her lecture came from another well-connected, high-profile woman:

> When Queen Mary, as Princess of Wales, visited the Vic three weeks before the death of King Edward VII she noticed various playbills in my Box, and one of the first things she said was "how interesting that a woman managed this theatre before" (that was a reference to Miss Vincent who managed the Old Vic for some years in the middle of last century).[42]

Baylis is particularly careful about listing several husband-and-wife teams in which she argues that the wife was the real manager: the Bancrofts, the Kendals, the Comptons, the Trees (she also celebrates the management career of Herbert and Maud Beerbohm Tree's daughter Viola), the Forbes-Robertsons, the Martin-Harveys, the Bensons.[43] Importantly, because they were always in a league of their own as far as Baylis was concerned, she also foregrounds the work of the husband-and-wife team of Matheson Lang and Hutin Britton, who really got Shakespeare started at the Vic. She applauds the work of Eliza Vestris, Sarah Lane, Sarah Thorne, Millicent Bandmann Palmer, Annie Horniman, Lady Gregory, Mary Moore, Gertrude Kingston, Mrs Henderson (who 'started at the Windmill 3 years ago the 1st non stop Variety'), Lena Ashwell, Sybil Thorndike (an odd choice, as Thorndike is not remembered as a director), Violet Melnotte, Nancy Price.[44] The rather dry list of women's names was clearly meant to be elaborated upon during the actual lecture: Baylis notes tersely that she should speak on the '[a]dvantages of a woman in the position – iron curtains and temperamental artists etc. Some of the difficulties, lack of space and storage, always trying to make ends meet.'[45] At this point the speech starts to head in the direction of one of Baylis's habitual pleas for donations to the Vic, which would make sense, given how wealthy some of the women in her audience were.

Baylis's speech was much mentioned in newspapers at the time and reported in full (it is claimed) in the *Era*.[46] Here she is quoted as stating:

> Women have done great things for the theatre, not only in our own times but in an almost unbroken line for over a century ...
>
> During the last sixty years one could mention a succession of outstanding women managers, not only in London, but in other great cities of England.

Baylis's lecture also offers further evidence of her phenomenal capacity for work. It is extremely impressive that with so little time on her hands, and with little formal training, she could produce such a history. It may be that the pressure of the occasion pushed Baylis into doing something she would not have done otherwise in constructing her hall of fame. However, her ongoing attempts to memorialise the work of Emma Cons, her care in keeping family papers over the years, her involvement in and authorship of a wide range of histories of the Vic, and her support for the Vic-Wells Association's attempt from 1931 onwards to construct an archive for the theatres, all suggest that Baylis did believe that developing alternatives to mainstream histories was an important activity.[47]

Baylis did not do all the research for this lecture entirely on her own: a series of supplementary notes exist, which are not in her handwriting, and which supply details as if replying to specific queries from Baylis.[48] The note-maker suggests some names to add to Baylis's list: Mrs Henry Beverley (at the Vic), Madame Beatrice (in the provinces), Mrs H.L. Batsman. The note-maker queries the inclusion of Fanny Stirling in the list, and confirms that Mrs Bancroft and not her husband 'was at all times the responsible manager'. Baylis has also scribbled on her notes the names of other women managers in London she might mention: Lillie Langtry, Olga Nethersole, Mrs Patrick Campbell, Gladys Cooper, and Alice Marriott at Sadler's Wells.

While in her notes Baylis doesn't conclude anything about the women managers' achievements, it is evident that she saw herself to a certain extent as heir to these foremothers, and a sister-in-arms with contemporary women theatre managers. Baylis takes a moderate feminist position in arguing that it was important not to forget these women's achievements. She was soon to discover, however, that as a theatre manager she could not afford to be too overtly political in her public statements. When she returned from the Paris conference excited and energised by her experiences, she wrote about it for the *Old Vic Magazine*.[49] Here she also describes a pre-conference event:

> Rachel Behrendt, whom some of you remember as Esther in "Caste", which we gave to celebrate the birthday centenary of her grandfather, Tom Robertson, took me to the People's Theatre on Sunday night to see Romain Rolland's "Le 14 Juillet", in which the leading characters were taken by well-known players from the Théâtre Français and the crowds played by the people. At the fall of the curtains the excitement rose to great heights; the players waved red streamers and green branches. A minute's silence was asked for and the huge audience stood, remembering their comrades who had fallen that week in Spain; I too stood and prayed for all who had died fighting. Then The Marseillaise was sung, and the great multitude stood with raised arms and clenched fists to sing their own anthem – The Red Flag – twice through,

everyone at the highest pitch of excitement. When the curtain finally fell the orchestra rose too and sang the anthem as the three thousand earnest, excited people left. It was most moving and I was thrilled from my toes to my hair.

In 1936, with fascism generally on the rise in Europe, and with Communists and Fascists at loggerheads in Spain, the admission of being 'thrilled from my toes to my hair' at the singing of 'The Red Flag' was guaranteed to generate controversy. In addition, *Le 14 Juillet*, written by Rolland in 1902, was a key work in the left-wing Théâtre Populaire movement and a celebration of Socialist values.[50] A furore followed, and the next issue of the *Old Vic Magazine* had to make a public statement that Baylis was not a Communist. The article declared:

> The Manager ... is a woman of one idea. There is no room in her life for Right, Left, Centre or anything but the Old Vic. and Sadler's Wells, and Full Houses at both Theatres.[51]

While Baylis the manager had to appear politically neutral, she was certainly not completely hostile to socialism: in January 1930, Baylis's *Old Vic Magazine* gave space to J.T. Grein to hold forth on the values of 'The Socialist Theatre', an idea being put forth then by the Independent Labour Party; Baylis had a close friendship with Ramsay MacDonald, Britain's first Labour Prime Minister; and, after her death, the *Daily Worker* claimed that Baylis was one of the Labour movement's 'deepest and most trustworthy friends', a 'far better friend of the gallery than the stalls'.[52] The *Daily Worker*'s claim seems slightly extravagant, but Patricia Don Young, in her record of her experiences of training as an actor at the Vic during 1936–8, was impressed by Baylis's insistence that the gallery was 'the most important part of the house'.[53]

In some ways Baylis's attendance at the 1936 Paris conference was the apotheosis of the way she liked to work: networking amongst women. So it is not surprising that during the 1930s she made it a priority to attend the luncheons and dinners run by the Women's Provisional Club, where she would continue to meet professional and successful women and hear about their work and the challenges they faced. The Women's Provisional Club was probably where Baylis reconnected with the woman who was later to become her companion at the Paris conference, Beatrice Gordon Holmes. Holmes was a suffrage activist, a stockbroker, an articulate and outspoken woman, and someone who admired Baylis intensely.[54] Holmes's uncle Jack had been in love with Baylis in South Africa, and Holmes herself portrays Baylis as wearing the willow for her lost lover for the rest of her life.[55] Holmes first met Baylis ('a young, attractive girl') when she began learning the banjo from her in Kennington, London; however, Holmes's 'temperamental grandmother' ordered the visits to stop.[56] The ban kept the two women apart until they met 'at a women's club'.[57] Once back within Baylis's orbit Holmes, despite her unconventional, high-powered city career and her thrilling adventures being driven through Europe by her girl chauffeuses, was soon having her car commandeered on Sundays to take performers to the St Giles home for lepers in Essex.[58] Holmes also frequently visited France and Belgium for the weekend with Baylis and Holmes's mother, 'whom [Baylis] adored', for a shopping spree.[59] Both Holmes and her mother, like most people, found Baylis's spoilt dogs a severe trial but Baylis had dinner with the two women every week, and Holmes describes Baylis as an excellent cook who often murmured in the middle of a public speech, 'Many's the proposal I've had over the frying pan!'[60] For Holmes, Baylis was 'shrewd, masterful, humorous', and remarkable for 'her casualness, her calm rudeness, her crooked smile, and her darling friendliness and personal affection'.[61]

During the 1930s Baylis also hit it off with another extraordinary (and unmarried) woman, Gertrude Stein. Ninette de Valois remembers

> Lilian Baylis and Gertrude Stein taking a call together – a delicious sight that was much to the liking of the audience. There was a great bond of sympathy between these two. "The Lady" found "the Stein" most intriguing.[62]

The occasion was the premiere of *The Wedding Bouquet,* a piece devised by Lord Berners and Frederick Ashton and based on Gertrude Stein's play *They Must Be Wedded to Their Wife,* which was produced at the Wells on 27 April 1937. Stein may not have been immediately identified by everyone in the Sadler's Wells audience as one of the most famous lesbians of her generation, although she had been living with Alice B. Toklas since 1907 and *The Autobiography of Alice B. Toklas* appeared in print in 1933. Nevertheless the expatriate, Paris-based American novelist, essayist and poet was associated with racy art-world figures such as Picasso, literary greats such as Hemingway, and *avant garde* taste makers and breakers of the literary salon circuit. The rapport between Stein and Baylis, for those who were not blinkered, would have added to the picture of Baylis as a woman at home with unconventional and assertive women, and for de Valois, even forty years after the event, this was 'a vision not easily erased!'[63]

Further light on Baylis's liking for working with successful and single women is shed by the autobiographical writings of Margaret Webster, who worked at the Vic as an actress before she departed for America to start a high-profile career there as a director. Webster was part of a leading theatre dynasty, a supporter of women's suffrage and an intelligent and articulate woman who turned down a place at Oxford in order to work in theatre.[64] Webster wrote extensively about her life experiences in several different books, but even when writing in the late 1960s she felt she could only hint at her lesbian identity.

Webster remembers Baylis as 'that dumpy, homely, rather comic aging woman with the peculiar cockney-colonial accent'.[65] She comments:

> Many of the stories about her are probably apocryphal, but everyone believed them immediately because it was impossible to exaggerate Lilian. However absurd the anecdote might be, it always cut to the heart of the matter.[66]

Webster in fact relates several Baylis anecdotes including one about actor Ernest Milton. When Milton told Baylis he was having a phone installed and he would phone her, Baylis replied, 'Very nice, dear … Come to me in your joys and come to me in your sorrows, but not in between because I've no time for chitchat' – a reasonable if abrupt response from an extremely busy woman.[67]

Baylis hired Webster after seeing her perform in Vanbrugh's *The Confederacy*. Webster felt she had not acted particularly well, and Baylis's comment was 'long part, dear – lot to do'.[68] However, Baylis then hired Webster to play a not dissimilar role – Toinette in Molière's *The Imaginary Invalid* – in which Webster had very considerable success. For Webster, Baylis had an uncanny ability to watch an audience and 'read the resulting graph to a hair';[69] the judgements that ensued 'were devastating, but they were shrewd'.[70] Baylis's pragmatism is also stressed: Webster relates how one night when Maurice Evans was onstage playing Iago in *Othello*, he realised that the theatre cat was onstage with him:

> Two seconds later Lilian's voice was heard from the wings. "Pussy, Pussy, pretty Pussy," said she in wheedling tones, and made alluring smacking noises with her lips. When this failed she tried poking at the cat with a broom. When that, too, proved useless, she reached firmly onto the stage, perfectly visible to the audience, seized the animal by the tail and yanked it off. It was typical Baylis technique, as applied to all problems.[71]

Webster also recalls that, after what Webster felt was her rather poor performance as Lady Macbeth, Baylis commented to her 'in a voice rough with commiseration … "Yes, dear. Just like giving birth isn't it?"' Webster reports she 'was grateful; though I didn't quite see how either of us should know'.[72] After her experiences of working at the Vic-Wells, Webster went on, in 1936, to begin a career in the United States, working as a director alongside performer Maurice Evans and designer David Ffolkes, producing Shakespeare on Broadway. All three had worked together at Baylis's Vic-Wells and they went on to break box-office records with a whole series of Broadway Shakespeare productions.

In 1934 Virginia Woolf wrote a letter to Ethel Smyth (who

besieged Woolf for some time) describing Baylis as a '[g]allant old bus horse ... a fine figure of a woman', and I would argue that seeing Baylis through the lens of her interactions with Woolf, Holmes, Gertrude Stein and Margaret Webster offers a useful corrective to the more antipathetic view of her put forward by Tyrone Guthrie or Edward Dent.[73] However, given the company Baylis kept, it is not surprising that the Vic-Wells acquired the reputation of being a 'lesbian stronghold'.[74] This worried some, and Richard Findlater's 1975 biography of Baylis is at pains to set the record 'straight' here. Findlater explains that although Baylis was often assumed to be lesbian because she was

> a dominating unmarried woman whose closest friends and colleagues (monks and clergymen aside) were mostly women (most of them unmarried); and because those who did not know her believed her, quite wrongly, to be mannish and butch[,]

nevertheless 'Lilian was, in fact, for all her brusqueness and bossiness, a very feminine woman.'[75] Findlater's nervousness here, and his eagerness to dissociate Baylis from lesbian women, originates in the testimonies of Kathleen Clark, the Vic box-office clerk, Baylis's secretary Evelyn Williams and her chauffeuse Annette Prevost. Indeed Findlater quotes Clark and Williams, who felt they had to warn Baylis not to hire a woman whom he excitedly describes as a 'proselytising lesbian' actress; they later claimed, in speaking to Findlater, that Baylis was deeply shocked by their revelations about this actress's sexuality. It is tempting to imagine what Holmes would have made of this story, and given that Baylis spent so much time with Holmes, socialising with her weekly, it is worth noting how forthright Holmes was on the subject of homosexuality. In her autobiography, Holmes labels Radclyffe Hall's 1928 novel *The Well of Loneliness* as disappointing in its lack of precise details concerning lesbian sex and declares unapologetically:

> Ordinary people who prate of homosexuality haven't the remotest idea what they are talking about, don't know that real homosexuality is an extremely rare thing. And, above

all, don't know that it's completely suitable and natural for all human beings to form deep and tender attachments, permanent or passing, irrespective of sex or age – and rather unnatural if they don't.[76]

It was possibly on Holmes's recommendation that Baylis listed Radclyffe Hall's novel *The Master of the House* as potential reading in her 1933 diary;[77] this novel actually finds Hall in fervent religious mode, which would have suited Baylis, but after the trial and subsequent suppression of *The Well of Loneliness* in 1928 it was impossible for anyone who read newspapers to be unaware of Hall's sexuality, and Clark and Williams seem here to have somewhat underestimated their manager.

In 1925 Baylis made a public statement that she had led a 'highly moral', which presumably means celibate, life.[78] However, Rosemary Auchmuty makes the point that in the 'lesbian witch-hunt' which followed *The Well of Loneliness* trial many women who might be read as lesbian became extremely wary and cautious in their behaviour.[79] Certainly, while some of Baylis's letters are intensely revealing, there is also clear evidence of censorship in her personal archive.[80] Baylis knew for a long time before her death that she was a potential stroke or heart-attack victim, and during the 1930s she was thinking about how she wanted her life presented to the public as she was engaged in collecting materials together for a biography. It is entirely possible that she destroyed some items which presented a side of her she did not want in the public domain.

Nevertheless, whatever her views on, and knowledge of, lesbians or bisexuals such as Beatrix Lehmann who worked in her theatre, it is absolutely beyond doubt that throughout Baylis's management the Vic constantly promoted the work of women. The theatre must have gained a reputation for being a place where ambitious women who were serious about their theatrical careers could set about creating important, if poorly paid, work. This was signalled in a variety of ways including the domination of all areas of work by women during the First World War and the various productions of Ethel Smyth's work. There was also the *Old Vic Magazine*, which crows when three

Lilian Baylis opening a new housing estate in Islington c. 1930.
Courtesy of the Getty Collection

out of four plays being performed at the Vic are by living
women authors – Cicely Hamilton, Rose Fyleman and
Clemence Dane – but complains in 1931 that 'this season
began with plays which scarcely gave the women of the
company a chance'.[81] Baylis not only had close friendships
with successful, professional women such as Holmes, Hamilton
and the pageant director Gwen Lally, but a month before her
death she was still contributing to the suffrage cause: on 15
October 1937 she wrote, as part of a public petitioning of the
Prime Minister, to request an honour be conferred on
Emmeline Pethick-Lawrence, the high-profile editor of *Votes
for Women* and founder of the Votes for Women Fellowship.
Baylis jotted a postcard to Miss Newsome, who had asked for
her support in this matter:

> Delighted to write as you ask re E.P.L. Can you give me
> points, details of activities, I know how she worked for the
> Suffrage and with her husband such a splendid Helpmeet

her charm and commitment etc.[82]

In asking for recognition of Pethick-Lawrence's suffrage work, as in constantly promoting the work of women in her theatres, Baylis was still holding true to the ideals of Emma Cons.

Emma Cons must also have been in Baylis's mind when she decided to offer full support to the 1937 summer theatre festival held at the Buxton Opera House. One reason Buxton – or the local aristocracy, the Dukes of Devonshire – deserved support in Baylis's eyes was because of her gratitude to their late relative Lady Frederick Cavendish. 'Lady Fred' had been a friend, a constant and extremely generous benefactor of Emma Cons. She was one of the original governors of the Vic, and through the early years of the twentieth century this former Maid of Honour to Queen Victoria inveigled royalty into attending important Vic events and badgered her rich friends into supporting the Vic in every way possible.[83] The Vic-Wells contribution to the Buxton Festival, however, was not without controversy. A local vicar, Canon Scott-Moncrieff, condemned the immorality of the Vic performing *Ghosts* and *Measure for Measure*, two plays focused very much on sexual immorality (the other play in the repertory was *Pygmalion*). Baylis went into print to defend *Measure for Measure*, picking up very precisely on Scott-Moncrieff's complaints:

> The moral of *Measure for Measure* seems to me to be "Judge not that ye be not judged" … if this play be … "disfigured by a persistent and exaggerated employment of the sex motive", the same disfigurement appears in the Old Testament and most of the works of St. Paul.[84]

This was a rather different Baylis from the one who, allegedly, after a dress rehearsal for *Measure for Measure* in which the Isabella was so chillingly chaste that the scenes with Angelo were becoming passionless, commented 'Well, dear – all we can do now is get on our knees and pray for lust.'[85] The Buxton season saw Baylis on top form in terms of anecdotes: one Baylis curtain speech blithely ignored the stalls and dress circle, which were packed with fashionable patrons, and reproved the house with the words 'I don't want to see the gallery looking like this again please. It is nearly empty.'[86] On discovering that the dressing rooms at Buxton were dirty, Baylis also countermanded a suggestion that two charwomen be sent for: 'Don't get two. Get one good one. Two will only waste time in talking.'[87]

The other major theatrical outreach that summer, however, kept Baylis's stress levels very high. In June part of the theatre company set off on a prestigious, profile-raising trip to play *Hamlet* at Kronborg Castle, Helsingør (Elsinore) in Denmark as part of the King of Denmark's silver jubilee celebrations. This trip was fraught with problems. Rehearsals in the castle itself were almost impossible because tourist visitors were there during the day. Bad weather hampered out-of-hours rehearsals in what was being set up as an open-air arena. Rehearsals had to run through the night and Baylis stayed up through it all to provide support and refreshment, some of it alcoholic, for the exhausted actors. When the local Danish band, which was providing the music, tried to get a share of the keg of rum she had secured for the Vic actors, Baylis slapped the bandleader's backside and told him the rum was only for 'her people'.[88] In the end, the performance in the presence of the King and Queen of Denmark had to be moved inside to the hotel ballroom because the weather was so bad that an outdoor performance would have been dangerous. The resulting performance was as bare-boards as the Vic used to be in the early days of the Shakespeare Company, it was in the round, and it was improvisatory, as there was not enough time to block the production properly before the gala performance. The excitement and energy this brought to the production inspired the director, Tyrone Guthrie, with new ideas (which he would promulgate for the rest of his life) on the virtues of the open stage.[89] For Baylis, however, this would have been a return to the performance style of the Gypsy Revellers back in the 1890s: flexible and responding to the crisis of the moment. It was also a style of performance Baylis had kept in touch with through the years: as part of her work with the leper community at St Giles's, Baylis asked stars of the Vic-Wells to perform on the most rudimentary of stages at East

Hanningfield, and she even, on one occasion, transported the entire theatre company away from their usual stage sets in order to present *Arms and the Man* in 'an old army hut' for the lepers.[90] Annette Prevost, writing in the *Old Vic Magazine* for September–October 1937 about the performance of *Hamlet* at Helsingør, certainly thought Baylis deserved some credit for what was already being considered an astonishing success. Prevost reports that as soon as it became clear that the performance could not take place outside as had been planned, Baylis began reconnoitring: 'Miss Baylis, long used to emergencies, had already spied out the hotel ballroom.'[91] While 'the same idea' came into 'Tyrone Guthrie's mind', Guthrie's published account of the event ignores Baylis's contribution to the crucial decision-making process.[92]

What was really distressing Baylis on the trip to Denmark, however, was the soap opera that was being flagrantly played out in the Vic-Wells company. While Laurence Olivier (Hamlet) and Vivien Leigh (Ophelia, who had been brought in, at Olivier's insistence, to replace the original Ophelia, Cherry Cottrell) canoodled very publicly, Alec Guinness was deployed to distract Olivier's wife Jill Esmond, in order, presumably, to delay the inevitable show-down. Annette Prevost tried to reassure Baylis:

> Someone mentioned that you were worrying yourself about a certain trio at Elsinore sorting itself out into the wrong 2 plus 1. But it's common knowledge that things were wrong *ages* before then and I'm convinced the same end would have been arrived at whether they'd gone with us or not. So *don't* worry please.[93]

More stress piled on after the company returned home and began rehearsals for the play that is seen as cursed, *Macbeth*. Baylis was particularly looking forward to a visit to the theatre by the new Queen, formerly Elizabeth Bowes-Lyon of Glamis. 'Glamis will see Glamis', Baylis was quoted as saying.[94] But by the time of the opening night, Olivier had flu and Guthrie judged that the director Michel St Denis had not got the production ready, so he postponed the first performance. This was a terrible blow to Baylis, brought up as she was on the 'show must go on' mentality. As Laurence Olivier puts it,

> I think the disgrace of a last-minute postponement in one
> of her theatres came as a terrible shock to her. Never in the
> history of the Old Vic under her management had such a
> thing happened.[95]

In fact opera productions had been postponed before this, but
the problem for Baylis was that the *Macbeth* opening had been
delayed on what for her were shaky grounds: the production
was not thought to be ready artistically. In her view, unless
artists were at death's door or had completely lost their voices,
they had a duty to their audience, and they ought to go on.
Indeed Prevost's account of the Elsinore *Hamlet* stresses
precisely this attitude to performance: the great success of the
event was not its artistic achievement but that 'we had refused,
against terrible odds, to let our public down'.[96]

It was in the period between the scheduled and the actual
opening of *Macbeth* that Baylis died. On 25 November 1937
Baylis died after collapsing with shock the previous day when
her sister Ethel came running into her home, yelling out that
one of Baylis's beloved dogs had just been run over and killed.
Her death certificate records the cause of death as angina
pectoris but she was also simply worn out.[97] Beatrice Gordon
Holmes went to see Baylis in her coffin and could no longer
find 'the streak of gamin in her crooked smile – but only an
old and very tired woman. I had not realized her age and how
much her tremendous work had aged her until then.'[98]

On a personal level, Baylis was well prepared for death.
Ninette de Valois remembered that

> [a]t the commencement of each season [Baylis] has always
> made a round of the dressing-rooms presenting the artists
> with a sprig of heather. This autumn [1937], for the first
> time, she gave everyone rosemary ... but she need not have
> made this change, for it is impossible that the English
> ballet could ever forget.[99]

Letters from Baylis to Prevost written on Baylis's last holiday
with Louie Davey in Wales during the summer of 1937 also
suggest a woman ready for, and accepting of, death. She

comments that 'Davey wants a boat & to take me for a row', while she herself just wants to rest; but because Prevost was about to have an operation, Baylis – despite her exhaustion – takes the time to discuss her own experiences of going under an anaesthetic:

> I've never felt much difference in waiting for an op, to having a tooth out, there is the possibility of passing on, & when, as you have always done, your duty and really tried to be thoughtful and helpful in everything, you can have no fears. My only fear has been in case I fail to face life bravely when one has to work again, that wants all one's courage. It really is an adventure and directly the 1st day or 2 of discomfort is over, just to be obedient, no other duty, is very wonderful and one has so much to thank God for, I've always grabbed my hanky and prayed I may breathe steadily and quietly as I lay down on the operating table, just the thought "To God I commend my spirit" and I close my eyes feeling *certain* God is close to me, really more at peace than any other time in my life.[100]

Baylis's great faith made her confident of the afterlife: for her, death was merely a transition.

After her death Baylis's body lay in state at St Agnes's church in Kennington, the church where she usually worshipped, where she had had a stations of the cross erected in memory of her parents, and where she had been district visitor until 1909. Her mentor Father Andrew conducted Baylis's funeral and recorded that

> Lilian's Requiem and Memorial Service were quite beautiful. Her dear ashes rest on Mrs. Bentley's grave in our Guild Ground in the Cemetery. There I laid her, and down came the rain; not a fragment would have been disturbed. I love to think that her grave is with us.
>
> She had the selfless, direct simplicity of a very high quality of sanctity, and never conventional, she was always orthodox.[101]

The Guild's base at Plaistow was well known to Baylis, who went there every year for St Philip's Day, and, on several occasions, for retreats. Donations in Baylis's memory were requested to be made either to the St Giles home for lepers or to the Vic-Wells completion fund. There were several remembrance services and requiems, including a service in St Martin's-in-the-Fields on 1 December, when the church – coincidentally, but appropriately – had a stage and backcloth erected around the altar, in preparation for that year's Nativity play. A service at St Edward's, Cambridge, was arranged at the request of actress Marie Ney, then on tour with the Vic theatre company.

Just before she died Baylis seemed to be at the peak of her success. The Vic-Wells finances were healthy: she had cleared the theatres of the massive debt that had been a source of worry and insecurity since the takeover of Sadler's Wells. Three days before her death the theatres were able to announce they were out of the red and had 'a respectable balance of working capital'.[102] Baylis also left a considerable personal estate – £10,037 11s 2d gross, £8,261 8s 8d net – a clear indication that by the end of her life she had become a woman of substance. She had at least two associates who may have been advising her on money matters: economist John Maynard Keynes, or stockbroker Holmes (who made a fortune on the stock exchange). But there were several squabbles over Baylis's estate. Annette Prevost and Baylis's sister Ethel fell out over Baylis's mandolin, both claiming that they had been personally promised it. Ethel argued that in 1932 Baylis had assured her she would get the instrument and that this was appropriate as Ethel's daughter, Gladys, had performed solos on the mandolin.[103] Ethel then offered to buy Prevost a replacement instrument. As Prevost was not known for her mandolin-playing talents, that was clearly not why she wanted to possess it. Prevost consulted lawyers, and her friends and relatives expressed disapproval of Ethel's lack of consideration for Prevost.[104] Although Prevost only met Baylis for the first time in 1932, she seems to have seen herself as indubitably the woman closest to Baylis at the time of her death, and the rightful guardian of the Baylis legacy.[105]

Ethel also got quite a shock when she found that she was not, as she had assumed she would be, the only beneficiary of Baylis's will. After small bequests to the Society of the Divine

Compassion, to William Townsend (a Vic stalwart who had
started working for Emma Cons when he was only twelve years
of age) and to employees in proportion to their years of
service, the bulk of Baylis's estate was left to Ethel (but only in
trust during her lifetime) and then to Baylis's nieces: Ethel's
daughter, Gladys Dunning, and, in Australia, Lillias Violet
Sebrah Bordas and her daughter, Shirley Bordas.[106] From
1934, when she moved to England from South Africa, Ethel
had become accustomed to living off her elder sister and, as
the settling of Baylis's final accounts reveals, Baylis had been
paying for the nursing of Gladys Dunning for some time. Ethel
did inherit Baylis's cottage at Hastings, but she had expected to
acquire 27 Stockwell Park Road as well. The London house,
however, was to be put up for sale, and Prevost was allowed to
live there until the sale went through. As Ethel and Gladys still
assumed they had the right to stay at Stockwell Road when they
were in London, this caused more friction with Prevost.

Ethel's expectations were not entirely unreasonable.
Indeed Baylis's earliest will, made in 1905, left her musical
instruments to her brother Willie but most other possessions
to Ethel and Liebe (except for trinkets given to Baylis by her
aunts, Emmie and Ellen, which her brothers Ray and Willie
were to have).[107] In her will of 6 February 1932, Baylis
instructs her sister, Ethel, to sort out Baylis's affairs and 'if very
good homes cannot be found for the dogs, they must be put to
sleep by Vet.'[108] Baylis specifies that she wants, like Emma
Cons, to be cremated at Golders Green crematorium and that
her ashes should be scattered in the East London Cemetery;
she asks for 'as little trouble as possible'. If she were to suffer
from a long, lingering illness Baylis requests that she be nursed
by Anglican sisters. Although Ethel was in the end
disappointed with the legacy she received, she did have her
sister Lilian to thank for the comfort in which she and her
daughter Gladys were able to live in the years after Ethel's
separation from her abusive husband.

With Baylis's death, a struggle to establish what her life and
achievements meant also began. This struggle was made all the
more complex simply because Baylis's personae were so
dazzlingly various: the comic manager telling off the audience

and calling them 'bounders' was nothing like the bereft niece writing to her parents, narrating the details of Emma Cons's death; the solemn, religious woman writing down careful accounts of her spiritual experiences after doing her best to test out their reality seems nothing like the woman who demanded to see Alec Guinness's legs and only then commented, 'You'll do',[109] the woman who hung out the train taking photographs of the Canadian Rockies seems little like the dignified woman responding on behalf of the honorary graduands at the Birmingham University ceremony. Baylis could on different occasions be the disingenuous old lady ('I'm just an ignorant woman'), or the canny beggar haggling over money with Keynes, or the confident, assertive professional addressing her peers at the Paris conference.

It was in the obituaries that the battle lines over how to remember Baylis were drawn up. Sybil Thorndike, writing for the true believers, the Vic-Wells faithful who read the *Old Vic Magazine*, maintains that Baylis 'was a mystic' with the fire of 'a St Joan'.[110] A few months later she adds:

> There was a real kinship between the peasant saint and her … one who has a real vision of God and of the work she is called to do – no thought of self – just a shouldering of a burden with never-ceasing courage – never sitting down and saying "I've done enough", asking nothing for herself – how like these two were! … Joan must have been as insistent – as irritating – as impossible in her demands as Lilian was.
>
> Lilian said to me one day: "Fancy a girl like that being able to face generals, kings and bishops and make them do what she knew was right – it's difficult enough with the Vic, but thinking of Joan is a help to me." Lilian would have faced anything if it had been asked of her. Like Joan she took every problem to the altar …

In dramatic contrast to the sentiments of Sybil Thorndike (a woman who, with Baylis's death, had lost a very dear friend and mentor) the *Observer* critic St John Ervine states in his obituary that Baylis was 'too much of an old maid in too many respects'; he claims that 'Many of the productions done at the Old Vic would have been booed off the stage of any other theatre'; and that Baylis 'generally did not know what she was talking about, so far as acting and the drama were concerned'.[111] And six months after Baylis's death Ervine resumed his attack. Baylis

> very conscientiously ... became a public character ... Saint Lilian and Shylock Baylis ... the Siamese Twins of the Waterloo-road ... She was a born boss, and nothing gave her greater pleasure than to domineer over other people ... She was a very bad business woman – a great deal of the financial trouble of the Old Vic was entirely due to her and her aunt's incompetence – and she made no bones about pushing a favourite on to the stage when that favourite's unfitness for the job was evident to everybody.[112]

In addition Baylis had a 'small shop-keeper's mind', and yet she

> succeeded in imposing upon the world a legend of herself as a mixture of Joan of Arc, Saint Teresa, and Florence Nightingale ... She was a pathetic, lonely figure, uneasy in company, and forced because of her shyness and disease to assert herself in a rough and often brutal manner. Her notions of herself were entirely romantic.

To a certain extent, Baylis's performance of the public persona of manager of the Vic, which entertained some and exasperated others, made this kind of battle almost inevitable. Very few people felt neutral about her – they either loved or loathed her – although it is also noticeable that women, in general, tended to be more appreciative of her, and men more aware of her shortcomings. And as Cicely Hamilton comments, in her *Time and Tide* obituary for Baylis, many found it

> hard to understand how, being what she was, [Baylis] had attained her goal and raised her two theatres to success. Being what she was: a woman with no looks to boast of, no natural graces of manner – who yet got work, and the best of work, not only from women but from men.[113]

She added, presumably as a riposte to St John Ervine, that there is no point in debunking someone who is not considered great.[114] Certainly the bare facts of Baylis's achievements remain undeniably impressive. In his obituary in *The Listener*, Harcourt Williams quotes Herbert Menges's bald summing up: 'No man has ever successfully run two theatres, presenting Shakespeare, Opera and Ballet, but a woman has done it.'[115]

NOTES

1 Weight recorded in Baylis's diary, 17 April 1931 (M&M).

2 Details recorded in Baylis's diary for 1932 (M&M). Backscheider, *Reflections on Biography*, p. 133 points to the importance of registering 'Women's Events' in a biography and Baylis's ability to run her theatres at this time must have been affected by this 'woman's event'.

3 OVLB/000160 – this typescript journal is not written by Baylis and refers to her as L.B.

4 Quoted in the *Yorkshire Post*, 26 November 1937.

5 'The Manager's Foreword', *OVM*, September–October 1934. Details of the holiday in Northern Ireland are in Baylis's diary for mid July 1934 (M&M). Baylis was accompanied by Davey on the holiday.

6 Diary, 2 September 1930 (M&M).

7 Diary, 9 June 1932 onwards (M&M).

8 See *South Wales Evening Post*, 25 November 1937. e.g. Neath in 1933 (*OVM*, January 1934), Fishguard in 1936 (*Daily Herald*, 26 November 1937).

9 For Cecil Leslie's career see B. Peppin and L. Micklethwait, *Dictionary of Twentieth Century British Book Illustrators* (London, 1983), pp. 182–3. Minutes of the Women's Provisional Club are held in the Women's Library, London.

10 Sketching sessions by Leslie are recorded in Baylis's diary (M&M) from 30 September 1931. The Old Vic and the National Portrait Gallery both have versions of this portrait. Ann Dalston's portrait hangs on a staircase at the Vic.

11 Baylis, 'Aims and Ideals of the Theatre'.

12 OVLB/000027/5, from Lilian junior to Lilian senior and written 1 December 1930, states that Lilian junior longs 'with all my heart to be doing a bit at Sadler's Wells' but she feels she cannot leave her mother, Katie.

13 Gielgud, *Early Stages*, pp. 111–12.

14 *OVM*, April 1932.

15 *OVM*, April 1932.
16 Baylis, 'A Greatest Hour'. The dinner was hosted by the OP Club on 15 March 1931 and was reported in *The Stage*, 19 March.
17 Executive minutes of 25 March 1931.
18 Baylis, 'A Greatest Hour'.
19 Lilian Baylis, 'The Old Vic and Sadler's Wells', p. 7. Her diary for 1931 (M&M) adds up the staff numbers and totals it at 259.
20 Baylis, 'A Greatest Hour'.
21 'The Diamond Jubilee of Sadler's Wells', broadcast 1991, includes reminiscences from three women who had been importuned by Baylis in this way whilst at school.
22 'The Manager's Foreword', *OVM*, September–October 1934.
23 Interview by Patricia Hyde, *Queen*, 8 October 1930.
24 Interview by Louise A. Coury, *Queen*, 24 February 1932.
25 *Queen*, 21 October 1937.
26 Baylis, '"The Old Vic" and "The Wells"', p. 108.
27 *Era*, 1 January 1936.
28 OVLB/000061.
29 *Yorkshire Observer*, 4 December 1937.
30 Baylis notes the opening of the Pankhurst memorial in her diary for 6 March 1930 (M&M). Baylis's Ascot visit is recorded in her diary for 19 June 1934 (M&M). Alicia Markova remembers that Baylis 'was not really interested in the race – so we ate strawberries and cream at the back of the box whilst everyone else was rather more concerned with spotting the winner' (Roberts, *Lilian Baylis*, p. 46).
31 This consisted of a boxed set of three disks (HMV RLS 707).
32 Letter from Cecil Madden, *The Stage*, 28 March 1974.
33 The portrait was exhibited by the Royal Society of British Portrait Painters. Executive Committee minutes of 11 February 1938 record that Gabain (or Mrs Copley) was giving the portrait to the Vic-Wells. See *OVM*, December 1936 for details of the exhibiting of the portrait. The portrait is now housed at Sadler's Wells.
34 Baylis, 'Busman's Holiday'.
35 Holmes, *In Love With Life*, p. 174.
36 Baylis, 'Busman's Holiday'.
37 OVLB/000151/2–5; the British Federation of Business and Professional Women Bulletin for May–July 1936 supplies some of these details in its report on the conference. The *Daily Sketch* in 1936 (unidentified clipping Box 13, Vic-Wells Association

collection, Blythe House) also mentions that in 'An Independence Night for Women' Baylis was one of the many women honoured in receptions in twenty-seven countries around the world all on the same night. Baylis was honoured for work in theatre alongside aviator Amy Mollison and Ellen Wilkinson for work in industry (Wilkinson campaigned for suffrage, and became a Labour MP in 1924; in 1936, as MP for Jarrow, she led the Jarrow march, and in 1945 she became the first woman Minister of Education).

38 OVLB/000009.
39 The Bristol archive holds notes, several drafts and correspondence concerned with this address: e.g. OVLB/000146; 000146/10; 000149.
40 OVLB/000146/2.
41 Lilian Baylis, 'Women and the Theatre; a Glowing Tribute', *Era*, 26 August 1936.
42 OVLB/000146/1.
43 OVLB/000146/3.
44 OVLB/000146/10.
45 OVLB/000146.
46 Baylis, 'Women and the Theatre'; however, the text reproduced in the *Era* differs from OVLB/000146.
47 The Vic-Wells Association first issued a call for help in constructing the archive (now lodged at the Theatre Museum, Blythe House) in the *OVM* for January 1932. They asked particularly for donations of programmes and *OVM*s pre-1924.
48 OVLB/000146.
49 *OVM*, September–October 1936.
50 My thanks to David Bradby for information about the French theatre.
51 *OVM*, November 1936.
52 *Daily Worker*, 26 November 1937.
53 Patricia Don Young, *Dramatic School* (London, 1954), p. 13.
54 Holmes, *In Love With Life*, pp. 141, 63. Rosemary Auchmuty (in 'By Their Friends We Shall Know Them') is the only commentator on Baylis who has previously taken Holmes's writing into account.
55 For Holmes's uncle Jack and his engagement to Baylis see Chapter 3.
56 Holmes, *In Love With Life*, p. 138. Baylis's diary for 22 June 1930 (M&M Theatre Collection) records Holmes visiting her hut at Betchworth, so the women had remet by then.

57 Holmes, *In Love With Life*, p. 138.
58 Ibid., p. 140.
59 Ibid.
60 Ibid., p. 141.
61 Ibid.
62 De Valois, *Come Dance With Me*, p. 118.
63 De Valois, *Step by Step*, p. 29.
64 Webster, *The Same Only Different*, p. 273.
65 Ibid., p. 337.
66 Ibid.
67 Ibid. Sometimes this anecdote is told in relation to Milton announcing his engagement to be married.
68 Ibid., p. 337.
69 Ibid., p. 333.
70 Ibid., p. 338.
71 Ibid.
72 Ibid., p. 356. Webster played Lady Macbeth in the 1932–3 season. For Baylis as motherer see, for example, Russell Thorndike, 'Lilian Baylis', p. 186; Evelyn Williams in Harcourt Williams, *Vic-Wells*, p. 32 records that in early years Baylis's nickname for the Vic staff was 'Mother' and this later became the rather stuffy 'The Lady'.
73 Virginia Woolf to Ethel Smyth, 29 July 1934.
74 Findlater, *Lilian Baylis*, p. 240.
75 Ibid., p. 241.
76 Holmes, *In Love With Life*, pp. 134–6.
77 Diary for 1933, preliminary notes (M&M). The 1933 diary is the one where Annette Prevost's handwriting starts appearing more and more, but this note is in Baylis's own handwriting.
78 'How to be Fit at Fifty', unidentified clipping (M&M).
79 Auchmuty, 'By Their Friends We Shall Know Them', p. 92. The 1920s was also a time when the notion of the frigid woman (that is, the not clearly active heterosexual woman) was demonised. The work of sexologists such as Havelock Ellis – whose publication *Sexual Inversion* classified all kinds of women as lesbian (Jeffreys, *The Spinster and Her Enemies*, p. 106) – was gaining popularity, and single women were being challenged either to identify with this 'inverted' state, or to dissociate themselves very clearly from it. Indeed in 1921 there was an attempt to make lesbianism illegal (Jeffreys, *The Spinster and Her Enemies*, p. 113).
80 For example, the letter from Baylis's close friend Louie Davey,

OVLB/000138/19. See also Baylis's reference to destroying personal papers belonging to Emma Cons (OVLB/000017).

81 *OVM*, May 1929; *OVM*, March 1931. (Amends were made later in the 1931 season with productions of *Twelfth Night, Antony and Cleopatra* and *Much Ado About Nothing*.)

82 Correspondence with Miss Newsome held in the Women's Library, London.

83 Lady Fred's beneficence towards the Vic extended beyond the grave: in 1935 a donation of £3,000 was made to the Vic-Wells in her memory (*The Times*, 4 December 1935).

84 *Daily Telegraph*, 27 August 1937.

85 Alan Strachan, *Secret Dreams: A Biography of Michael Redgrave* (London, 2004), p. 121: Michael Redgrave is identified as the source of this story.

86 *Buxton Daily Despatch*, 31 August 1937.

87 *Birmingham Post*, 26 November 1937.

88 Crimp, 'Opera at the Vic', radio broadcast, 1985.

89 Robert Shaughnessy, *The Shakespeare Effect: A History of Twentieth Century Performance* (Houndmills, 2002), p. 114 points out that contemporary reviews actually suggest rather more problems than most accounts admit to and that the 'finale was a shambles, but not quite in the way the author intended'.

90 *Nottingham Evening Post*, 25 November 1937.

91 *OVM*, September–October 1937.

92 *OVM*, September–October 1937. Shaughnessy, *The Shakespeare Effect* examines Guthrie's, and others', myth-making in relation to this performance.

93 OV/M/000076/7.

94 *Yorkshire Post*, 26 November 1937.

95 Quoted in Roberts, *Lilian Baylis*, p. 30.

96 *OVM*, September–October 1937.

97 OVLB/000351.

98 Holmes, *In Love With Life*, pp. 141–2.

99 De Valois, *Step By Step*, p. 34.

100 OV/M/000041/3–4.

101 Quoted in Burne, *The Life and Letters of Father Andrew*, p. 153. The grave is in the East London Cemetery, in ground belonging to St Philip's Guild, square 44, grave number 31227. Louisa Mary Bentley died on 16 June 1931, aged seventy-nine.

102 *Daily Telegraph*, 26 November 1937. Unfortunately, after Baylis's death the Vic-Wells promptly went back into loss: 'At the end of the season of 1938–39 both theatres showed losses of

considerably over £6,000' (Dent, *A Theatre For Everybody*, p. 85).

103 OV/M/000089/23.

104 OV/M/000089.

105 Prevost is first noted in Baylis's diary on 9 September 1932 (M&M).

106 Baylis's relatives in South Africa did not do well: her nephew Robert Dunning, who remained close to his father, did not benefit, and neither, in the end, did Baylis's niece, Lilian, who had married on 20 April 1937 (OVLB/000060).

107 OVLB/000338. Nothing was specified as being left to Baylis's sister Violet.

108 OVLB/000349. A 1934 codicil to this will, however, leaves most of Baylis's property to Ethel in trust for Gladys Dunning, Lilian Baylis junior, and Shirley Bordas. The codicil hopes the hut at Betchworth can be sold, with fittings, for £100.

109 Roberts, *Lilian Baylis*, p. 23.

110 Sybil Thorndike, *OVM*, December 1937. It is worth remembering that early in the twentieth century, St Joan was much in the public consciousness as a heroine to the suffragette struggle; Baylis was not the only person to be compared to St Joan for battling away in what seemed like an impossible cause.

111 *Observer*, 28 November 1937. Ervine had changed his views from 1926 when he was singing Baylis's praises in an article entitled 'Pioneer Work of Women Who Manage Theatres', *Good Housekeeping*, April 1926.

112 Findlater, *Lilian Baylis*, p. 286 makes the point that Ervine's attitude was possibly coloured by the experience of having a play rejected by the Vic. Ervine also tried, via his *Observer* column, to fundraise for the Vic in 1922 before George Dance saved the day. Ervine's attack appeared in the *Observer*, 8 May 1938.

113 *Time and Tide*, 4 December 1937.

114 Ibid.

115 *The Listener*, 1 December 1937.

[11]

The Baylis Legacy

Baylis's legacy consists of her theatres, her theatre companies and the questions she raised about theatre practice. Some of these questions still pose urgent challenges today. This is especially true of her claim that those on low incomes have a right to high art, and that building a working-class audience base is an unquestionable priority for producers of drama, opera and ballet. Her commitment to the lowest possible prices for tickets remains a source of reproach to many theatre managements, although some have tried to follow her lead: Joan Littlewood, at Stratford East, attempted, like Baylis, to serve her theatre's working-class local constituency, but Littlewood, again like Baylis, found it difficult to weather invasions by the West End at the first hint of artistic success.

Of course the question does need to be posed as to whether Baylis was correct that opera, Shakespeare and ballet were what the Lambeth and Islington poor needed. Like Emma Cons, Baylis always sought to alleviate existing social conditions rather than trying for a radical, fundamental change in society.[1] Indeed Baylis's missionary work in bringing high art to the masses could be read as maternalist, perhaps as providing bread and circuses to the detriment of more far-reaching social change. However, Baylis's Vic-Wells was always about far more than theatre. The support activities that accompanied the theatre performances, especially in the early days, were vital here: parties, games and presents for children; community celebrations such as remembrance day, St Patrick's Day, Shakespeare's birthday; fundraising for St Giles's; even the fact that anyone willing to help the Vic without much financial reward could simply walk in off the street and join a close-knit community – all of these aspects offered far more to locals than most theatres do now.

Baylis also raised important questions aesthetically. For example, her insistence on performing all operas in English helped revolutionise opera production and force the issue on translation and, eventually, surtitles. Audiences at the Vic got used to hearing a libretto they could understand and they acquired a taste for this. Performers got used to audiences laughing at jokes, which they had ignored when operas were sung in Italian or German, and began to enjoy what was at first a startling experience.[2] In the realm of theatre, the bare-boards aesthetic which Baylis helped foster – particularly in the 1920s Shakespeares under Robert Atkins – continued to impress and influence theatre workers, and can be seen alive and flourishing in some of the work produced at Shakespeare's Globe in London. And after his conversion at Helsingør, Tyrone Guthrie spread the gospel of the open stage all over the world – to Stratford Ontario, Minneapolis, and Chichester. And while in relation to dance Baylis's questions were even more fundamental – how can we nurture British dance? how can we build an audience for a permanent ballet company? – it is her success in answering those questions that makes them slightly redundant now. Certainly British dance has flourished and developed in a way that would have seemed incredible in 1931, when Baylis opened Sadler's Wells with a 'company' of only six female dancers.

Pragmatically speaking, however, Baylis's legacy initially consisted of two theatres, the Vic and the Wells, and three companies, the opera, the ballet and the Shakespeare Company; and the man who inherited control of these companies was Tyrone Guthrie. The Vic-Wells under Guthrie was soon facing the critical challenge of how to respond to the worsening situation as Britain edged towards war in 1939. The policy adopted was one of boosting morale by entertaining as many people as possible, and touring extensively, but the first drama company tour, sponsored by the British Council, was controversial. This 1939 tour of the Mediterranean, led by Lewis Casson and Esmé Church, was welcomed by Mussolini; indeed Casson reported back that the Duce was 'a great admirer of "Hamlet"'.3 And the ballet company, under Ninette de Valois, were actually performing in the Netherlands in 1940 when Germany invaded, and only struggled home after having abandoned most of their possessions.

For the rest of the war, the ballet company continued to tour, playing anywhere they could, accompanied at first only by two pianos – played by Constant Lambert, their music director, and Hilda Gaunt, their rehearsal pianist – and later on, after the Vic-Wells Association made a guarantee against loss in 1941, with a good-sized orchestra. The New Theatre became the ballet's London base, and they staged an extraordinary amount of work during this period, something which significantly raised their profile and extended their audience base.4 Meanwhile, the Old Vic building was bombed on 10 May 1941, and the theatre company moved its administrative headquarters to the Victoria Theatre, Burnley, for the period of the war, while the company toured the UK. In effect, this marked the beginning of subsidy, as the company tours were seen as part of the war effort and supported by the Council for the Encouragement of Music and the Arts. The Sadler's Wells Theatre also went off limits as far as production work was concerned when the building was temporarily commandeered to house 180 local people made homeless by bombing raids, although the rehearsal rooms continued to be used by the ballet company and the ballet school.5 The opera company carried on with leadership variously provided by Sumner Austin, Guthrie, and Joan Cross, and also toured, using the New Theatre as its London home.

Although Guthrie inherited ultimate control of the theatre, opera and ballet companies, he soon divided up that empire, and the companies went their very separate ways. Guthrie also offered implicit criticism of Baylis's legacy in the major changes he instituted in Vic-Wells policies. Women's opportunities at the Vic declined; the theatre ceased to be a matriarchy and moved steadily away from its founding, social-work principles, while high-profile, director-centred, critically acclaimed productions that would pull in the West End audience that Baylis professed to despise became *de rigueur*.6 The Vic-Wells became less concerned with its local parishes, the working-class districts of Lambeth and Islington, and the *Old Vic Magazine* was tamed. After celebrating women's successes raucously for over twenty years, the September issue for 1939 announces that as the magazine is seen (presumably by the new regime) as one-sided and as it tends 'to ram opinions down the throats of an audience without giving them a chance to reply', this will now change. What actually happened was that the *Old Vic Magazine* ceased publication. Some rationalisation was probably unavoidable because of the war, but it does seem very significant that Baylis's outspoken mouthpiece was reined in so quickly. Perhaps Baylis's most significant legacy here is simply to have proved how successfully a matriarchal theatre could flourish.

After the Second World War, Baylis's companies reopened brilliantly. The Sadler's Wells Opera, led by Vic stalwart Joan Cross, moved back to the Wells and opened with an historic performance, the premiere of *Peter Grimes*, by the young Benjamin Britten, with Peter Pears and Cross creating the leading roles. In his liking for chamber opera, Britten in some ways linked back to work by Charles Corri at the Vic in the early years of the twentieth century, when even Wagner got reduced down to a chamber scale.[7] The opera company, however, disliked *Peter Grimes*, and responded by pressuring Cross into resigning her leadership. Meanwhile the Sadler's Wells Ballet moved to Covent Garden and opened in 1946 with Margot Fonteyn dancing Princess Aurora in *Sleeping Beauty*. Also in 1946, an Old Vic company led by Sybil Thorndike opened at the Theatre Royal in Bristol, thus laying the foundations for what became known as the Bristol Old Vic. The Vic Theatre Company itself, based at the New Theatre, began a glamorous period under the artistic directorship of the triumvirate of Laurence Olivier, Ralph Richardson and John Burrell, while the actual Old Vic building housed the Young Vic, under George Devine, which for five years offered a training ground for young performers and an opportunity for them to stretch themselves in demanding roles on tour.

The Vic then went on something of a roller-coaster ride. In 1949, the contracts of Olivier, Richardson and Burrell were, controversially, not renewed, and Hugh Hunt was appointed artistic director. In 1950 the Old Vic reopened, after the bomb damage had been repaired, with a gala performance, but by 1953 Hunt had departed and Michael Benthall became artistic director, working closely with his long-term partner Robert Helpmann, who had danced for Baylis in the 1930s before concentrating on acting and directing. Benthall decided to follow Baylis's example in staging all the plays of the Shakespeare First Folio, but whereas Baylis took nine years, Benthall aimed to achieve it in five. The focus on Shakespeare attracted rising stars such as Richard Burton, Claire Bloom and John Neville, while Judi Dench began her professional career with a series of lively performances, among them a feisty Ophelia, that got traditionalist critics, including Richard Findlater (already by then at work on his Baylis biography) into a lather of indignation.

During this period the Sadler's Wells Ballet at Covent Garden was dominated by the dancing of Margot Fonteyn, partnered first by Robert Helpmann and then by Michael Somes; Fonteyn achieved international star status, particularly after the 1949 tour of the US. The Sadler's Wells Ballet became the Royal Ballet in 1956, and in 1962 Fonteyn first danced Giselle with Rudolf Nureyev as partner, something which ushered in a new period of excitement and glory for the company. Choreographer Frederick Ashton, who from 1935 onwards had been creating new works for Fonteyn, became director of the Royal Ballet in 1963 when Ninette de Valois retired, and under Ashton and his successors such as Kenneth MacMillan, the Royal Ballet carried on growing in reputation and prestige. Meanwhile at the Wells the dance tradition was carried on by the Sadler's Wells Opera (later Theatre) Ballet, the second, more junior, company which toured the UK and in 1990 relocated to Birmingham, becoming the Birmingham Royal Ballet. The Wells began bringing in a wide range of touring and international dance companies, including productions by seminal figures such as Pina Bausch, although Margot Fonteyn felt 'The disapproving spirit of Lilian Baylis was definitely hovering' about the Wells when a nude ballet was performed.[8]

Opera continues to be performed at the Wells; indeed

when the new building opened there in 1998, it was explicitly dedicated to opera and dance. However, the Sadler's Wells Opera Company relocated to the Coliseum Theatre in 1968 and the company was renamed the English National Opera in 1974. ENO retains a commitment to several of Baylis's ideals, such as outreach, but most crucially it performs opera in English, something absolutely central to Baylis's vision. ENO's productions also tend to be more alternative, more risk-taking and more controversial than opera at Covent Garden, with concept directors regularly relocating and updating the action, as well as branching out into works that are not conventional opera company territory, such as Gilbert and Sullivan or *On the Town* or Kurt Weill's *Seven Deadly Sins*.

In 1963 Baylis's Old Vic Theatre became home to the National Theatre, and what Laurence Olivier described as the 'marriage' between the Vic and the National became official.[9] While many made the claim that Baylis was a founder of the National Theatre in all but name, in fact she was very specific in her support for a national theatre. She did not want just any old national theatre; she wanted the Vic-Wells acknowledged as the *de facto* National Theatre and for funding to come her way, funding which was already in existence and yet not being used. Baylis's major contribution to the National Theatre movement was not her rhetoric – others put the case far more eloquently – but her practical demonstration that a theatre offering stimulating and demanding productions could attract broad-based support. But it was really Baylis's tenacity, her extraordinary perseverance and her cheerful exploitation of her workers that, more than anything, helped her create and maintain the nearest thing to a National Theatre that London had seen.

By 1976, with the National Theatre's move out of the Vic and into its new building on the South Bank, many were wondering what would happen to the Vic building. The South Bank area – which when Baylis started working there was effectively off limits and seen as downright dangerous by most people working in art and culture – was, partly as a result of Baylis's work at the Vic, now turning into a major arts complex. But the Vic was on the periphery of this complex and having to compete with its own offspring, the National. Indeed, Paul Rogers emotively claimed that the way in which the National had used the Vic and then tossed it aside after thirteen years was a kind of rape.[10] Certainly the Vic took some time to recover from the occupation by the National. Initially the theatre played host to Prospect Productions, headed by Toby Robertson, which staged many star-studded productions, but overall Prospect did not manage to balance the books. Timothy West eventually took over from Robertson and made a brave attempt to rescue Prospect, but he also was eventually defeated by finances. In 1982, Toronto-based Ed Mirvish purchased the Vic, refurbished it, reopened it in 1983, and nobly lost money on it for several years. The Vic then became a receiving theatre for a while until Kevin Spacey took over as artistic director and began attempting to resurrect the Vic's reputation as a producing theatre.

Although Baylis herself also plumbed the depths of financial despair, her overall success in running her theatres contrasts starkly with the doldrums, in economic terms, encountered by some of her successors. Of course much of Baylis's success was based on exploitative levels of pay, compensated for by opportunities that were not to be had elsewhere. The fact that Baylis, via the Royal Victoria Hall Foundation, and courtesy of benefactors such as Samuel Morley, George Dance and the Carnegie Foundation, in effect owned her theatres – that the buildings had been purchased and that she had to pay rent to nobody – also freed her from challenges faced by many current theatre managements. However, there is one skill that none of Baylis's successors have perfected as she did, and that skill was absolutely critical to her theatres' success: begging. Baylis nagged, wheedled and begged for her theatres all her working life. On one occasion when Ninette de Valois just couldn't bear to think of Baylis begging the audience for more money, 'I told her to say anything she liked but not to ask for money. She threw me a look of sheer agony and gasped, "My dear, I must ... "'[11] The success of her theatres was in no small part due to the fact that Baylis became such a consummate, habitual and entertaining beggar.

This talent for begging actually created one of Baylis's most challenging legacies because by begging so successfully she demonstrated that it *was* actually possible to stage opera, ballet and theatre without state subsidy – the subsidy of course came from the workers instead. This may be why many of Baylis's co-workers, who preferred not to beg and not to subsidise the companies out of their own pay packets, very much espoused the cause of subsidy in the middle and latter years of the twentieth century. For example, Edward Dent, who personally subsidised the opera companies by never demanding royalties for his libretti, argued extensively in his history of the Vic-Wells that government should support the arts. However, Ethel Smyth offers a fascinating insight into the subject of subsidy and Baylis. Smyth is arguing that subsidy should have no strings attached; as an idea it is 'Excellent – so long as it means a guaranteed income for Miss Baylis, *coupled with a free hand.*'[12] She also implies that were subsidy available to the Vic, Baylis would have to fight a lot harder to keep control there, as she would be under threat from those seeking a share of the cake: as Smyth vividly puts it, 'the crows come flocking and swooping from all quarters of the compass'.[13] Smyth is suggesting that one reason Baylis, an unconventionally educated, driven and eccentric woman, was able to run the Vic so successfully for so long was *because* there was no subsidy, and no one else thought it worth their while to try and muscle in on her work. Baylis was working in the margins that others could not be bothered to colonise and this gave her freedom, even though the price of this freedom was that for a long time many refused to take her work seriously.

Crucially, also, Baylis never had to face an interview panel to get her job. The matriarchal Emma Cons passed her theatre on to her niece and so bypassed the conventional work practices which, in 1898, would have favoured men. Peter Hall, someone who, like Baylis, drove himself to near breakdown in the name of theatre, draws attention to the importance of Baylis's privileged position here:

> She was *obviously* mad, she would *never* have been employed by the Arts Council, no feasibility study by an Arts Council

sub committee would have *possibly* allowed Lilian Baylis to run a theatre and had she been running it she would have been removed as quickly as possible ... She was a law unto herself ... One has to celebrate her pottiness.[14]

While celebrating Baylis's 'pottiness' runs the risk of forgetting her effectiveness, Hall is right to warn that those who best fit Arts Council expectations are not necessarily the most inspirational in terms of running theatres.

A particularly challenging aspect of Baylis's legacy as a pioneering woman is that although, as she herself demonstrated in her lecture in Paris in 1936, women had run theatres before her, Baylis is still exceptional when measured in terms of the scale, status and longevity of her enterprise. While she, like her friends in the Women's Provisional Club, achieved so much more than was expected of her in a man's world, she also dared other women to follow in her footsteps. But Baylis has had relatively few successors: women have run major theatre companies – Jude Kelly at the West Yorkshire Playhouse in Leeds, for example – but no woman has come near to equalling Baylis's power and success in so many different areas of theatre. W.J. Turner really spelt out the standard Baylis set in his obituary for her in the *New Statesman and Nation*:

> Miss Baylis started in 1898 as the manager of a very inferior, ill-equipped theatre in one of the most sordid and depressing parts of London, and having survived every other theatrical manager in London without exception, ended by being the manager in 1937 of two excellent and well-equipped theatres, one (Sadler's Wells) being entirely new, the freeholds of which are in the possession of the management, all this having been achieved by the most austerely artistic policy conceivable – namely, the performing throughout nine months of the year of Shakespeare's plays and classical opera.[15]

It is also important to acknowledge that while Baylis radically changed the face of English theatre, opera and dance, to a large extent her achievements in opera and dance are more impressive than those in the area of drama: Baylis's success in starting the Old Vic Shakespeare tradition should never be underestimated, but there is an expectation that the English can 'do' Shakespeare. When Baylis started her opera and dance companies there was not an expectation that the English could 'do' opera or dance.

Baylis's commitment to outreach can still be seen flourishing in the work of her companies' descendants. The ENO outreach department is actually named after Baylis, and theatre historian Sarah Lenton comments that it

> works to make the resources of ENO accessible to a wide range of people. The department engages with about 12,000 people annually, getting them to see shows and participate in opera at a school or community level. For most of them it will be their first experience of the art form. Recently the Baylis Department has commissioned an opera (*Bake for One Hour*), which is fun, musical and full of large gestures, which they tour round schools (with professional singers) to get kids to realise how hugely enjoyable opera can be.[16]

Meanwhile the Royal Ballet's outreach

> follows directly from Lilian Baylis's LCC matinees. The Royal Opera House put on 6 Schools' matinees a year, (3 ballet, 3 opera), they play to full houses, the kids pay £6 wherever they sit, first time schools are given priority and state schools predominate. They get about 12,000 people in total.[17]

The Royal Opera House has also had great success with the Big Screen, which relays free performances into the Covent Garden market area, and, like the Coliseum, runs schemes which keep the cheapest seats in the house very cheap.[18] Lenton vividly sums up:

> For me it's the Robin Hood angle that seems the strongest link with Baylis. Both the Royal Ballet and the ENO are ruthless in their pursuit of the rich and/or corporate members, and their money subsidises the rest of the house.[19]

Baylis also continues to inspire support for the arts in other areas: the Lilian Baylis Trust Fund was for many years run by the Vic-Wells Association for the promotion of opera, drama and ballet at the Vic and the Wells;[20] the Wells runs the Lilian Baylis Over 60s Performance Group; the studio theatre at the Wells is named after her; and the Royal Victoria Hall Foundation continues to award scholarships to students training at the London acting academies. However, Baylis's legacies also include the non-theatrical: a London school bears her name; a rose is named after her; after her death, Oakley Street in south London was renamed Baylis Road.

Finally, the question has to be asked: 'How did she do it?' Baylis's autobiographical writings offer the answer 'God, and her family.' But her success was undoubtedly also founded upon personal characteristics as well: her extraordinary energy and capacity for work; her utter conviction that her work was important; her phenomenal memory, which enabled her to remember over many years tiny details about people who might one day be useful to her;[21] her ability to inspire people to slave for her cause; her ability to beg. But most of all it was Baylis's connection with – her wooing and seduction of – her audiences as well as her exploited theatre workers that enabled her to perform so successfully her role of 'Manager of the Old Vic *and* Sadler's Wells'.

NOTES

1   See Vera Gottlieb and Robert Gordon, 'Lilian Baylis: Paradoxes and Contradictions', *Themes in Drama*, 'Women in Theatre' issue (1989), pp. 155–75, for criticisms of Baylis as Victorian in her thinking in relation to charity.
2   Dent, *A Theatre For Everybody*, p. 87 records that '[s]uperior members of the audience' used to Italian opera at Covent Garden were also startled by this experience.
3   *Guardian*, 21 April 1939.
4   The New Theatre is now named the Albery.
5   Evelyn Williams, 'The Old Vic and Lilian Baylis', Report of the Annual Address given by Miss Evelyn Williams 20 July 1951, *Royal Academy of Dancing Gazette*, August 1951.
6   See Peter Roberts, *The Old Vic Story: A Nation's Theatre*

1818–1976 (London, 1976), p. 132 for comments on these changes.

7   See White, *The Rise of English Opera*, p. 159 for this argument.

8   Fonteyn, *Margot Fonteyn: Autobiography*, p. 51.

9   'Farewell to the Vic', BBC radio, 15 June 1963. The programme was written by Christopher Venning.

10 *Omnibus*, 1983.

11 De Valois, *Come Dance With Me*, p. 83.

12 Smyth, 'Lilian Baylis', p. 178.

13 Ibid., p. 179.

14 Peter Hall in 'Lilian Baylis – a Portrait of "The Lady"'.

15 *New Statesman and Nation*, 4 December 1937.

16 Sarah Lenton, private communication, March 2006.

17 Ibid.

18 The Paul Hamlyn Foundation and Travelex (who support the National Theatre in a similar way) subsidise hugely popular and over-subscribed low-price ticket schemes.

19 Sarah Lenton, private communication, March 2006.

20 Charity Registration Number 208371. This is now the Ninette de Valois Fund.

21 For Baylis's phenomenal memory see e.g. the *Reading Evening Gazette*, 26 November 1937.

Appendix
Afterlives

Baylis has been discussed, analysed, celebrated and impersonated many times since her death. What follows is a brief record of some of her afterlives.[1]

1938 Sybil and Russell Thorndike, *Lilian Baylis*. A hagiography which states: 'This is a humble tribute to the memory of the most courageous woman that was ever associated with the Theatre.'[2] Sybil Thorndike elaborates her view of Baylis as a latter-day St Joan, a view she continued to promote all through her lifetime.

1938 Harcourt Williams, *Vic-Wells: the Work of Lilian Baylis*, a series of brief essays by a variety of people who knew Baylis in different capacities: contributors range from Kathleen Clark, the box-office manager, to Sir Hugh Walpole. The book closes with a fulsome discussion of Baylis's spirituality, written by Father Andrew, who compares Baylis to St Theresa of Avila, and constructs a holy, humble Baylis that few of her exploited, overworked employees would easily recognise.[3]

1938 *Observer* critic St John Ervine denounces Baylis vitriolically on the weekend of what would have been her birthday.[4]

1939 7 May: a memorial to Baylis is unveiled by the Bishop of Kingston at St Agnes, Kennington. This church, which housed the stations of the cross donated by Baylis in memory of Emma and Ellen Cons, Newton, Liebe and Willy Baylis, was badly bombed during the Second World War. (The church website www.saintagnes.org.uk includes pictures of the old church Baylis would have known.)

1939 September: Baylis's contribution to the Buxton Festival is acknowledged in a plaque placed in the Opera House: 'This tablet is a tribute to Lilian Baylis C.H., M.A., LL.D., and the 'Old Vic' who did much to advance dramatic art and to whose inspiration and enthusiasm the success of the Buxton Festival is largely due.'

1944 Dora Northcroft, 'A Theatrical Genius – Lilian Baylis', a chapter in Northcroft's book *Girls of Adventure*.[5] Northcroft's agenda includes demonstrating to girls and young women of 1944 that they have the potential, like the 'Girls of Adventure', to be remarkable; Baylis's career is held up as something to admire and emulate.

1944 Beatrice Gordon Holmes's autobiography *In Love With Life*. Baylis is identified as a role model for Holmes as she fought to succeed in the male-dominated profession of stockbroking.[6]

1945 Edward Dent, *A Theatre For Everybody*. Ostensibly a history of the Vic-Wells, this book is also lobbying for the companies' continuation after the upheavals of the Second World War, and putting the case for government subsidy of the arts in general. Dent's Baylis is a predominantly comic character.

1947 The tenth anniversary of Baylis's death is marked with a service at Southwark Cathedral.

1947 Evelyn Williams (Baylis's secretary) gives a talk entitled 'I Knew Lilian Baylis', on *Woman's Hour*. It repeats much material from her essay in Harcourt Williams's 1938 book, *Vic-Wells*. Williams consistently tries to argue that Baylis 'had no patience at all with the aggressive feminist point of view', but this belief seems difficult to reconcile with Baylis's support for women's suffrage, or her close friendships with outspoken – and occasionally strident – feminists such as Holmes, Ethel Smyth and Cicely Hamilton.[7]

1949 22 March: Baylis's 'ghost' appears in 'Citizenship', a schools radio programme, as part of a series entitled 'Great Citizens'. In the period of post-war reconstruction, Baylis's hard work and 'can do' spirit should be emulated.

1949 30 October: 'Return to the Old Vic', a radio programme reminiscing primarily about the theatre company, which at that time was basking in the glory of the years under the artistic directorship of Olivier, Richardson and Burrell.

1950 Film cameras record the reopening of the Old Vic on 14 November. The intention is to use the footage in a feature film about Baylis's life, starring Edith Evans as Baylis, and directed by Herbert Wilcox.[8] The film did not materialise.

1952 25 July: ex-Vic stage manager Malcolm Baker-Smith broadcasts 'A Portrait of a Great Lady' on radio, a largely celebratory collage of reminiscences from friends and colleagues.

1952 A blue plaque is unveiled at 5 and 6 Moreton Place, commemorating the fact that Baylis and Emma Cons lived there. The *Guardian* (30 October 1952) reproduces a drawing of the houses.

1957 Ninette de Valois, in *Come Dance With Me* (as in all of her writings over the years), argues that Baylis was not a joke, registers her deep respect for Baylis, and her admiration for her as a trailblazer.9

1963 'The Old Vic 1914–1963', written and produced by Christopher Venning, is broadcast on 9 June to mark the metamorphosis of the Old Vic into the National Theatre. So many people declare that Baylis would have approved that it is difficult not to wonder if this is really true.

1965 Tyrone Guthrie, *In Various Directions*, includes a portrait of Baylis. For Guthrie Baylis was 'cosy rather than glamorous, odd rather than elegant', she swore a lot, and she used 'rather out-of-date, schoolboyish slang – "old bounder", "dirty little rotter", "a swizz", or "a priceless lark"' and an accent 'far from aristocratic'.[10] It would be using a sledgehammer to crack a walnut to go through Guthrie's inaccuracies, but one example is Guthrie's claim that Liebe Baylis was 'a soprano of meagre attainment', when Liebe actually sang contralto.[11] Guthrie was born in 1900 and Baylis's parents gave their last professional performance in the UK in 1891, so how he arrived at this verdict is not clear. The fact that Guthrie also met Baylis thirty years after her professional musical career was over did not stop him opining that 'no one could say that [Baylis] was either a very gifted or at all a cultured musician'.[12] Although he was twelve years old when she died and never met her, Guthrie also ludicrously describes pioneering suffrage campaigner Emma Cons as 'a very mousy little person indeed'.[13] Guthrie's agenda needs to be contextualised by the fact that Baylis acolytes considered that he had dismembered her empire and betrayed her most dearly held principles.

1968 Margaret Webster, *The Same Only Different*, celebrates Baylis and Emma Cons as 'remarkable women' whose legacies should be remembered with respect.[14]

1968 Playwright R.C. Sherriff describes Baylis in his autobiography:

> She looked untidy and dishevelled, with something bewildered
> and scatterbrained about her. She talked in a fevered, disjointed
> way, switching from one thought to another so abruptly that you

found yourself answering something that she had already discarded and forgotten. You wouldn't have thought she could have got anywhere without losing her way, but she managed to get where she wanted to go much more quickly than most other people did, and those who worked for her revered her.[15]

1970 Moreton Place, Baylis's former home, is demolished. As no-one is allowed more than one blue plaque, Baylis's joint blue plaque here, shared with Emma Cons, has been preventing a blue plaque being granted to Baylis's later home at 27 Stockwell Park Road. This obstacle is now removed.

1974 The centenary of Baylis's birth.
• Annette Prevost writes a two-page article entitled 'A Great Lady and her People: Lilian Baylis and the Vic-Wells Era'.[16]
• Peter Roberts edits a souvenir booklet full of photographs, anecdotes, chatty interviews and shamelessly partisan reminiscences.
• 5 May: A commemoration service is held at Southwark Cathedral.
• 6 May: *Tribute To The Lady*, devised by Val May, is performed at the Vic with Peggy Ashcroft as Baylis and Laurence Olivier as narrator and with guest appearances by John Gielgud and Ralph Richardson. This gala performance, in the presence of the Queen Mother, the Mayor of Lambeth and Sir Max and Lady Rayne, is broadcast on radio the same night. Baylis is the eccentric, outrageous but entertaining caricature. The tribute includes a set-piece Baylis curtain speech entitled 'Keeping up attendances'.
• 9 May: the Greater London Council has a blue plaque unveiled at 27 Stockwell Park Road to mark the fact that Baylis used to live there.
• 9 May: an exhibition on Baylis opens at Leighton House.
• 12 May: Judi Dench, Barbara Leigh-Hunt, Margaretta Scott, Ian Charleson, Robert Harris and William Squire perform in a celebration piece entitled 'Theatre', devised by John Carroll, at the Young Vic.
• 14 and 15 May: the Royal Ballet and Ballet for All celebrate the early years of the Vic-Wells ballet, and the work of de Valois and Ashton, at the Wells.
• 17 May: a tree is planted in Baylis's memory outside the Wells Theatre.
• 17 May: Joan Cross directs *The Marriage of Figaro* for the London Opera Centre at the Wells. The performance is

conducted by Lawrance Collingwood.
- 19 May: opera gala attended by Princess Margaret at the Wells.
- 20 May: English Opera Group concert performance of Britten's *Rape of Lucretia*.
- 22 May: Evening of operetta including work by the Lilian Baylis Festival Orchestra.
- 23 May: the Baylis Festival closes with a fancy dress ball taking the period of Baylis's life, 1874–1937, as its theme.
- 26 May: 'The Lady', a compilation of reminiscences by Old Vic stalwarts, broadcast on Radio 4.
- The Royal Ballet revives the Ashton/Stein/Berners piece *A Wedding Bouquet* especially for the Festival.
- Ninette de Valois and Joan Cross address the City Literary Institute on the subject of 'The Lady'.
- St Paul's, Covent Garden unveils a plaque to Baylis.
- Away from London, *In Despair I Turned to Shakespeare*, devised and directed by Christopher Denys, is performed at the Bristol Old Vic. The cast includes John Nettles and stars June Barrie as a Baylis who made 'bossy headmistress speeches' without descending into caricature.[17]

1975 Richard Findlater's biography of Baylis published. Findlater explains that it took him over twenty years to write and that in the meantime his car, containing 'notes on interviews and library research', was stolen.[18] Presumably this is why much of the book does not document Findlater's sources.

1975 John Barber, reviewing Findlater's biography in the *Daily Telegraph*, deduces Baylis was

> [an] impossible woman. Richard Findlater does not minimise Lilian Baylis's awfulness. The funny, frightening, omnipotent but remote eccentric who managed the Old Vic for 25 years was large and ugly, with untidy hair and dreadful clothes. When Miss Baylis spoke, one side of her red face slipped. She gave off the aura of a brusque parish visitor or a bossy seaside landlady. Typically, she also kept nasty little dogs in her poky office ... she was not only stingy, dowdy and insensitive. She was uneducated. She could be instantly unjust and irrationally offensive...[19]

1976 *Tribute To The Lady* revived on 28 February 1976 as the final show to be performed at the Vic Theatre, before the National Theatre Company moved into its new South Bank building.[20] The production again features Peggy Ashcroft as a comic-caricature Baylis. It was broadcast 6 April 1976.

1976 Peter Roberts publishes a history of the Old Vic, which builds on his Baylis centenary souvenir brochure and on Findlater's biography, and adds little that is new to the public perception of Baylis.

1976 The medium Leslie Flint claims to channel Baylis's voice, in a radio programme.

1976 6–23 October: *Lilian*, a revival of Denys's *In Despair I Turned to Shakespeare*, produced in Northampton.[21]

1977 *Auntie's Niece*, a play by Jack Rosenthal, is aired on BBC2, as part of a series, entitled *The Velvet Glove*, looking at powerful and effective women including Edith Cavell and Elizabeth Fry. 'Auntie's Niece' stars Annette Crosbie as Baylis. Baylis frequently speaks to God (by addressing the theatre gods), and also to Emma Cons long after she is dead. She has a decided passion for Father Andrew, and the play is heavily dependent on Findlater.

1978 14 September: The National Theatre inaugurates the Lilian Baylis Terrace with a plaque including the words 'Her work laid the foundations for a National Theatre'.

1981 Plaque in memory of Baylis unveiled by Joan Cross and the Earl of Harewood at the entrance to the fully licensed bar of the Coliseum.

1981 'The Baylis Connection', an exhibition in the foyer of the Olivier Theatre.

1983 6 May–4 June: 'From Waterloo Road to King Street: Treasures for the Old Vic' exhibition mounted by the Bristol Theatre Collection at the Theatre Royal, King Street, Bristol.

1983 The *Evening Standard* (5 October) reports that workmen renovating the Vic for the new owner Ed Mirvish have seen a female ghost, presumed to be Baylis, prowling around the theatre. Mirvish renames the gods the 'Lilian Baylis Circle'.

1983 30 October: 'Omnibus' features the history of the Vic in anticipation of its reopening after renovations.

1984 Douglas Hankin's play *Beauty and the Bounders: a Remembrance of the Old Vic*, which is actually dedicated to Findlater (such was the biography's influence on the play), appears at the 1984 Edinburgh Festival Fringe, featuring Polly March as Baylis. The play is revived at Sadler's Wells in December 1987 to mark the fiftieth anniversary of Baylis's death.

1987 30 September: Vera Gottlieb and Robert Gordon's *Waterloo Road* plays at the Young Vic Theatre.[22] The role of Baylis is played by Barbara Kinghorn, who also works as a guide

showing tourists around the Vic, and who explains that
Baylis's ghost puts in an appearance at the Vic '[w]henever
anything structural is done' to the building.[23] However, the
focus of the playwrights, Gottlieb and Gordon, is on Baylis's
legacy in terms of the public funding of the arts: Baylis is
seen to have sold out by the end of her life, and indeed is
rebuked for abandoning her working-class parish by a
representative of that group, Bob Baker. The play also
situates Baylis as a woman participating in professional
women's networks, represented here by Cicely Hamilton and
Ethel Smyth.

1985 11 August: Bryan Crimp broadcasts 'Opera at the Vic',
reminding radio listeners of Baylis's pioneering work in
opera, and interviewing Joan Cross and Powell Lloyd.

1989 Gottlieb and Gordon publish the research behind their play,
Waterloo Road, and raise important questions about the Baylis
myth. Of Guthrie's comments that Baylis 'sublimated
personal life for the sake of the Old Vic' they ask to what
extent

> would this be an issue if she had not been a woman? – no
> 'peculiarity' or 'mystery' is attached to Baylis's male colleagues,
> Tyrone Guthrie, Ben Greet, Granville-Barker, whose
> commitment to their work was no less than hers.[24]

1989 Lesbian feminist historian Rosemary Auchmuty calls for a
complete overhaul in the way Baylis is perceived. Auchmuty
finds Findlater's biography sexist, anti-feminist and
heterosexist. Auchmuty herself sees Baylis as happily
functioning at the centre of a major lesbian theatre network,
and closely connected with lesbian networks in medicine and
social housing.

1993 George Rowell publishes a scholarly history of the Old Vic
Theatre in which he accepts everything that the 'wise and
well read' Findlater says about Baylis and is seemingly
oblivious of, or impervious to, Auchmuty's criticisms.[25]

1990 The *Daily Mail* (2 June) trumpets that there is an 'Uproar
over "Lilian Baylis lesbian" slur'. An Islington Council
'What's On' information sheet advertising gay pub walks is
quoted as stating: 'Islington boasts two famous figures in gay
history – Lilian Baylis and Joe Orton.' Ninette de Valois's
opinion is sought and she retorts 'I've never heard such
nonsense.'[26]

1991   The Diamond Jubilee of Baylis's reopening of Sadler's Wells in 1931 is celebrated with a radio programme, presented by Sheridan Morley.

1996   *'Monday Nights Have Got to be Better'*, a one-woman show written and performed by Anthea Preston, tours. The performance features Preston making forays into the audience and interacting with them in true Baylis style.

1997   17 August: to mark sixty years since Baylis's death, Donald Sinden hosts a radio programme, entitled 'Lilian Baylis – a Portrait of "The Lady"'.

1998   The centenary of the beginning of Baylis's management of the Vic is remembered in a radio broadcast of a lecture on Baylis by Joy Melville

2001   12 November: a tribute entitled 'Celebrating Lilian Baylis' is staged at the Linbury Studio for the Friends of Covent Garden. Devised and presented by Sarah Lenton, the tribute includes contributions from former prima ballerina Pamela May, remembering her early days with the Sadler's Wells Ballet. Lenton comments that some terms often associated with Baylis's work – 'parish', 'Sunday school', 'mission' – would, in 2001, be used to sneer at it, but that, at the time Baylis was actually doing this work, they suggested something 'rather heroic'.

2005   14 and 15 December: drama students at Royal Holloway, University of London, revive Gottlieb and Gordon's *Waterloo Road*.

2006   10 February: *Woman's Hour* marks the seventy-fifth anniversary of Baylis reopening Sadler's Wells, which was also celebrated by the Vic-Wells Association on 6 January 2006.

Baylis also has an extensive presence on the web, although most of the results of a search on 'Baylis' refer to events at the Lilian Baylis Studio, Sadler's Wells, or the Lilian Baylis School in London.

NOTES

1   The survey of writings about Baylis offered here cannot be exhaustive. Many, many people who worked at the Vic (and some who did not) relate Baylis anecdotes in their biographies, and I have selected the most influential and the most challenging.

2   Sybil and Russell Thorndike, *Lilian Baylis*, p. 7. The memoir is

extremely partisan but it is almost unique in taking Baylis's South African adventures seriously, in being sympathetic towards her mother, Liebe, and in acknowledging, quite rightly, that Baylis's connections in Australia really were VIPs, although Sybil Thorndike (pp. 10–11) doesn't get the Australian family tree quite right.

3   Andrew Hardy in Harcourt Williams, *Vic-Wells*, pp. 103, 104.

4   Findlater, *Lilian Baylis*, p. 286 points out that one of Ervine's plays had been rejected by the Vic and that this may have coloured his attitude to Baylis. Ervine's attack appeared in the *Observer*, 8 May 1938.

5   Other 'Girls of Adventure' included the following: Margaret Bondfield, the first woman in the British Cabinet, and a pioneer trades unionist; Hertha Ayrton, the physicist and inventor; artist Laura Knight; surgeon and maternity hospital reformer Elsie Inglis; Salvation Army General Evangeline Booth; explorer and travel writer Mary Kingsley; aviator Amy Johnson; composer Ethel Smyth; and housing reformer Octavia Hill.

6   For Beatrice Gordon Holmes see also Chapter 3 and Chapter 10.

7   Evelyn Williams in Harcourt Williams, *Vic-Wells*, p. 33.

8   See e.g. *News Chronicle*, 8 November 1950; *Daily Express*, 15 November 1950.

9   *Invitation to the Ballet* appeared in 1937. De Valois also went into print in 1977 when she published *Step by Step*, a history of the Vic-Wells and then Royal Ballet.

10   Guthrie, *In Various Directions*, p. 145.

11   Ibid., p. 147.

12   Ibid., p. 149.

13   Ibid., p. 146.

14   Webster, *The Same Only Different*, p. 247.

15   R.C. Sherriff, *No Leading Lady: An Autobiography* (London, 1968), p. 301.

16   *Country Life*, 9 May 1974, pp. 1144–5.

17   *Guardian*, 24 May 1974.

18   Findlater, *Lilian Baylis*, pp. 11, 13.

19   *Daily Telegraph*, 7 August 1975. In the previous year Barber had denounced Baylis for being 'physically unprepossessing, a homely, dumpy person in spectacles, speaking cockney out one side of a mouth twisted by a slight stroke', and 'ill-educated, stingy, domineering, rude, prudish, and a bad business woman' (*Daily Telegraph*, 22 April 1974).

20 Ironically the move to the National left Baylis's Vic very vulnerable and the theatre has had a chequered career since.

21 The play was part of a 'Feminist' season, which included *Hedda Gabler* and *The Prime of Miss Jean Brodie*. Information courtesy of Richard Foulkes.

22 My thanks to Robert Gordon for making the script available to me. Images from the production are reproduced in Gottlieb and Gordon, 'Lilian Baylis'.

23 *Hampstead and Highgate Express*, 2 October 1987.

24 Gottlieb and Gordon, 'Lilian Baylis', p. 157.

25 Rowell, *The Old Vic Theatre*, p. 71.

26 The *Mail* also quotes from 'Miss Baylis's current biographer, Angela Patmore', but Patmore's biography has not appeared in print.

Bibliography of works cited

Agate, James, *Ego 2: Being More of the Autobiography of James Agate* (London, 1936).

Allen, Percy, *The Stage Life of Mrs. Stirling: with Some Sketches of the Nineteenth Century Theatre* (London, 1922).

Arundell, Dennis, *The Story of Sadler's Wells, 1683–1964* (London, 1965).

Atkins, Robert (ed. J.C. Trewin), 'The Lady of Waterloo Road', *The Times*, 30 March 1974.

Auchmuty, Rosemary, 'By Their Friends We Shall Know Them: The Lives and Networks of Some Women in North Lambeth, 1880–1940' in Lesbian History Group (ed.), *Not a Passing Phase: Reclaiming Lesbians in History 1840–1985* (London, 1989).

Backscheider, Paula R., *Reflections on Biography* (Oxford, 1999, reprinted 2001).

Barlee, Ellen, *Pantomime Waifs or, a plea for our city children* (London, 1884).

Barber, John, '"St Joan" of the Old Vic', *Daily Telegraph*, 22 April 1974.

Baylis, Lilian, Letter on the death of Emma Cons, 1912 (OVLB/000017).

  'The Royal Victoria Hall', *The Shakespeare League Journal*, July 1915.

  'Things Near My Heart', *OVM*, May 1921.

  'At "The Old Vic"', *Home Chat*, 14 June 1924.

  'The Manager's Letter' (from Cape Town), *OVM*, October–November 1924.

  'What the Old Vic Stands For', typescript, M&M (broadcast 9.40 p.m., 3 December 1924).

  'Reminiscences', 2 typescripts, M&M, file labelled 'Talks by Lilian Baylis', 1924.

  'The Manager's Letter', *OVM*, September–October 1925.

  'The Art of Living – the Need for the Theatre', M&M, BBC, 1925.

  'The Last of the Cons Family', obituary for Liebe Cons Baylis (probably written by Baylis), *OVM*, December 1925.

'Foreword' to Westwood, *These Players*.

'Emma Cons, the Founder of the Vic', in Hamilton, *The Old Vic*.

'Aims and Ideals of the Theatre', 3 typescripts, M&M (broadcast
    9.15, 24 October 1928).

'Prayer – and One's Hour of Destiny', *Daily Sketch*, 13 July 1931.

'The Work of the Vic-Wells Association', typescript speech,
    c. 1931 (OVLB/000144).

'The Old Vic and Sadler's Wells', typescript article, c. 1931
    (OVLB/000145).

Typescript speech on the Old Vic, c. 1931 (OVLB/000146).

'Shakespeare for the People', typescript/manuscript speech,
    c. 1931 (OVLB/000147).

'The Old Vic and Sadler's Wells', typescript article, c. 1931
    (OVLB/000148).

'In Memory of "Bob"', *OVM*, February 1931.

'Stories of the "Old Vic". A Chapter of Experiences', *Southwark
    Diocesan Gazetteer*, 31 December 1931.

'Why We Wanted Sadler's Wells', *The Sadler's Wells Book, A Souvenir
    of Sadler's Wells Theatre Past, Present and Future* (London, 1931),
    pp. 9–10.

'"The Old Vic" and "The Wells"', *Toc H*, March 1933, pp. 108–13.

'A Greatest Hour', *John Bull*, 10 February 1934.

'The Manager's Foreword', *OVM*, September–October 1934.

'Preface' to Kate Neatby, *Ninette de Valois and the Vic-Wells Ballet*, ed.
    Edwin Evans (London, 1934).

'Women's Contribution to the Modern World in the Field of
    Theatre Management', address to the International Federation
    of Business and Professional Women Congress, Paris, 27 July – 1
    August 1936 (OVLB/000149).

'Women and the Theatre; a Glowing Tribute', *Era*, 26 August
    1936.

'Busman's Holiday', *OVM*, September–October 1936.

'The Home of Repertory: Old Vic's Policy: Team Work and the
    Star System: Art and the Box Office', *Glasgow Herald*, 1 April
    1937.

'Romance of the Vic-Wells Opera', the *Star*, 16 November 1937.

'The Old Vic and Sadler's Wells', autobiographical typescript
    article for All Saints parish magazine, undated
    (OVLB/000139).

'St Giles', undated manuscript article on the home for lepers
    (OVLB/000154).

'Autobiography', autobiographical essay dictated to Annette
 Prevost, c. 1936 (OVLB/000156).

'Myself When Young', autobiographical essay dictated to Annette
 Prevost, c. 1936–7 (OVLB/000157).

'"Light" Shows and the Classics', unidentified and undated
 clipping, Vic-Wells Association Box 6, Theatre Museum, Blythe
 House.

Baylis, Lilian, social events diaries for 1924, 1928, 1930, 1931,
 1932, 1934 (M&M).

Baylis, Lilian, interviewed in:

Time and Tide, 15 July 1921.

'How to be Fit at Fifty', *Daily Chronicle*, 30 May 1925.

'WOAD! Celebrities in Undress: XLVI – Miss Lilian Baylis',
 interview with Beverly Nichols, *Sketch*, 9 February 1927, p. 258.

'At the Old Vic', by F.W. Thomas, pictures by Low (part of series
 'Low and I'), the *Star*, 5 October 1925.

Westminster Gazette, 28 April 1930, interview with J.L. Hodson.

'The Soul of the Old Vic: An Interview with the Creator of
 England's National Theatre, Miss Lilian Baylis, whose
 Indomitable Enthusiasm, Energy and Courage have made Stage
 History in this Country', interview with Patricia Hyde, *Queen*,
 8 October 1930.

'The Woman Who Has Made Stage History: Miss Lilian Baylis
 Talks About the Theatre of Yesterday and To-day', interview with
 Louise A. Coury, *Queen*, 24 February 1932.

'The Greatest Englishman of All', interview with Louise Morgan
 on the subject of Shakespeare, *Everyman*, 22 April 1933.

'The Theatre of To-day and To-morrow: Lilian Baylis Wants An
 Old Vic in Each Town', interview with Margery Rowland, *Era*,
 5 September 1934.

'Lilian Baylis and the National Theatre', interview with Elizabeth,
 Lady Kilbracken, *Queen*, 21 October 1937.

Bell, E. Moberly, *Octavia Hill: A Biography* (London, 1942).

Bettany, F.G., *Stewart Headlam: A Biography* (London, 1926).

Booth, John, *The 'Old Vic': A Century of Theatrical History. 1816–1916*
 (London, 1917).

Boyd, Nancy, *Josephine Butler, Octavia Hill, Florence Nightingale: Three
 Victorian Women Who Changed Their World* (London, 1982).

Brandreth, Gyles, *John Gielgud: An Actor's Life* (Stroud, 2000).

Bratton, Jacky, *New Readings in Theatre History* (Cambridge, 2003).

Brown, Ivor, 'Lilian Baylis: Old Vic Directress and Empressario',
 Theatre Arts Monthly, February 1938.

Browne, Stanley, *Leprosy in England: Yesterday and Today*, pamphlet in East Hanningfield collection, 1977.

Brunsdon, Ann, 'Introduction' to Mary Norton, *The Bread and Butter Stories* (London, 1998).

Burne, Kathleen E., *The Life and Letters of Father Andrew S.D.C.* (London, 1948).

Carlson, Susan, 'Comic Militancy: the Politics of Suffrage Drama' in Maggie B. Gale and Viv Gardner (eds.), *Women, Theatre and Performance: New Histories, New Historiographies* (Manchester, 2000), pp. 198–215.

Clarke, Mary, *The Sadler's Wells Ballet: A History and Appreciation* (London, 1955).

Cole, Marion, *Fogie: the Life of Elsie Fogerty* (London, 1967).

Coleman, J., *Charles Reade as I Knew Him* (London, 1904).

[Cons, Emma], 'The Royal Victoria Coffee Music Hall: Rules [for Artistes]' (M&M).

Cons, Emma, 'Women and the County Council', letter to *The Times*, 1 December 1890.

'Armenian Exiles in Cyprus', *Contemporary Review*, 70 (July–December 1896), pp. 888–95.

Corathiel, Elisabethe H.C., 'Old Vic Memories', *The Stage*, 9 November 1950.

Cross, Joan, manuscript autobiography, Britten-Pears Library.

'The Bad Old Days' in Anthony Gishford (ed.), *Tribute to Benjamin Britten on his Fiftieth Birthday* (London, 1963).

Curtis, Geoffrey, *William of Glasshampton: Friar: Monk: Solitary 1862–1937* (London, 1947).

Daneman, Meredith, *Margot Fonteyn* (London, 2004).

Darley, Gillian, *Octavia Hill* (London, 1990).

de Valois, Ninette, *Invitation to the Ballet* (London, 1937, reprinted 1953).

Come Dance With Me: A Memoir, 1898–1956 (London, 1957).

Step by Step: The Formation of an Establishment (London, 1977).

Denning, Vere, 'Women who Count in the Theatre: The Power behind the "Old Vic": an Impression of Lilian Baylis', *Theatre World*, December 1931, p. 293.

Dent, Edward, *A Theatre For Everybody: The Story of the Old Vic and Sadler's Wells* (London, 1945).

Denys, Christopher, *In Despair I Turned to Shakespeare*, performed at the Bristol Old Vic May 1974.

Devlin, Diana, *A Speaking Part: Lewis Casson and the Theatre of his Time* (London, 1982).

Dolin, Anton, *Markova: Her Life and Art* (London, 1953).

Elsom, John and Tomalin, Nicholas, *The History of the National Theatre* (London, 1978).

Ervine, St John, 'Pioneer Work of Women who Manage Theatres', *Good Housekeeping*, April 1926.

Evans, Maurice, *All This … and Evans Too! A Memoir* (Columbia, South Carolina, 1987).

Faderman, Lillian, *Surpassing the Love of Men: Romantic Friendship and Love between Women from the Renaissance to the Present* (New York, 1981, reprinted London, 1985).

Fagg, Edwin, *The Old 'Old Vic'; A Glimpse of the Old Theatre from its Origins as 'The Royal Coburg' First Managed by William Barrymore to its Revival under Lilian Baylis* (London, 1936).

Findlater, Richard, *Lilian Baylis: The Lady of the Old Vic* (London, 1975).

Fonteyn, Margot, *Margot Fonteyn: Autobiography* (London, 1975).

Forbes, Bryan, *Ned's Girl: the Authorised Biography of Dame Edith Evans* (London, 1977).

Foss, George, *What the Author Meant* (London, 1932).

Gale, Maggie B., 'From Fame to Obscurity: in Search of Clemence Dane' in Maggie B. Gale and Viv Gardner (eds.), *Women, Theatre and Performance: New Histories, New Historiographies* (Manchester, 2000), pp. 121–41.

Gale, Maggie and Gardner, Viv, *Auto/biography and Identity: Women, Theatre and Performance* (Manchester, 2004).

Gielgud, John, *Early Stages*, 2nd revised edition (London, 1987, third impression 1988).

Gottlieb, Vera and Gordon, Robert, 'Lilian Baylis: Paradoxes and Contradictions', *Themes in Drama*, 'Women in Theatre', 1989, pp. 155–75.

Guinness, Alec, *Blessings in Disguise* (Harmondsworth, 1997).

Guthrie, Tyrone, *A Life in the Theatre* (London, 1959, reprinted 1961).

'A Portrait and Two Profiles: Lilian Baylis' in *In Various Directions: A View of Theatre* (London, 1965).

Hallett, Nicky, *Lesbian Lives: Identity and Auto/Biography in the Twentieth Century* (London, 1999).

Hamilton, Cicely, *The Old Vic* (London, 1926).

Life Errant (London, 1935).

Haskell, Arnold, *Ballet Since 1939* (London, 1946).

Hill, William Thomson, *Octavia Hill: Pioneer of the National Trust and Housing Reformer* (London, 1956).

Hodder, Edwin, *The Life of Samuel Morley* (London, 1887).

Holledge, Julie, *Innocent Flowers: Women in the Edwardian Theatre* (London, 1981).

Hollingshead, John, *Ragged London in 1861* (London, 1861).

Hollis, Patricia, *Ladies Elect: Women in English Local Government 1865–1914* (Oxford, 1987).

Holmes, Beatrice Gordon, *In Love With Life: A Pioneer Career Woman's Story* (London, 1944).

Huckerby, Martin, 'Half a Century of Sadler's Wells', *The Times*, 6 January 1981.

Isaac, Winifred F.E.C., *Ben Greet and the Old Vic, A Biography of Sir Philip Ben Greet* (London, 1964).

Jeffreys, Sheila, *The Spinster and her Enemies: Feminism and Sexuality 1880–1930* (London, 1985).

'Does It Matter If They Did It?' in Lesbian History Group (ed.), *Not a Passing Phase: Reclaiming Lesbians in History 1840–1985* (London, 1989), pp. 19–28.

Kersley, Leo, 'A Reminder of the Past', *The Dancing Times*, January 1998, pp. 351–3.

Keynes, Milo (ed.), *Lydia Lopokova* (London, 1983).

Leighton, Judith, 'An Analysis of the Life and Work of Emma Cons (1838–1912), Manager of the Old Vic Theatre, London', M.Phil. dissertation, Middlesex University, 1996.

Leonard, Maurice, *Markova: The Legend* (London, 1995).

Levine, Philippa, *Feminist Lives in Victorian England: Private Roles and Public Commitment* (Oxford, 1990).

Littlewood, Joan, *Joan's Book: Joan Littlewood's Peculiar History as She Tells It* (London, 1995).

Mander, Raymond P., 'The Old Vic Fifty Years Ago', *The Vic-Wells Association Newsletter*, 82 (November 1953).

'Forty Years On, Part One', *The Vic-Wells Association Newsletter*, based on the memories of Mrs Matheson Lang, Mrs Napper, Miss Estelle Stead and Mr Andrew Leigh (August 1954).

Mangan, Richard (ed.), *Gielgud's Letters* (London, 2004).

Marshall, Norman, *The Other Theatre*, 2nd impression (London, 1948).

Martineau, Caroline, 'A History of the Royal Victoria Hall and Morley Memorial College', pamphlet reprint of article first published in the *Morley College Magazine*, October 1894.

Martineau, Violet (compiler), *Recollections of Sophia Lonsdale* (London, 1936).

Maurice, C. Edmund, *The Life of Octavia Hill As Told in Her Letters* (London, 1913).

May, Val, *Tribute To The Lady*, performed 1974.

Neatby, Kate, *Ninette de Valois and the Vic-Wells Ballet*, ed. Edwin Evans, with a preface by Lilian Baylis, C.H. (London, 1934).

Newton, H. Chance, *The Old Vic And Its Associations: Being My Own Extraordinary Experiences of 'Queen Wictoria's Own Theayter'* (London, 1923).

Northcroft, Dora, *Girls of Adventure* (London, 1944).

Oldfield, Sybil, *Spinsters of This Parish: The Life and Times of F.M. Mayor and Mary Sheepshanks* (London, 1984).

Peppin, B. and Micklethwait, L., *Dictionary of Twentieth Century British Book Illustrators* (London, 1983).

Poel, William, 'The "Vic" fifty Years Ago', *OVM*, December 1930.

Phillips, Eric, 'Memories of the Old Vic', *The Listener*, 14 February 1957.

Prevost, Annette, 'A Great Lady and her People: Lilian Baylis and the Vic-Wells Era', *Country Life*, 9 May 1974, pp. 1144–5.

Raymond, Harry, *B.I. Barnato: A Memoir* (London, 1897).

Rhondda, Margaret Haig, Viscountess, *This Was My World* (London, 1933).

Richards, Denis, *Offspring of the Old Vic: A History of Morley College* (London, 1958).

Roberts, Peter (ed.), *Lilian Baylis Centenary Festival 1974: Souvenir Programme* (London, 1974).

   The Old Vic Story: A Nation's Theatre 1818–1976 (London, 1976).

Rosenthal, Jack, *Auntie's Niece*, episode in *The Velvet Glove* series, BBC2, 1977.

Rowe, Reginald, 'Twin Theatres; Sadler's Wells Again', *The Times*, 6 January 1931.

Rowell, George, *The Old Vic Theatre* (Cambridge, 1993).

Royde-Smith, N.G., 'Lilian Baylis: An Impression', *The Weekly Westminster*, 12 January 1924.

Sadie, Stanley (ed.), *The New Grove Dictionary of Music and Musicians*, 20 vols. (London, 1980).

Salter, Elizabeth, *Helpmann* (London, 1978).

Schafer, Elizabeth, *Shakespeare in Production: 'The Taming of the Shrew'* (Cambridge, 2002).

Shaughnessy, Robert, *The Shakespeare Effect: A History of Twentieth Century Performance* (Basingstoke, 2002).

Sherriff, R.C., *No Leading Lady: An Autobiography* (London, 1968).

Smith, Iain R., *The Origins of the South African War, 1899–1902* (London, 1996).

Smyth, Ethel, *Streaks of Life* (London, 1921).

A Final Burning of Boats (London, 1928).

'Lilian Baylis: a Sketch' in *Female Pipings in Eden* (London, 1933).

Speaight, Robert, *William Poel and the Elizabethan Revival* (London, 1954).

Sprigge, Elizabeth, *Sybil Thorndike Casson* (London, 1971).

St John, Christopher (Christabel Marshal), *Ethel Smyth: A Biography* (London, 1959).

Strachan, Alan, *Secret Dreams: A Biography of Michael Redgrave* (London, 2004).

Thorndike, Russell, 'Lilian Baylis: As I Knew Her' in Sybil and Russell Thorndike, *Lilian Baylis* (London, 1938), pp. 109–97.

Thorndike, Sybil, 'Lilian Baylis: As I Knew Her' in Sybil and Russell Thorndike, *Lilian Baylis* (London, 1938), pp. 21–105.

Twain, Mark, *Following the Equator: A Journey Around the World*, vol. I (London, 1899).

Walker, Kathrine Sorley, *Ninette de Valois: Idealist Without Illusions* (London, 1987).

Webb, Beatrice, *My Apprenticeship*, vol. II (Harmondsworth, 1938).

Webster, Margaret, *The Same Only Different: Five Generations of a Great Theatre Family* (New York, 1969).

Westwood, Doris, *These Players: A Diary of the 'Old Vic'*, (London, 1926).

White, Eric Walter, *The Rise of English Opera* (London, 1951).

Whitelaw, Lis, *The Life and Rebellious Times of Cicely Hamilton: Actress, Writer, Suffragist* (London, 1990).

Whitworth, Geoffrey, 'The People's Theatre: Lilian Bayliss's [*sic*] Great Work at the "Old Vic"', *John O'London's Weekly*, 18 February 1922.

Williams, Evelyn, 'How They Began: I: The Sadler's Wells Ballet', *The Dancing Times*, July 1950.

'The Old Vic and Lilian Baylis', Report of the Annual Address given by Miss Evelyn Williams, 20 July 1951, *Royal Academy of Dancing Gazette*, August 1951.

Williams, Harcourt, *Four Years at the Old Vic 1929–33* (London, 1935).

Vic-Wells: the Work of Lilian Baylis (London, 1938).

Old Vic Saga (London, 1949).

Williamson, Audrey, *Old Vic Drama: A Twelve Years' Study of Plays and Players* (London, 1948).

Old Vic Drama 2: 1947–1957 (London, 1957).

Woolf, Virginia, *The Sickle Side of the Moon: The Letters of Virginia Woolf, Volume 5: 1932–1935*, ed. Nigel Nicolson (London, 1979).

Young, Patricia Don, *Dramatic School* (London, 1954).

Sound and film archive material

1936 March, vinyl record of Lilian Baylis talking about the Old Vic and Sadler's Wells.

1937 Lilian Baylis interviewed by Leslie Mitchell, BBC television *Picture Page*, 29 September.

1944 'Useful Citizens' number 8, featuring the work of Emma Cons and also mentioning the work of Lilian Baylis, BBC Home Service, 10 March.

1949 'Great Citizens', a schools radio programme on Baylis's work.

1949 'Return to the Old Vic', radio broadcast, 30 October. Written and produced by W. Farquharson Small.

1952 'Lilian Baylis: A Portrait of a Great Lady', radio broadcast, 25 July. Produced by Malcolm Baker-Smith.

1963 'The Old Vic 1914–1963', BBC Home Service, 9 June. Written and produced by Christopher Venning.

1963 'Farewell to the Vic', BBC radio, 15 June.

1974 'The Lady', Derek Parker introduces a compilation tribute to Baylis, Radio 4, 26 May 10.15 p.m. Produced by Denys Gueroult.

1974 'Tribute to the Lady', by Val May, broadcast of the gala evening at the Old Vic, 6 May. Produced by Ian Cottrell. Typescript in the National Theatre archive.

1983 *Omnibus* on the Old Vic, A Film by Cyril Frankel, 30 October 10.25 p.m. Narrated by Richard Baker.

1985 'Opera at the Vic', Brian Crimp talks to Joan Cross and Powell Lloyd, Radio 4, 11 August.

1991 'The Diamond Jubilee of Sadler's Wells', presented by Sheridan Morley, Radio 2, 1st Sunday in January.

1997 'Lilian Baylis – a Portrait of "The Lady"', by Joy Melville, introduced by Donald Sinden, Radio 2, 17 August 11 p.m. – 12.05 a.m. Produced by Tamsin Collison.

1998 'A Centenary Celebration of Lilian Baylis', by Joy Melville, introduced by Ronald Harwood.

2001 'Celebrating Lilian Baylis', Linbury Studio, 12 November 2001, devised and presented by Sarah Lenton for the Friends of Covent Garden, audio tape, Royal Opera House archive.

N.B. Some newspaper articles cited were read in cuttings collections. Dates may not always be exact when this is the case.

Index